1

WAR, STATE AND SOCIETY

By the same author

MARXISM AND SOCIAL SCIENCE: The Roots of Social Knowledge
MARXISM VERSUS SOCIOLOGY: A Guide to Reading
SOCIALISM AND MILITARISM

WAR, STATE AND SOCIETY

Edited by
Martin Shaw

MACMILLAN PRESS
LONDON

First published 1984 by
THE MACMILLAN PRESS LTD
London and Basingstoke
Companies and representatives
throughout the world

ISBN 0 333 33992 4 (hardcover)
ISBN 0 333 35810 4 (paperback)

Printed in Hong Kong

Contents

1 – 11S rec²

Acknowledgements

This book is based on a conference held at the University of Hull in 1981, at which the papers were first delivered. I wish to thank all the contributors and participants for making this a stimulating occasion, the results of which can usefully be made available to a wider audience. I also wish to thank my colleagues in the Department of Sociology and Social Anthropology for making the conference possible. In particular, my gratitude goes to Valerie Hurst for her help in organisation, and to her and Teresa Weatherston for typing my own contributions. Finally, I thank Glynis Clemo, my wife, for her support and encouragement during the preparation of both conference and book.

Martin Shaw
Hull

Notes on the Contributors

Andrew Cox is Lecturer in Politics, University of Hull.

Michael Cox is Lecturer in Political Science, Queen's University, Belfast, and an editor of *Critique*.

John Hall is Lecturer in Sociology, University of Southampton.

Stephen Kirby is Lecturer in Politics, University of Hull.

Michael Mann is Lecturer in Sociology, London School of Economics and Political Science.

Ralph Miliband is Professor of Sociology, Brandeis University.

Martin Shaw is a Lecturer in Sociology, University of Hull.

Dan Smith is the author of *The Defence of the Realm in the 1980s*.

Nigel Young is Reader in Peace Studies, University of Bradford.

Introduction: War and Social Theory

MARTIN SHAW

The experience of war in our Northern industrial civilisation is a strange phenomenon. After two world wars, the nature and effects of which were unprecedented in human history, we have lived through nearly four decades without global conflict. This period, usually described as one of peace, has been overhung by the fear of warfare of unimaginable horror, and accompanied by the 'noises off' of an unending series of lesser but still very bloody wars, almost all of them in the South. The 'peaceful' North has been the site of preparations for a Third World War, as well as sending forth its armies or its weapons and (important for our psychological participation) its television cameras to each phase of Third World war.

No period of 'peace' has been as dominated by warfare as that of recent times. Preparations for war have reached ever higher levels: world military expenditure was probably approaching $700 billion in 1982, and growing at three per cent per annum in real terms. High levels of armaments are becoming more universal among states: the share of Third World countries (excluding China) in world military spending rose from nine per cent to sixteen per cent between 1971 and 1981.[1] All the signs are that a major proliferation of nuclear weapons may not be far away, as a weapon-capability becomes available to many of the forty or so states with nuclear power programmes. If there has been some tendency, as a recent study suggests, for the number of wars to fall off,[2] the growth of the arsenals means that the potential damage from even 'local' wars is much greater.

Public awareness of issues of war and peace has varied enormously in its intensity during the period since 1945. In the 1950s and early

1

1960s, the Cold War and arms race were highly manifest and much debated, at least in the West. In the late 1960s and early 1970s, at the height of 'détente', the nuclear danger began to fade from the public mind. Particular wars, notably in Vietnam but more briefly others such as those in the Middle East, were centres of public attention. In the later 1970s, a new escalation of the arms race and the outbreak of wars between 'socialist' states in Asia both received less attention than they should as Western societies turned in on themselves with the onset of economic crisis. Only in the 1980s has a dramatic series of events – the NATO decision on theatre nuclear 'modernisation', the Polish crisis and the Soviet occupation of Afghanistan, the unending explosions in the Middle East, the Falklands War – brought about a new consciousness of the danger of war. The popular literature on nuclear weapons has suddenly flourished, and 'scenarios' of possible wars have been endlessly debated.[3]

It would be nice to think that social science had transcended the limitations of popular consciousness and sustained ongoing theory and research into war in modern civilisation. And yet most of the mainstream academic writing about war dates back to the 1950s and early 1960s, if not before. The great social science boom of the later sixties and seventies almost wholly neglected the issue. The intellectual revolution which produced so much radical and Marxist social theory bypassed this most fundamental of problems. C. Wright Mills' other writings were pivotal to the changes in sociology, but his appeal for a study of war went almost completely unheeded. Even the work in which it is contained, alone among his books, has long been out of print.

Only on the margins of the social sciences have strategic analysis and its radical counterpart, peace research, established a body of knowledge about the contemporary military situation. Work carried out very much unrecognised over a decade or so has now become a focus of wider attention. It has taken the 'new Cold War' and the related popular consciousness to stimulate this interest. In this new military and political situation, the debates of the strategists and peace researchers can contribute to a wider understanding of the social causes and consequences of warfare.

It was with the aim of bringing together such contributions with some of the perspectives on power in society which are emerging from within social science, that a conference was organised at Hull University in 1981, on which the present volume

is based. The intention was to discuss both the most general
questions – the role of war in society and the state, especially in
modern industrial societies – and some of the more specific issues
raised by the new debate about nuclear war. These concerns, although broadly distinguishable, intersect particularly because one
of the most important theses put forward recently about nuclear
war (E. P. Thompson's account of 'exterminism') challenges one
of the most widely-held intellectual assumptions about war in
modern society in general (the orthodox Marxist belief that war is
the product of capitalism). Although the range of the contributors is much wider than this particular argument, the issue
tends to recur in one form or another, and from contrasting
points of view. At the conference, we had the benefit of contributions from Thompson himself, Mary Kaldor and Michael
Kidron, who helped to focus the argument about capitalism and
warfare, and from David Holloway, who extended our field of
analysis to Soviet militarism. Some of this work has been
published elsewhere, and readers may wish to consult it in order
to complement the articles in this book.[4]

Many (but not all) of the contributors generally support the
new movement for European nuclear disarmament, and some of
us are actively engaged in its work. This book certainly reflects
the new concern about nuclear weaponry, and some of the papers
deal with problems of perspective which are of direct relevance to
the anti-nuclear movement. At the same time, we aim to go
beyond the immediate problems, to stimulate debate on more
general issues in the way we theorise about war, the state and
society. What this volume brings out is that those who share an
active concern about the issues of war and peace may approach
them from very different intellectual standpoints, which in turn
produces a different emphasis in the way they express their
practical concern. In this book there are contributions from
sociologists and political scientists, Marxists and non-Marxists,
peace researchers and defence analysts.

The aim of this introduction is to provide a brief general survey
of the treatment of war in two of the main intellectual traditions
which are at work in this book, academic sociology and Marxism,
and then to outline the parameters of two current issues which are
very central to the papers which follow: the relationship of war
and capitalism, and the social causes of the drive towards nuclear
war. The purpose is not to provide a comprehensive overview of

the literature on war, the state and society, nor to survey the arguments of the later papers. The goal is to provide some points of common reference – a very selective introduction to the arguments and literature – for the main body of discussion in this book.

CAN THERE BE A SOCIOLOGY OF WAR?

yes

Social science has identified two main sorts of problem in dealing with war, particularly in its modern manifestations. The primary issue has been to produce an account of the causes of war and its significance for society. The secondary one is to explain particular features of war and war-preparation in social terms.

A great deal more effort has been devoted, and with more success, to the latter than to the former. Defence analysts have produced close accounts of the institutional contexts and political pressures influencing military policy.[5] Military sociology has been primarily concerned with institutional analysis, with the social organisation of armed forces and the way this influences their goals.[6] It must be said, however, that even this tradition has had few recent exemplars in Britain: very little of any sort of sociology of war has been produced.[7]

The larger questions of the nature, causes and effects of war have proved more intractable. There may be a general rejection of biological or physiological explanations for human aggression, a point which anthropologists have argued.[8] But there is little agreement beyond such very basic points. A major reason for this is that the main sources of the wider sociological tradition provide so little of the framework needed for a sociology of war. Nineteenth century sociology was much imbued (as Michael Mann and John Hall discuss) with the evolutionary optimism of the age: Comte for example believed that industrial society was replacing military society. Even Marx, while articulating the contradictions of industrial capitalism, shared in this failure to anticipate the modern problem of war. Durkheim had little to offer which bore directly on the subject; Weber produced a definition of the state which laid stress on its monopoly of armed force (discussed by Nigel Young), but very little towards a substantive sociology of warfare. Several mid-twentieth century writers have done substantial work, often of a sweeping comparative kind. But the work of men like Pitirim Sorokin, Quincy Wright, and in Britain, Stanislav Andreski, is largely obscure to modern sociologists.[9] Indeed there is evidence that, even in their day, the impact on sociology as a whole was marginal: Alvin Gouldner surveyed twenty-five introductory textbooks published between 1945 and 1954, and found that only 275 out of a total of 17 000 pages dealt with some aspect of the causes or effects of war.[10] A similar survey today could only show the persistence or exacerbation of relative neglect.

The mid-century studies we have mentioned ranged very widely across the centuries. Sorokin attempted statistical comparisons from Ancient Rome and Medieval Europe to the First World War; Wright (less strictly in a sociological tradition) suggested a multi-factor institutional, legal, political, social and psychological theory of war; Andreski amassed huge evidence behind his particular typology of societies, based on their 'military participation ratio'. To the extent that these studies receive continuing attention, it has generally been critical. A recent American writer, concerned with sociology's contribution to peace research, criticises Wright and Sorokin for having done little more than demonstrate 'the frequency, persistence, and increasing intensity of war'.[11] An economic historian comments from a scholarly standpoint that 'many of these studies are ambitious in scope and in claims of predictive value, but there is at least some question about their usefulness to students of particular wars'.[12] The sociologist might throw back the criticism that many economic and social historians' work on war has been so narrow in focus that its value even for a general account of a particular war, let alone a wider social theory of war, is open to question.[13] We are back to the old dilemma of 'grand theory' versus 'abstracted empiricism'.[14]

There can be little doubt that the most useful social-scientific writing on war has involved bridging this particular gap. Arthur Marwick, for example, opened new ground with his studies of British society in war, exemplifying Trotsky's thesis that 'war is the locomotive of history'.[15] He has recently applied, and modified, Andreski's thesis of the 'military participation ratio' (that is the proportion of a society mobilised for war) as the key to the effects of war on society. Marwick argues that it is not military but general wartime participation which is the key to social change. Analysing the experience of a number of societies in the two world wars, he identifies four aspects of the effect of war: the destructive (war as disaster), the test (of the institutions of a society), participation (of the population, leading to social changes both 'guided' and 'unguided') and the psychological. Suggesting a number of major dimensions of change: in social geography, economics, social structure, social cohesion, social ideas, welfare policies and politics, Marwick sees these as developing chiefly in proportion to the participation of the population in war. This basic cause is not exclusive to the 'total wars' of the twentieth century, but can be sought in earlier wars and in modern guerilla wars, in different degrees.[16]

This sort of socio-economic historical writing, with the enormous merit of producing grounded assessments of broad and general issues, has however left two major problems.[17] First, it has lent itself more, as Marwick admits, to study of the consequences than of the causes of war. Second, it is in a sense outmoded by the development of massive nuclear arsenals. The 'progressive' reforms and radical, even revolutionary, social changes wrought by the First and Second World Wars are unlikely to be repeated in the event of a third world war. Nuclear war would bring catastrophic change, of a kind only glimpsed in the most nightmarish episodes of previous wars, on a wholly unprecedented scale. There is little in modern sociological and historical writing which prepares us for this decisive shift in the social character of war.

Among social theorists who have confronted this issue, Raymond Aron, who is discussed in the paper by John Hall, sees the modern arms race, like previous ones, as the inevitable outcome of the system of sovereign states. He argues not for sweeping measures of disarmament, but for recognition that nuclear war is unwinnable, and differentiating strongly between different types of war.[18] C. Wright Mills, whose appeal was not just for the study of war but for critical intellectual activity against it, argues more radically that nuclear war is 'irrational', 'absurd', 'obsolete as a means of any policy save that of mutual annihilation'. Wright Mills linked the war danger to the emergence of a society dominated by a power élite, in which thinking, participating publics were being transformed into powerless masses. Despite the obsolescence of war, the preparation for World War III was being built into the economics and politics of both East and West. The 'inertial thrust' of which

E. P. Thompson now warns was first identified in this tract of
Wright Mills. Sociological explanation consisted not in reducing
militarism to prior socio-economic causes, but in analysing the
permeation of social process and social institutions by war-
preparation. For Mills, as for Thompson (who acknowledges the
debt), 'The immediate cause of World War III is the military
preparation of it'.[19]

CAN MARXISM UNDERSTAND WAR?

The targets of Mills' polemic were (apart from the power élite
itself) the intellectual technicians and apologists of the war
machine. It is a symptom of the change in intellectual life, as
well as of the difference between Europe and America, that
Thompson's modern version is directed immediately not against
latter-day NATO propagandists but at the Marxist left. They,
more than anyone else, are accused of intellectual complacency
(or in a grander word, 'immobilism') in the face of the nuclear
threat.

The legacy of Mills (who died tragically young in 1962) to sociology was a curious one. This most courageous and articulate of
radicals opened up the cleavage in social science, demystifying
functionalism, clarifying social conflicts and analysing the
mechanisms of power. He also brought the Marxist tradition to
sociological attention, although he was clearly opposed to a
dogmatic Marxism. The rapid effect of radicalisation in social
science was to lead, however, to the development of specifically
Marxist schools. The gains in theoretical precision which these
have involved have been accompanied by a loss of vision, not to
mention clarity, compared with the earlier work of Mills.[20]

The development of Marxist approaches in the social sciences
coincided exactly with the period of détente, in which war as a
general intellectual and political problem almost disappeared
from social consciousness. The new Marxism did not know, or at
least forgot, about nuclear war; it readily embraced civil, revolutionary and guerilla war (in the Third World, if not in its own
societies).[21] These 'silences' can be related to a one-sided
emphasis in Marxist theories of imperialism and the state, as I
suggest in a later paper in this volume.

The Marxist tradition contains a number of contradictory

strands in its theorisation of war. The problem never figured centrally in Marx's theory of capitalism, or in the materialist account of historical development in general (it was left to the non-Marxist sociologist Werner Sombart to suggest that war had created many of the conditions for the development of capitalism in Europe[22]). However Engels, a military specialist, laid the foundation for an economic interpretation of war. Both the technology and the social organisation of militarism, he argued, were dependent on the economic structure of society. Engels' account was not mechanical or fully technologically-determinist, as it allowed for the effect of morale as well as of weaponry. He was, moreover, conscious of contradictions emerging within militarism: he was one of the first to suggest, over-optimistically, that the perfection of modern warships made them 'both outrageously costly and unusable in war'. He also looked forward to when 'the armies of princes become transformed into armies of the people', leading to 'the bursting asunder of militarism from within'.[23]

Marx and Engels were impressed by Clausewitz, and did not question the view that war was the continuation of politics (hence also, in their view, of economics) by other means. They felt no need for a critical attitude towards war as such, and were contemptuous of pacifism. They had no difficulty in supporting whichever side in a war seemed most likely, through its victory, to aid the cause of democracy or, later, socialism.[24] The problems have arisen when these essentially nineteenth-century attitudes have been maintained in the drastically changed conditions of twentieth-century warfare: for example by German socialists supporting their government in 1914, or by Soviet theorists justifying possible nuclear war against the West today.

Engels laid the foundations both for a matter-of-fact, Clausewitzian-Marxist approach to military strategy, and for the more critical approach of radical Marxists before and during World War I. Karl Liebknecht saw militarism in general as a product of class society, and the impending European war (he was writing in 1907) as the expression of competitive rivalry between capitalist states. He formulated the law that large-scale militarism more and more influences the internal structure of capitalist society, becoming 'the final regulator, now secret, now open, of all class politics, of the tactics in the class struggle not only of the capitalist classes, but also of the proletariat'.[25] According to Liebknecht,

Rosa Luxemburg, V. I. Lenin and Nikolai Bukharin, militarism undermined parliamentary democracy, leading to 'bureaucratic-military dictatorship' in Western societies.

The contradictory nature of war was emphasised by Lenin, who saw it as creating the conditions for revolution, and expounded theoretically by Bukharin, who saw capitalism as thoroughly militarised and war, therefore, as the prime source of crisis in the system (displacing the crisis of overproduction on which Marxist analysis had hitherto hinged).[26] Certainly, the First World War did see the rise of proletarian revolution on a scale conspicuously lacking in times of purely economic crisis. Trotsky expressed the revolutionary potential of war in his phrase 'the locomotive of history', although in theoretical terms this must be considered too neat. The changes which wars bring include reform as well as revolution, as Marwick has shown, and they are by no means all changes which would have occurred anyway and are merely accelerated by war.[27]

Even the radical-Marxist concepts of war, like much of the wider sociological and historical literature, are too closely based on the experience of past wars to be a clear guide to the understanding of the nuclear age. Indeed Marxists generally have an additional handicap in the legacy of the Russian Revolution. One result of this is often a falsely dichotomous view of states and social formations, which sees only (Western) capitalism as imperialist or militarist. Thus a widely used text, Baran and Sweezy's *Monopoly Capital*, suggests that the arms race is entirely a matter of US imperialism seeking to contain its essentially peaceful socialist rival.[28] This misses the reciprocal (if not symmetrical) logic of the East-West conflict. Another result is that within large parts of the Marxist tradition, the critique of militarism has been lost, in a celebration of socialism as armed struggle. A recent commentator was not entirely wrong when he talked of a 'triumph of military science over Marxism'.[29]

Classical Marxism has provided a mixed legacy of hypotheses about the socio-economic causes and revolutionary effects of modern war, of dubious applicability to late twentieth-century militarism. Contemporary Marxism has shared in the predilection of the social sciences for system, equilibrium, and 'normal' processes of change, even if it has reinterpreted these as class structure, class compromise and class struggle. For example, the arguments about reform and revolution as roads to socialism have ırgely been conducted without reference to war, although that has been the context in which both reformist and revolutionary movements have had most impact in this century. Even where contemporary Marxism has recognised militarism at the centre of the capitalist system, it has curiously neutralised the phenomenon. Discussion of the military expenditure, which was stressed by writers of the 1960s as diverse as Baran and Sweezy, Michael Kidron and Ernest Mandel, centred on the effects of this expenditure in 'stabilising' the capitalist economy. The sense of nuclear weaponry as extremely dangerous to the stability of every form of society, indeed to modern civilisation itself, was lost when it was seen as just another form of state expenditure.[30]

A THEORY OF WAR AND CAPITALISM?

War, as a social process, has the characteristic of cutting through most of the barriers that exist in social life. The study of war, likewise, cannot help but cut across the disciplinary barriers in the social sciences. Although this or that particular aspect of warfare may be encompassed in a narrowly economic, psychological or sociological view, any general treatment of the problem must be more catholic and wide-ranging. This is all the more true, given the relative neglect of war in many fields.

If the study of war is too important to be left to the strategists, social scientists must clearly come to terms with the documentation and research which has come primarily from those concerned with the inner logic of modern warfare. On the other hand, a great deal of research into the 'half-life' world of defence would clearly benefit from a closer integration with the main traditions of social, economic and political analysis. Whether one believes, fairly conventionally for social science, that it is a matter of finding clear social causes for war, or whether one sees the issue more radically as one of the militarisation of society, the 'war-society interface' is a crucial one.

A social theory of war, in general, is certainly a tall order. The tension we have noted, in applying concepts developed for pre-nuclear wars to the nuclear age, is one instance of a more general problem. The development of war, from the localised conflicts of tribesmen to the great armies of antiquity and medieval times and the industrialised navies of the late nineteenth century, shows immense changes. Clearly a general social theory of war would suggest that these changes have been closely related to wider changes in social relations, state systems and technology. But the very gulfs which exist between different stages in the history of war and society raise a very large issue of 'historical specificity' in social theorising about war.

The chief substantive focus of this methodological issue is the debate about capitalism and war. Classical Marxist theory suggested that modern warfare is specifically connected to the nature of capitalism, and most recent sociology has analysed various aspects of social reality within the framework of a theory of capitalist society. It is natural, therefore, that explanations for war should be advanced again in this context. Three dimensions that we have mentioned are central to such explanations: the expansionist, and more specifically imperialist, tendency of capital; the economic interest of capitalism in war production; and the development of specifically capitalist forms of weaponry (weapon-systems).

Two main sorts of objection may be raised to the whole attempt to link capitalism and warfare in this way. From one historical end, it may be argued that, granted that modern industrialism has changed the scale and technology of warfare, the continuities are still very marked (see Michael Mann's paper). Imperial expansion has been a tendency of states throughout the history of civilisation, and is not specific to capitalism: while the imperial expansion of modern 'capitalist' states is not to be so closely linked with economic expansion or capital export.[31] From the other historical end, it is not obvious that 'socialist' states are any less militarist than 'capitalist' ones. The elements of imperial expansion, arms economy and weapons-systems are all more or less common to modern industrial states, East and West. The non-Marxist will argue that there is little specifically 'capitalist' about modern militarism.

The argument about capitalism and warfare is still relevant, however, for two main reasons. On any definition, the world economic system is predominantly capitalist, and the most powerful single sector of it is the Western capitalist group of states. The economic and military policies of all states are powerfully influenced by these realities, a point which is recognised in most studies of Russia and Eastern European states (however little

agreement there may be on the precise sociological definition of
such states). In addition, war and war-preparations are now
major economic realities: the study of these phenomena in
capitalist societies must take into account the specific nature of
their economies. This approach does not exclude study of the role
of war-preparations in Soviet-type economies: on the contrary, the
recognition of the depth of the 'arms economy' in the West has
prompted much of the interest in the parallel 'military-industrial
complex' in the USSR.

A sophisticated attempt to articulate a theory of 'Warfare and
capitalism' is made by Mary Kaldor.[32] Her starting point is the
specific character of war: the 'mode of warfare' and the 'mode of
production' may be analagous – as in Clausewitz's view that battle
is to war what cash payment is to commodity exchange – but they
are not the same. War, she argues, 'is in one sense antithetical to
capitalism...in that it constitutes a potential interruption to
commodity production', but at the same time it is 'an inevitable
consequence of the working out of capitalism'. In order to explain
the *role* of war, she attempts a difficult distinction between a
dominant imperial state acting on behalf of capital accumulation
as a whole (Britain in the mid-nineteenth century, America after
1945), and the 'regressive' militarism of competing and especially
decaying national capitalisms. The *mode* of warfare she sees as
something which can never reproduce itself and is therefore
essentially parasitic on capitalism. Defence industries, including
the great modern arms corporations, share in this parasitism,
which accounts for the form that innovation takes in modern
weapon systems. Huge increases in complexity and sophistication,
for diminishing utility, amount to what she has elsewhere
described as a 'baroque' technology.[33]

Kaldor's analysis raises the issue, which concerns several contributors to this book, of (although she does not actually use the
term) the 'relative autonomy' of warfare and the state in capitalist
society. It has the advantage of trying to show how the mode of
warfare is relative to the mode of production, as well as how it is
autonomous from it. Of particular interest is the extension of her
analysis to the Soviet Union, where she argues that 'war has been
the main form of commensuration' in economic affairs:

Could we not [she asks] describe the Soviet Union as itself
the warfare state embodying the antithesis of warfare to

capitalism? Such a system would be dependent upon and yet opposed to capitalism. The mode of production would take on the characteristics of the mode of warfare; indeed it would be shaped by the need to reproduce the mode of warfare rather than the other way round.

In the West, the dominant sector, the source of accumulation, of social dynamism, is the capitalist sector. The warfare sector emerges to serve the capitalist sector although, as we have seen, it takes on its own dynamic properties which can impose a brake on accumulation. In the Soviet Union, it could be the other way round, that the mode of production is subservient to the mode of warfare, and that social dynamism comes from war.[34]

In these rather tentative comments, the potential for the autonomy of mode of warfare from mode of production is taken to the point where we begin to ask instead: is the mode of production autonomous from that of warfare? This question can ultimately be asked, not only about the USSR, but of the West as well.

A LOGIC OF EXTERMINISM?

Kaldor's analysis of warfare and capitalism leads naturally into the specific debate about nuclear war which has influenced most of the authors of this book. Kaldor's argument is that capitalism needs states, which need war, but that war is 'a burden on and a potential interruption to capitalism'. It is 'the tension between warfare and capitalism' which explodes periodically in war itself. War is 'an act of desperation', which could now result from the economic and political tensions of a world in which the 'mode of warfare' has undermined the 'mode of production'.

Kaldor's argument is an attempt, at a fairly high level of generality, to show the structural links between socio-economic crisis and the development of warfare, as possible causes of global war. Her approach can be seen as overcoming the one-sidedness both of much strategic and peace research, with its overwhelming emphasis on developments in weaponry and strategy, and of much socio-economic and political writing, with its emphasis on causes external to the dynamic of war-preparation. This is highly

important in the context of the Marxist debate following E. P.
Thompson's celebrated 'Notes on Exterminism, the Last Stage of
Civilisation' (to which Ralph Miliband's paper in this volume is a
contribution).

Thompson's polemic is directed against those who believe that
the dangers of war can be explained (and thus controlled) by the
logic of capitalism; it is imbued with an urgent warning of global
catastrophe. But it is also a reasoned historical argument, which
relies a good deal on concepts as well as information produced
within peace research. Thompson argues that we cannot explain
the arms race and its possible outcomes in terms of the economic
interests and political intentions of states and ruling élites. The
arms race has a logic of its own, the secret of which is to be found
in its products. Bombs are not just things, but 'components in a
weapons-*system*: and producing, manning and supporting that
system is a corresponding social system . . . .'. The competition of
war-producing societies in the US and USSR leads Thompson to
propose that

> There is an internal dynamic and reciprocal logic here which
> requires a new category for its analysis. If 'the hand-mill gives
> you society with the feudal lord; the steam-mill, society with
> the industrial capitalist', what are we given by those Satanic
> mills which are now at work, grinding out the means of human
> extermination? I have reached this point of thought more than
> once before, but have turned my head away in despair. Now,
> when I look at it directly, I know that the category which we
> need is that of 'exterminism'.[35]

This logic has been attacked by Raymond Williams as a form of
'technological determinism', which

> is, if taken seriously, a form of intellectual closure of the com-
> plexities of social process. In its exclusion of human actions,
> interests and intentions, in favour of a select and reified image
> of their causes and results, it systematically post-dates history
> and excludes all other versions of cause. This is serious every-
> where, but in the case of nuclear weapons it is especially
> disabling. Even when, more plausibly, it is a form of short-
> hand, it steers us away from originating and continuing causes,
> and promotes (ironically, in the same mode as the ideologies

which the weapons systems now support) a sense of helplessness beneath a vast, impersonal and uncontrollable force.[36]

Williams argues that while nuclear weapons have assisted in the rise of superpower domination, 'the central thrust of this deadly competition has not been primarily military-technological but, in the broadest sense, political'. And while there have indeed been 'dramatic increases in the levels of surveillance and control' in Western societies in the nuclear era, these relate as much to internal social conflicts as to the arms race.[37]

'Exterminism' is clearly not to be taken in any narrowly technologically determined sense. Thompson's updating of Marx is not even strictly shorthand – more a metaphor, which he has vowed to discard, should it mystify more than it enlightens.[38] His concept of 'weapons system' derives from recent peace research, and clearly refers to the social relations of modern warfare. Ulrich Albrecht and Mary Kaldor, for example, locate the weapons system in terms of the development of the 'industrial army', dating from the Anglo-German naval race before World War I. The rise of the weapons system marks a crucial change in the social character of war:

> Formerly, the weapon was the instrument of the soldier. Today, the soldier appears to be the instrument of the weapons system. The resulting organisation is hierarchical, atomistic, and dehumanising. It reflects the importance accorded to industrial products, particularly machines, in society as a whole.[39]

The concept is therefore, in one sense, an extension of the Marxian critique of alienation to the sphere of war. It has been used, moreover, to analyse the socio-economic and political as well as military significance of transfers of arms technology to the Third World.[40]

Nuclear weapons systems come in a line of industrialised weapon systems developed over the last hundred years. Their origins clearly lie in the transformation of warfare by industrial capitalism – but their end? Thompson is raising the issue of how not just a complex of nuclear systems, but the military-political thrusts which they embody, have come to dominate capitalism as well as to reflect it. He shows that his point is not simply about the technology when he suggests that it is necessary

> to see Western imperialism as a force which originated in a
> rational institutional and economic matrix, but which, at a
> certain point, assumed an autonomous self-generating thrust
> in its own right, which can no longer be reduced by analysis to
> the pursuit of rational interests – which indeed acted so
> irrationally as to threaten the very empires of its origin and pull
> them down.[41]

The thesis of the irrationality of the arms race, central to
Thompson's argument, is profoundly attractive from a human
point of view but arouses immediate social-scientific suspicion.
Deeply wedded to the view that political and military activity
must reflect rational economic interests, social scientists in-
stinctively dismiss any suggestion of fundamental incongruence.
Thus an economic historian of World War II insists that

> War not only continued to meet the social, political and
> economic circumstances of states but, furthermore, as an in-
> strument of policy, it remained, in some circumstances, eco-
> nomically viable. War remains a policy and investment
> decision by the state and there seem to be numerous modern
> examples of its having been a correct and successful decision.
> The most destructive of modern technologies have not changed
> this state of affairs.[42]

It is hardly likely that this claim, even if we accept it (with qualifications) for the 1939-45 war, would remain true for an all-out
nuclear exchange. There are of course those who argue that the
rational economic interests of East and West, particularly in the
context of growing *Vodka-Cola* trade and investment, effectively
exclude this military outcome. The 'New Cold War', on this view,
will not be as permanent or dangerous as is feared.[43] Such a
reading seems highly complacent, however, when one is
confronted with the evidence of developments in strategic
thought and weaponry.[44]

THE FALKLANDS WAR AND BRITISH SOCIETY

The Falklands War occurred as this book was being prepared. In many ways it has been a textbook conflict, so neatly confined in time and space, and certainly many a textbook will seek to perpetuate its military 'lessons'. It has brought war to the forefront of the British (and Argentine) national consciousness, and may be expected to stimulate a considerable number of new studies by social scientists. It is early to draw full lessons, but it may be useful to outline some of the issues which seem to have arisen.

The global significance of the Falklands War is not as great in many respects as other wars which have taken place since 1945. From a simple human point of view, the number of casualties was small (relative to other wars), and the number of civilians directly involved almost uniquely tiny (on the same day as the British media expressed concern for the 600 civilians trapped in Stanley, the International Red Cross claimed that 600000 may have been rendered homeless by the Israeli invasion of Lebanon). From a geopolitical and strategic standpoint, the fact that the war was between two major allies of the United States served to restrict possible escalation along East-West lines.

In other senses, however, the war could prove an important case. Unlike many other 'Third World wars' involving advanced Western states this was not a colonial war, in the classic sense of involving a conflict between a colonial or neo-colonial power and an insurgent people or liberation army. Instead it was a war between a major Northern industrial power and a relatively advanced Southern state, the latter armed well, if not well enough, with advanced Western weapons. The relative lack of people on the Falklands (no colonised Argentinians, very few English colonists) served to clarify the fairly novel character of the war; although an interesting precedent is to be found in the US-Iran conflict of 1979-80, which was probably saved from significant escalation when the American helicopters crashed before reaching Teheran. Taken together with other developments of recent years – wars between 'socialist' states (e.g. China/Vietnam) and between relatively rich and well-armed 'Third World' states (e.g. Iran/Iraq) – this 'new' type suggests a global pattern of warfare of growing complexity.

Looked at in isolation, this limited war has been welcomed by some strategists, politicians and professional soldiers as proof that an advanced Western state can still use military force in a rational way to achieve political goals. In the global context, however, it can equally be seen as powerful confirmation of a new sort of unpredictability in international relations, which makes nuclear wars, even an East-West nuclear war, more likely in the longer term.

The assumption of 'rationality' in the Falklands fighting requires analysis. Whatever the long-term economic potential of the Falklands, the surrounding sea-bed or the Antarctic, it is not evident that this played a major role in the rationale of either side. In relation to the actual economy and population of the islands, it can well be claimed that the human and financial cost was 'disproportionate', and the war in that sense 'irrational'.[45] The most obvious sense in which 'rationality' works is that of politics, and chiefly domestic politics. For each government the main possible gain, against which large economic costs had to be offset, was the maintenance or enhancement of its domestic position. Only in this sense was the war 'rational', in a way that an unlimited nuclear war could never be.

The effects of the war on the societies involved have broadly confirmed the thesis of the 'wartime participation ratio' as the key to social change. The demands made on Argentine society by the war were far more profound than any made on British society; taken together with the initial intensity of feeling about the 'Malvinas' and the destabilising effects of defeat, this explains the greater upheaval in Argentina (although the full scope of this is far from clear at the time of writing). For British society, the participation ratio thesis would suggest that a war conducted 8000 miles away, in which only a few tens of thousands of troops, sailors and islanders were directly involved, and in which even media coverage was exceptionally controlled, would have little fundamental effect. Nevertheless, there is no exact comparative calculus of military participation: the effects of war are always proportional to the initial condition of the societies involved. In a society like Britain, embroiled in the economic, political and military contradictions of a long imperial decline, and deprived of open inter-state warfare for decades, the effects of a successful limited war may be apparently disproportional to the marginal 'real' gains of the state.

It is only possible to speculate about the deeper impact of the Falklands War on British society: about how far it has evoked 'the atavistic moods of violence' lying close to the surface of daily life, or stirred the 'nationalist sediment which will cloud our political and cultural life'.[46] The froth may settle quite quickly. It is easier to estimate the short-term effects on institutions, and especially the state, which the war has produced. The performance of the media will keep the *Bad News* school of sociologists busy for months to come;[47] the effect on defence policy choices, discussed in Dan Smith's paper, and the role of parliament in influencing these, documented by Stephen Kirby and Andrew Cox, will be closely watched. Above all, in the short term, is the question of how far it was the war which clinched a second term for Mrs Thatcher's brand of Conservatism. The Falklands War, which produced like most wars a high degree of superficial national unity, may have played a crucial part in deepening the already profound divisions in British society in the 1980s.

If nothing else, the Falklands War must surely have completed the process of alerting British social scientists to the crucial importance of war to the modern state and society. One can confidently predict that the discussion in this book will be taken up in future volumes, and that many more detailed studies will be made in the years to come.

NOTES

1. Figures based on SIPRI (Stockholm International Peace Research *Institute*), 'The Arms Race & Arms Control' (London: Taylor & Francis, 1982) pp. 2, 63. The 1982 figure for world arms expenditure is an extrapolation, allowing for real increase estimated of about 3%, plus inflation, from the 1981 SIPRI estimate of 'about $600–650 billion'.
2. Istvan Kende, 'Local Wars 1945–76', in Asbjorn Eide and Marek Thee (eds), *Problems of Contemporary Militarism* (London: Croom Helm, 1980) pp. 263–64, 279–80.
3. For examples, E. P. Thompson and Dan Smith, *Protest and Survive* (Harmondsworth: Penguin, 1980); Lawrence Freedman, *Britain and Nuclear Weapons* (London: Macmillan, 1980); Robert Neild, *How to Make Your Mind Up about the Bomb* (London: Deutsch, 1981); Jonathan Schell, *The Fate of the Earth* (London: Picador, 1982).
4. For E. P. Thompson, 'Notes on Exterminism, the Last Stage of Civilisation', see *New Left Review*, 121 (1980), and his *Zero Option* (London: Merlin, 1982); for further discussion of this paper, together with Mary Kaldor, 'Warfare and Capitalism', see Thompson *et al.*, *Exterminism and Cold War* (London: New Left Books/Verso, 1982); for David Holloway, 'War, Militarism and the Soviet State', in Thompson and Smith, op. cit. is an article relating to the themes on which he spoke at Hull. Michael Kidron is the author of a classic on the 'arms economy': *Western Capitalism since the War* (London: Weidenfeld & Nicolson, 1968). His contribution at Hull

reversed his earlier view that arms lead to capitalist stability; he has yet to explain his new position in print.

5. For examples, see the literature cited by Dan Smith, *The Defence of the Realm in the 1980s* (London: Croom Helm, 1980).

6. For a classic collection, see Morris Janowitz (ed.), *The New Military* (New York: Norton, 1969). This narrow definition of military sociology is specifically rejected by Kurt Lang, *Military Institutions and the Sociology of War* (London: Sage, 1972) p. 12, although the evidence of his bibliography is that sociologists have concentrated a large part of their work on military organisations. This is confirmed by a recent survey, Gwyn Harries-Jenkins and Charles C. Moscos Jnr, 'Armed Forces and Society', *Current Sociology*, 29, 3 (Winter 1981).

7. This is illustrated by the paucity of entries under 'Military' in the bibliography in J. T. Eldridge, *Recent British Sociology 1960–1980* (London: Macmillan, 1981). A notable exception is a new study by Tony Ashworth, *Trench Warfare 1914–18: The Live and Let Live System* (London: Macmillan, 1981).

8. Most recently, Richard Leakey, *The Making of Mankind* (London: Michael Joseph, 1981); but the case has frequently been argued, see e.g. Margaret Mead, 'Warfare is only an Invention – Not a Biological Necessity', in Leon Bramson and George W. Goethals (eds), *War: Studies from Psychology, Sociology, Anthropology* (London: Basic Books, 1964).

9. Pitirim Sorokin, *Social and Cultural Dynamics: Vol. 3 Fluctuation of Social Relationships, War, and Revolution* (London: Allen and Unwin, 1937) pp. 259–382; Quincy Wright, *A Study of War*, 2 vols. (University of Chicago Press, 1942); Stanislav Andreski, *Military Organisation and Society* 1954 (2nd edn, Berkeley: University of California Press, 1968).

10. Alvin W. Gouldner, Introduction to Emile Durkheim, *Socialism and Saint-Simon* (London: Collier-Macmillan, 1962) p. 10.

11. Ruth Harriet Jacobs, 'Sociological Perspectives in the Etiology of War', in Martin A. Nettleship, R. Dalegivens and Anderson Nettleship (eds), *War, Its Causes and Correlates* (The Hague: Mouton, 1975) p. 30.

12. J. M. Winter, 'The economic and social history of war', Introduction to Winter (ed.), *War and Economic Development* (Cambridge University Press, 1975) p. 2.

13. This is certainly the impression gained from most of the papers, and also from the lengthy bibliography in the collection edited by Winter.

14. C. Wright Mills, *The Sociological Imagination* (Harmondsworth: Penguin, 1970).

15. Arthur Marwick, *Britain in the Century of Total War* (London: Bodley Head, 1968); see also *The Deluge* (London: Bodley Head, 1965).

16. Marwick, *War and Social Change in the 20th Century* (London: Macmillan, 1977) Introduction and Conclusion.

17. Alongside Marwick's work here, we may particularly mention Alan S. Milward, *War, Economy and Society 1939–1945* (London: Allen Lane, 1977).

18. Raymond Aron, *On War* (London: Secker & Warburg, 1958).

19. C. Wright Mills, *The Causes of World War Three* (London: Secker & Warburg, 1958) p. 85.

20. I have commented on this in *Marxism and Social Science* (London: Pluto, 1975) esp. pp. ix–x, 105–106.

21. Martin Shaw, *Socialism and Militarism* (Nottingham Spokesman, 1981).

22. Werner Sombart, *Krieg and Kapitalismus*, 1913, summarised by Winter, op. cit., pp. 4–5.

23. Friedrich Engels, *Anti-Dühring*, Moscow 1954, Part II, ch. III; extracts in Bernard Semmel (ed.), *Marxism and the Science of War* (Oxford University Press, 1981) pp. 49–57 (for criticism see also Semmel's Introduction, pp. 3 – 12).

24. E. H. Carr, 'The Marxist Attitude to War', in *The Bolshevik Revolution 1917–1923*, Vol. 3 (Harmondsworth: Penguin, 1966) pp. 541–560.

25. Karl Liebknecht, *Militarism and Anti-Militarism* (London: Writers and Readers, 1979).

26. Nikolai Bukharin, *Economics and Politics of the Transformation Period*, ed. K. J. Tarbuck (London: Routledge & Kegan Paul, 1979).

27. Marwick, *War and Social Change in the 20th Century*, op. cit., Introduction.

28. Paul A. Baran and Paul M. Sweezy, *Monopoly Capital* (Harmondsworth: Penguin, 1968) ch. 7.

29. Semmel, op. cit., pp. 39–41.

30. Baran and Sweezy, op. cit.; Michael Kidron, op. cit.; Ernest Mandel, *Marxist Economic Theory*, Vol. 2 (London: Merlin, 1968).

31. cf. D. Fieldhouse, 'Imperialism: An historical revision', *Economic History Review*, 1961.

32. Mary Kaldor, 'Warfare and Capitalism', op. cit.

33. Kaldor, *The Baroque Arsenal* (London: Deutsch, 1982).

34. Kaldor, 'Warfare and Capitalism', op. cit.

35. Thompson, op. cit., pp. 6–7.

36. Raymond Williams, 'The Politics of Nuclear Disarmament', *New Left Review*, 124, p. 28, and in Thompson *et al.*, op. cit.

37. Williams, op. cit., p. 30.

38. In a contribution to the Conference at Hull, May 1981.

39. Ulrich Albrecht and Mary Kaldor, Introduction to *The World Military Order* (London: Macmillan, 1979) p. 10.

40. See the papers in the book edited by Albrecht and Kaldor; for a brief statement, Mary Kaldor, 'The Significance of Military Technology', in Eide and Thee, op. cit., pp. 226–229.

41. Thompson, op. cit., p. 23.

42. Milward, op. cit., p. 3.

43. Charles Levinson, *Vodka-Cola* (London: Levinson, 1981).

44. See the evidence and analysis in recent volumes of the SIPRI Yearbook, annually (London: Taylor & Francis); or the analysis in Dan Smith, *The Defence of the Realm in the 1980s* (London: Croom Helm, 1980).

45. See Peter Jenkins' column in *The Guardian*, April-June 1982.

46. E. P. Thompson, 'The War of Thatcher's Face', *The Times*, 29 April 1982, reprinted in his *Zero Option*, op. cit., p. 195. See also Anthony Barnett, *Iron Britannia* (London: Allison & Busby, 1982).

47. The Glasgow University Media Group, authors of *Bad News* (London, Routledge & Kegan Paul, 1976) and related studies, seem to have been

beaten to it by the excellent study of Robert Harris, *Gotcha! The Media, the Government and the Falklands Crisis* (London: Faber & Faber, 1983).

Part I

Capitalism, Militarism and the State System

1 Capitalism and Militarism

MICHAEL MANN

INTRODUCTION: THREE THEORIES

The aim of this paper is less to write a history of the relationship between capitalism and militarism than to analyse their present relationship in the light of history. More specifically, I seek to answer the questions: what difference, if any, has capitalism brought to the nature and degree of militarism in modern society? And to what extent, if any, is the threat of militarism which, in its nuclear form, leans so terrifyingly over our society, to be blamed upon capitalism?

I define capitalism later. *Militarism is here defined as an attitude and a set of institutions which regard war and the preparation for war as a normal and desirable social activity.*

To these questions, social theory gives three types of answer. The first, which I shall call *the theory of militaristic capitalism*, asserts that whatever militaristic tendencies lay in earlier societies they were boosted considerably by the advent of capitalism. The second, *the optimistic theory of pacific capitalism*, asserts on the contrary that capitalism (or often, industrial capitalism) is inherently pacific, and as it is also *the* central structure of modern (Western) society, we can be optimistic about the likelihood of militarism declining. The third, *the theory of geopolitical militarism*, argues that militarism is due fundamentally to other, more permanent aspects of the international relations of states, to which capitalism has brought little change. I shall criticise all three but argue that the last, suitably amended, has most to commend it.

Of course, these are not just theoretical questions. They have great bearing upon contemporary politics (and, indeed, upon our very survival). Hence the theories, or popularised versions of them, have had great impact upon political movements and world leaders. This is necessarily so: in order to make the world safer, we have to decide which fundamental elements of our social structure contribute to militarism. Then, perhaps, we can reform or overthrow them.

It is particularly important to clarify the role of capitalism in militarism. For there is a clear political carry-over between attitudes to the two. Those active in peace movements, who are probably more concerned than anyone else about militarism, tend to be anti-capitalist. Sometimes explicitly, more usually implicitly, they tend to blame capitalism for nuclear militarism, because they tend to blame it for the other ills of society. Political activists all over the Western world denounce capitalism and militarism not as separate, but as essentially conjoined, enemies.

Such political denunciations are usually supported by the theory of militaristic capitalism. Capitalism is the keystone of our society and it is fundamentally militaristic, it is argued. Hence militarism cannot be eliminated unless we eliminate capitalism. Naturally, to this argument must be added a specific explanation of militarism in the Soviet Union which I will not enter into here. Indeed this theory has many particular strands which cannot be discussed in a paper of this length. I will not discuss the 'military-industrial complex' variety associated particularly with C. Wright Mills and American radicals. Nor will I enter into the controversy started by radical economists arguing that militarism in the form of high military expenditure is functional for the capitalist economy. A third strand not discussed here is that militarism is useful in diverting the attention of the working class from the facts of their exploitation by capital. A fourth emphasises that militarism is necessary to keep down the even more exploited peoples of the Third World. These two last-mentioned generally unite in the Marxist theory of imperialism, associated with some of Marx's successors, especially Hilferding and Lenin (discussed in this volume by Martin Shaw). I will discuss this, albeit briefly. Nevertheless, all these detailed controversies can, to an extent, be bypassed by a more general 'historical analysis enquiring what difference capitalism seems to have made to the contours of militarism.

But blaming capitalism has been a minority tradition in main-stream social science theory. In economics and sociology, and in liberal and some social-democratic political rhetoric, the second theory, the optimistic theory of pacific capitalism, has pre-dominated. Like the radicals, this has seen capitalism, or often industrial capitalism, as the keystone of modern society, but it is a pacific keystone because it is *transnational*. It brought to an end the militaristic states of previous historical epochs. Whatever else divided such theorists as Adam Smith, Bastiat, Carey and Schumpeter or St Simon, Comte, Spencer, Marx himself and Durkheim, on one prediction they united. Contemporary mili-tarism between states was 'archaic', the declining residue of an earlier epoch (to which they often gave a militaristic name; for example Spencer's militant society or Bastiat's, Carey's and Schumpeter's age of imperialist plunder). The modern era was to be pacific, because its keystone, industrial capitalism, was trans-national.

These views, prevalent in the nineteenth and early twentieth century in England, America and France, did not go unchal-lenged. Writers like Gumplowicz, Ratzenhofer, Schmitt, Hintze, Mosca and Pareto stressed the continued vitality of militaristic currents in contemporary society. But several of them seemed to actually approve of militarism. And as, ironically, they all belonged to the defeated powers of the two world wars, their memory was largely suppressed. By and large the Anglo-Saxon and Gallic victors in the West preferred to forget their ideas. The dominant liberal, and a surprising proportion of the Marxist-socialist tradition, have continued to believe that capitalism and industrialism are pacific – often struggling heroically against the overwhelming evidence of modern history to do so. Here, for example, is Perry Anderson, struggling more than most Marxists to understand warfare, discussing the prevalence of war in about every other year in the sixteenth and seventeenth centuries. He concludes, '. . . that does not correspond to a capitalist rationality: it represents a swollen memory of the medieval functions of war. . . Such calendars are foreign to capital, although. . . it even-tually contributed to them'.[1] After 95 million dead in two world wars, almost all of whose protagonists were mature capitalist powers, this is a little difficult to believe!

But in both post-war periods, liberals and socialists alike seem to have decided that it would be best to wish militarism away by ignoring it. For example, in the Marxist tradition, in the 1960s and 1970s came a flurry of theories of the state. Dozens of books and hundreds of articles have poured forth on 'the capitalist state'. Almost none of them have contained a single word about what has been one of the principal activities of most capitalist states – preparing for, and conducting, war.[2]

More or less the same would be said of liberal theory, in which pluralist theories of the state have competed in silence on militarism (Mills' 'élite theory' crops up again here as the principal opponent which does deal with militarism).

However, in very recent years changes are occurring, especially among Marxists. E. P. Thompson has most notably broken with orthodoxy in his suggestion that we are now confronting a new, post-capitalist 'exterminist mode of production' which unites capitalism and the Soviet system.[3] Militarism is at the centre-stage but it is not necessarily connected to capitalism, he argues. Unfortunately, it is not clear what it does relate to. Thompson is better at demolishing traditional leftist slogans concerning the nature of what he calls 'the logic of exterminism', than he is at constructing his own theory.

Thompson's sensitivity to contemporary militarism has been paralleled by our own neo-Marxist editor, Martin Shaw. He has also moved considerably since his 1974 article on the state, which largely maintained the then normal silence on militarism in Marxist state theory.[4] His present contribution to this volume calls for a new Marxist theory of militarism. Neither of these writers, starting *theoretically* from a belief in the centrality of capitalism in modern society but then noting *empirically* the importance of militarism, has yet been able to locate the essential causes and nature of militarism today.

This is not surprising because capitalism and militarism are both core features of our society but they are only contingently connected. In contrast to both these traditional views on the relation between capitalism and militarism, I will make the following three points:

1. Militarism *is* a central part of modern society.
2. But its centrality does not derive principally from either capitalism or industrialism.
3. Instead militarism derives from geopolitical aspects of our social structure which are far older than capitalism.

Thus my argument is initially congenial to the third theoretical tradition, *geopolitical militarism*. In academe, the traditional home of this tradition has been in political science and more recently in departments of International Relations. Within sociology, Raymond Aron's notable contributions to this theory (ably discussed elsewhere in this volume by John Hall) have been largely ignored. But the major impact of the approach has been felt outside academe, in the rather more important power relations of militaristic states themselves. Thus, for example, the author of an academic book on Metternich, which was written entirely from this viewpoint, became an actual successor of Metternich in the geopolitical arena – Henry Kissinger.[5]

On the other hand, this tradition has an obvious weakness: it is so obsessed with geopolitical relations that it takes the existence and future destinies of states as the only significant actors upon the stage as 'givens'. But states are not the only collective actors in societies, and their influence waxes and wanes in the historical process. I ask here how and why the modern geopolitical system arose, and, more specifically, to what extent it was a part of the rise of capitalism.

On this basis I will add three further points to the three listed above.

4. Militarism became contingently associated with the rise of capitalism.
5. This association had the effect of greatly increasing both technically and socially the menace of militarism.
6. But in the twentieth century both menaces became the general property of expansionist industrial societies and are no longer specific to capitalism.

To demonstrate all six points, I proceed in two stages. First I will take various indices of militarism and examine their secular tendencies. Have they noticeably altered in the period of capitalism's emergence and development? On that basis I turn to the second stage, to see whether there is a causal relationship between capitalism and the changes which do emerge.

SECULAR TENDENCIES IN MILITARISM

Have war and militarism been a constant in human experience: the reflection, perhaps, of our own aggressive natures and/or of the essence of social co-operation? Such a view is often found, especially as a kind of pessimistic base for geopolitical theory. But studies of war among primitive peoples enable us to refute these notions in two ways. It is perfectly true that the vast majority of all known societies engage routinely in war-like activities. But, firstly, the mere fact that a minority do not (in Otterbein's study four out of fifty primitive peoples[6]) silences the fear that war is *essential* to our individual or social natures. Secondly, most war-like activity does not actually involve systematic killing: in most primitive societies a ritualised brandishing of weapons and ferocious intent sufficiently deters further escalation. In these 'wars' it is considered disastrous if anyone does get killed – which happens perhaps once in a generation.[7]

We of the nuclear age should look longingly at even this second level of pacific primitivism – let Ronald Reagan annually drive a (disconnected) ICBM to the East German border, there to make rude gestures at Yuri Andropov! The causes of *dangerous* militarism do not lie in our inevitable natures, but in historical developments, which are therefore potentially reversible.

Yet the emergence of systematic warfare happened very early in our history and has become nearly universal among more civilised peoples. Thus it is ultimately impossible to fully explain it. A number of inter-connected factors appear to have been involved.

1. When the surplus extracted from Nature increased, the spoils of plunder became more desirable. Some could live without working.
2. Associated with this was an increase in territorial fixity of the surplus and of the human labour invested in it. This made it impossible to run away with one's resources if threatened (as hunter-gatherers could). One stayed to fight.
3. Also associated with this was an increase in the fixity of social co-operation as labour was invested in co-operation with a particular and permanent social group with whom one then fought in co-operation.
4. All these tendencies encourage the rise of organised, centralised social co-operation, territorially and socially fixed – that is the state.

The consequence is clear: where we find socially and territorially fixed groups with states and surpluses, we find systematic killing in organised wars. Not all such killing is undertaken by states – though it is rare to find a situation where none of the combatant groups is state-organised – but all states undertake such killing. Geopolitical factors are essential to an understanding of historical militarism.

Indeed, though states have other purposes too, they have been *principally* concerned throughout recorded history with warfare. This is revealed in relatively advanced states in their financial accounts. In previously published research I showed that in the period 1130–1815 the English state spent the bulk of its revenue (and normally between 75 per cent and 95 per cent of all revenues spent on public functions) on war and preparations for war.[8] In this, it was typical of the European states of these centuries. And in research still in preparation, I find more or less the same devotion to war by states in classical Greece, Rome, imperial China and indeed throughout recorded history. So militarism is largely the province of – and the largest province of – the state. Capitalism arrived so late on this scene that it might seem that the mould was relatively firmly set.

So let us now examine the incidence of war. Has it greatly changed in the period of the emergence and development of capitalism? Here we can turn to the various compilations made by social statisticians. The first great study was Sorokin's *Social and Cultural Dynamics*, Vol. III, originally published in 1937.[9] For the nineteenth and twentieth centuries, especially outside of Europe, I have supplemented Sorokin with Singer and Small, and have checked the main trends against those reported in Wright and Richardson.[10]

Throughout the whole history of the West from 500 BC to the present day, the average state has been engaged in at least one open, organised war with another state in about 50 per cent of years. No states have a predominantly peaceful history: unexpectedly, Germany/Prussia has been the most peaceful modern state on this measure, engaged in war in only a third of the years from 1651 to the present day. But the fluctuation between states is only between one-third and just less than two-thirds (between Prussia and Spain, from 1476 onwards). A century of peace is unique to the case of Holland: 1815 to 1914. Since 1815, non-European states have enjoyed slightly more peace than the European states. There has been no tendency for the incidence of war to either increase or decrease throughout the period. In fact, measured just by the frequency of war, the eighteenth century was unusually warlike, the nineteenth century unusually peaceful, and the twentieth century just about average so far. Apparently, warfare has been a normal way of conducting international relations throughout recorded history. But *always* in conjunction with peace: war and peace succeed each other as the characteristic instruments of inter-state relations. These are therefore carried on in relatively rational, calculative forms, with an eye to the particular advantages in any situation of either war or peace. To these historic patterns of diplomacy, capitalism cannot have contributed much, one way or another.

A further sign of this is the recurrence of certain basic patterns of diplomacy enduring right through the period in which capitalism emerged. I will mention two such patterns. The first is found where no one state predominates in a multi-state system. In self-defence, and with an eye to its own potential aggressions, each power becomes embroiled in a fluctuating alliance system which is invoked particularly when one power seeks to attain hegemony. Thus certain characteristics of the diplomacy and wars which greeted the advent of Charles V and Philip II, of Napoleon and of Hitler were very similar. This is despite the many social-structural changes occurring between the early sixteenth, nineteenth and twentieth centuries, including the emergence of capitalism. The end result was the same of course: the humiliation of the would-be hegemoniser.

But it is an example of a second pattern which threatens us today: the rise and confrontation of two super powers. Here we must go back further for close parallels – to Rome and Carthage, or to Greece and Persia. In such cases, the two rivals hegemonise their neighbours until no neutral space is left between them. Then they encourage subversives in each other's domains and client-states, claiming, of course, that they stand for certain eternal verities – individual freedom against despotism, citizenship against oligarchy, progress against reaction, order against anarchy (of the four classical cases we lack only the Carthaginian version of the justice of their cause). Indeed, the final conflagration is part thrust upon, part provoked by the super powers, normally through the agency of the disorderliness of the subverted client-states (the revolt of some of the Greek colonies of Asia Minor against Persia; or faction fighting in Greek and Carthaginian city-states of Sicily). This is still the probable way in which the world will end – the contradiction of the uncontrollable clients. It is difficult to see in the modern version of the pattern much of a contribution from capitalism (or indeed from socialism). Imperialism, yes – but that is as old as the well-ordered state.

There are many other patterns besides these two. They are the staple diet of the theory of geopolitical militarism. They are also part of the consciousness of state élites themselves. They are, as the title of one academic text puts it, *Games Nations Play*.[11] They are the *same* games as we can see played out in the rather older texts of Herodotus and Polybius (which concern the two earlier cases mentioned of super power confrontation). In these respects little has changed.

In the sphere of war, the metaphor of 'the game' may seem in rather bad taste, like black comedy. One reason why the comedy keeps repeating itself is that the victors survive to dominate the next period, and usually to write history. When states neglect their militarism they perish: where are the Burgundies and Bavarias of yester-year? The consequence is that at any one point in time, the major states are almost certain to have benefited considerably from militarism. It is asking a lot of the United States and the Soviet Union to abandon their nuclear arsenals when their super power status emerged through two world wars which finished off their rivals. Thus the militaristic patterns are actually self-fulfilling prophecies. That is the main force of the theory of geopolitical militarism, one that still endures today.

But not all our militarism is patterned by such a long time perspective. In certain respects the geopolitical struggle *has* been revolutionised in our modern era. This is obviously true of the techniques of war and diplomacy. Here capitalism provided one of the major initial impetuses. No one would dispute this. In the last few centuries successive revolutions have occurred in the technology of weapons. More precisely this has led to an exponential growth in what military specialists call 'lethality indices'. Until the development of gunpowder, the capacity of armies to kill did not greatly increase through recorded history. The first jump, attributable to artillery in the fifteenth to eighteenth centuries, was not caused principally by the emergence of capitalism. But when capitalism pioneered industrialism, it proved capable of generating repeating rifles, heavy bore field guns, high explosives, tanks, ironclad battleships, fighter and bomber aircraft, submarines, rockets, and nuclear weapons. In the century from the 1870s to the 1970s, the lethality of weaponry increased a *billion-fold*, according to Robinson's estimates.[12] Luckily, the last and major part of this rise is still only potential. But in actual warfare casualty rates have nevertheless rocketed, though this tended to occur in two stages, rising almost three-fold in both the seventeenth century and the twentieth century. As we are nowadays well aware, the arsenals of the super powers are now sufficient to kill everyone on the planet in a matter of hours. Because of this we live in fear. Without capitalism's historical contribution we would probably not live in fear, but in poverty, in poor agrarian societies incapable of destroying each other.

In addition, by penetrating the whole globe, capitalism revolutionised international diplomacy. Nowhere is now outside of the diplomatic system or the military striking range of the super powers; and they have nowhere to expand which does not bring them into contact with each other. The entire world is a client-state system, threatened as a single entity by militarism. And again, without capitalism's historical contribution, this would not be so. Israelis and Arabs, black and white southern Africans, Cambodians and Vietnamese, would be threatened only by each other (plus, perhaps, the activities of any greater power adjacent in territory to them).

Third, these two changes have had an impact on the culture of militarism. It is a necessary part of militarism to value highly whatever qualities are thought useful to military efficiency. For most of history, these qualities centred upon martial physical valour. Thus physical violence was glorified. The fact that this no longer occurs to any significant extent should not blind us to the continued existence of high regard for military efficiency. Our sports may not be dominated by chariot races, gladiatorial combat or races in full battle gear, but our culture is permeated by the desirability of team discipline, of mathematically precise logistical planning, of split second timing: all qualities which are most closely paralleled in our society by the requirements of warfare. Similarly, as Randall Collins has brilliantly demonstrated, the era of trigger and push-button warfare has fostered the development of different emotional supports: from *ferocity* and *cruelty*, useful for killing people in physical combat, to *callousness*, useful for remote control killing.[13] Our militarism is impersonal, not in the service of gods against devils, but in the service of rational necessity.

Fourth, the capitalist era has directly implicated not just military personnel but the whole population in its militarism. Indeed, the military figures alone conceal this. Historical statistics exist as to the proportion of the size of the army to total population: the military participation ratio (MPR).[14] For what it is worth, the MPR in the West appears high in classical Greece, highest of all in the Roman Republic and Empire, and varies in the subsequent historical period – lowest in the twelfth century, growing considerably from the twelfth to the fourteenth, dropping in the fifteenth, rising in the sixteenth and seventeenth, dropping slightly in the eighteenth, greatly in the nineteenth, and then rising again in the first half of the twentieth century (but only back to the level of the thirteenth). Throughout the period from the twelfth to the twentieth century, the highest century's ratio (the seventeenth) is about three times that of the lowest (the twelfth). Variations in militarisation thus seem erratic and not attributable in simple fashion to the emergence and development of capitalism. Nevertheless this conceals two trends.

The first concealed trend is that if we were also able to include in the MPR 'civilian participation' through armament industries, then industrial capitalism would have a far more pronounced effect, especially in war-time. Here the only rivals would be ancient ones, some Greek city-states and the later Roman Republic and the Roman Empire. The second concealed trend is that the degree of total resource mobilisation (not just manpower) for militarism is also higher in the modern period than in previous European history. Even in peacetime, though our states today spend only half the proportion of their budgets on defence as their medieval counterparts did, as a proportion of Gross National Product it is assuredly far higher. What is often forgotten is how puny the medieval states were, and how marginal they were to the lives of most of their inhabitants. Not until the seventeenth century would any of them have spent as much as two per cent of estimated GNP; not until the Napoleonic Wars were they up to ten per cent. Now they disburse anywhere between thirty per cent and fifty per cent of GNP. And in the two major twentieth century wars, the major combatant states actually spent this proportion of GNP on war alone.[15]

With these two corrections made, there is only one historical period whose level of militarisation of social life in general approaches our own. It is the classical age, from the rise of Sparta and Athens to the triumph of Rome, especially the latter. Obviously even then a far higher proportion of total social resources than today would be spent on mere subsistence rather than on a 'luxury' like militarism. But in another sense their militarism exceeds ours – in its relentless stability. For around six centuries the Roman state spent about 75 per cent of its annual resources on its legions and navies, geared its 'class' structure, its citizenship, its political offices, its conception of virtue and honour to military exigencies.[16] If our militarism has the potentiality to so endure until AD 2500, it will assuredly destroy the world beforehand.

To even begin to regard our militarism as comparable to Roman militarism is to draw attention to its extraordinary strength and threat. For there is a similarity between our militarism and theirs which is most profound and terrifying – their capacity for popular mobilisation. In between these two eras, war was a matter for state élites and their clients and their clients' dependants – it was not diffused to the whole population. The citizen army, the mobilised economy, are to be found *only* then and now. (The exceptions are the armies of a few small city-states or tribal groupings. It is equally sobering to reflect that the only comparable pre-classical quasi-citizen army may have been the Assyrian. Read the Old Testament or visit the British Museum to catch the two main available glimpses of the terror *that* inspired.) The modern version of this level of mobilisation is *the nation-state*. This is the infrastructure of modern militarism which requires explanation.

We have found militarism to be highly traditional in society, probably caused by factors connected with the initial rise of the state and soon taking on patterns which have endured right through history up to today. Nevertheless, there are some modern characteristics of militarism. It mobilises the population as a whole – as it did previously only in classical Rome and to a lesser extent in classical Greece. And the techniques of militarism now encompass all populations everywhere. Thus something requires explanation from outside of the theory of geopolitical militarism. It seems to concern the relationship between the nation-state and capitalism. I turn to the second stage of the argument.

MILITARISM NECESSARY FOR CAPITALISM

It is time to define capitalism. The capitalist mode of production contains three main inter-related elements.

1. *Commodity production* – every factor of production is treated

as a means, not as an end in itself, and is exchangeable with every other factor. This includes labour.

2. *Private possession of the means of production* – the factors of production, including labour-power, belong formally to a private class of capitalists (and not to the state, the mass of labourers, the community, God or anyone else).

3. *Labour is free and separated from the means of production.* This is implied by 1. and 2. above. Labourers are free to sell their labour-power and withdraw it as they see fit; they receive a wage but have no claims over the surplus produced.

The definition itself contains nothing about states or militarism – and nor does any other definition of which I am aware. But do these characteristics presuppose militarism?

It is not difficult to see why these elements would have implications for states and militarism. Firstly, commodity production presupposes a set of universal rules defining the terms under which values are to be established and exchanged. The flow of comodities cannot be interrupted by numerous local rules and customs assigning fixed values to things. Thus, an unusual degree of long-distance political regulation backed up by force is required by capitalism. Second, private possession of the means of production and the full separation of labour are, in historical terms, extremely unusual. It is normal to find a multiplicity of overlapping individual, familial and communal rights to the means of production. Specifically, free labour is rare (and often confined to soldiers and foreigners). We should also note that full private ownership of the means of production runs counter to common sense. A large enterprise is worked co-operatively by workers, by those with managerial or scientific expertise, and by those who provide risk capital (to say nothing of also presupposing others who work in educational, communications and health infrastructures). Thus it is positively bizarre to regard those who provide the land or the capital as the sole proprietors! It is surely a safe bet that capitalism would need a large degree of political and military support to be introduced into regions where multiple property rights existed. It presupposes wholesale expropriation by military force.

Yet have these two functional requirements led capitalism to a higher level of militarism than any other historic form of imperialism? This seems doubtful. *Any* conquest requires the imposition of rules – whether relatively universalistic, as in the case of capitalist imperialism, or particularistic, as in most previous cases – and the expropriation of property. It is not capitalism's form that particularly encourages militarism, but its *success*. The European capitalist powers have provided the world with imperialism on a global scale – and extremely rapidly. Is this the source of the similarity with Rome, which had hitherto provided the most successful and rapid conquests in Western history?

But there is a problem confronting this analogy. Unlike Roman imperialism, capitalism, once institutionalised, seems to require relatively *little* maintenance by force. If basic rights to property are established then value can be set by the operation of supply and demand in markets. Furthermore, once capitalism entered its industrial phase, two other cases of force common in pre-industrial societies diminished. First, in agrarian societies increasing economic productivity usually meant increasing the intensity of labour. The usual means was to step up the level of coercion through slavery, serfdom or *corvée* labour. Through industrialisation, machinery increased the quality of labour and this did not usually entail coercion. Second, in agrarian societies the local peasantry is 'in possession of' the means of subsistence. If non-producers extract the surplus from them, this requires coercion. But after industrialisation, with an extensive division of labour and exchange of commodities, very few local groups are potentially self-sufficient. Extensive interdependence generally replaces local coercion (as Marx noted). In both respects, industrial capitalism diminished the significance of a form of militarism that had so far escaped my notice – local, non-state militarism. It is true, of course, that like any form of expropriation, capitalism will be defended by force if necessary by its dominant classes. Nowadays that is largely force wielded by the state. But in this respect it differs only from a wholly non-exploitative system of production. 'Class militarism' is not specific to capitalism – indeed it is less evident there than in most historic societies.

This combination of tendencies has led to the 'core-periphery' differences so typical of the development of capitalism. In each phase of its development, capitalism has contained an institu-tionalised, relatively non-coercive core and an expropriated, militaristic periphery. Its core has widened from the 'Home Counties' around the capital of countries like England, France and Spain from the late fourteenth to the sixteenth centuries; thence to the 200–400 mile diameter 'national' extensions of such counties, and to the 'Home Counties' of their client-states and imitators in the sixteenth to the early nineteenth centuries; thence to their entire national territories and to wider cores of their clients, imitators and 'white' colonies in the nineteenth and early twentieth centuries; thence to neo-colonial enclaves all over the world in the mid-twentieth century; and thence, most recently, to the emerging 'middle class' countries of South East Asia in the 1970s and 1980s. All the while, more and more of the globe has been caught up in the transition from 'backwardness', through an era of massive expropriation, coercive labour forms and military violence, to a more institutionalised integration into capitalism and free wage labour. The earlier phases of this movement have all been thoroughly charted by Wallerstein.[17] But it still continues today.

Thus we can begin to appreciate why capitalism has been regarded so variously as militaristic and pacific. It all depends where you look, and at what point in that locality's history. Furthermore, the unevenness has been heightened by particular military and geopolitical chronologies. As European capitalism expanded, it tended to encounter less and less advanced peoples (though the penetration of the Far East does not fit such a chronology). And simultaneously its own weapons were becoming exponentially more lethal. The military superiority of the core over the periphery became more and more pronounced. Quite small numbers of troops, ships and colonial garrisons were sufficient to dictate the terms of trade and expropriate property rights and labour, either directly or through local native élites. Thus militarisation of the periphery did not usually have major repercussions on the core. No European power required a high level of military mobilisation to sustain the capitalist part of its global imperialism. This cannot be the source of our society's closest resemblances to Roman imperialism.

MILITARISM NECESSARY TO THE MULTI-STATE SYSTEM

We must now discuss a second aspect of the militarism of the capitalist era. So far I have discussed the expansion of capitalism as if there were a 'one-to-one' relationship between capitalism, the state and military force. But there were, of course, *many* capitalist states. The overwhelming mass of military activity was not directed outwards by one capitalist state. Nor was it even directed by many capitalist states outwards against peripheral areas and states. Instead it was directed by capitalist states against each other. Why should this be so?

One point must be made clearly – there is nothing in the capitalist mode of production which itself 'requires' a multi-state system. The two are contingent. Indeed, the requirements for political regulation and military expropriation mentioned above would be met more efficiently by a single, universalistic state, at first European-wide, then global in scope. It is true that many historians argue that the multi-state system encouraged the competitive dynamism of capitalist development; that is competition between states, as well as enterprises, encouraged growth. I accept this argument. But if so, this was an empirical fact, not a functional requirement. The multi-state system was in place well before capitalism emerged. So, too, were the cores of about half the actual major powers of mature capitalism. And though the process of capitalist industrialisation encouraged the disintegration of some, and the growth of others, the personnel change among the leading powers was not noticeably greater or slower in the period of capitalist development and domination than it had been earlier. The multi-state system cannot be reduced to the requirements of industrial capitalism. Nor, therefore, can the fact of warfare between them, which we also saw earlier was a constant right through European history.

This point is rarely denied by the theory of militaristic capitalism. Instead it is ignored. Versions of this theory start with the individual geopolitical state as a given. They note, often correctly, the influence of capitalism upon its foreign policy and so conclude that war is inherent in the structure of capitalism. But that is only if we first assume that capitalism is structured by the boundaries of states. For example, the Marxist theory of imperialism argues that inter-capitalist rivalry under certain economic conditions will take a militaristic turn and precipitate wars, like the First World War. Regardless of the correctness of the economic arguments – which are usually disputed by historians – there is one large gap in the argument. Why should rivalry between capitalists be between 'national' blocs of capital?

Not a word in Marx, in Hilferding, in Lenin or in the rest of the orthodox Marxist tradition serves as an explanation of these factors. The most important point of all in the conflagration of 1914–1918 – that it was fought between nation-states: Germany, Austria-Hungary and allies against Britain, France, Russia (and later the US) and allies – is not explained at all. Nation-states are *presupposed* in the Marxist theory of imperialism.

Where do they come from? They need explaining, after all, for they were not there in medieval Europe. If we take, for example, the twelfth century states of Henry I in England, or Louis VII of France, or Frederick Barbarossa in Germany, we are not dealing with states with clearly defined territorial boundaries, with monopolistic powers over their people, or indeed with *any* direct relationship to the people as a whole. They were 'feudal' or 'patrimonial' states existing by virtue of particularistic, voluntaristic contracts made between sovereigns and lords, only reaching the people *through* such lords. Yet over the next centuries, through slow, unsteady and variable rhythm, they gradually became 'modern states' in Max Weber's sense, possessing universalistic, rule-making powers, backed up by a monopoly of the means of legitimate violence over a given territorial area. This territorial area began to be known in the sixteenth to nineteenth centuries as a 'national' area, and in the seventeenth to twentieth centuries the core people inhabiting them became a nation. (Obviously, the exact relations between 'nations' and 'states' have been complex and varied; some became multi-national rather than national; in other cases 'nations' existed before states.) These nation-states are the perpetrators of our era's extraordinary militarism.

I have discussed elsewhere, and at some length, the rise of these states.[18] There seem to have been two main, connected causes of their emergence and dominance up to the early nineteenth century: developments in military technology, and an economic expansion that became increasingly capitalistic in form. The feudal state's military function was to co-ordinate the levies 'freely' offered by its lords together with its own core (usually professional) retainers. Relying on the stone castle and the heavily-armoured horseman, it was well-suited to defending relatively small spaces against outside barbarians. But gradually it became obsolete in the later middle ages as first mercenaries, then trained mixed infantry/cavalry/archery armies, and finally armies with guns, successively wasted the lords' levies. Professionals, training and equipment required more central organisation and, above all, more money. Only states could eventually undertake this role. Those states – hitherto puny – that happened to be around became strengthened, if they could master the additional resources. This depended upon economic expansion, the second factor. Economic expansion disproportionately increased realisable wealth, that is, trade and money visibly entering market-places, and river and road toll-gates. It could be taxed more easily than land itself could be. The persons involved in such trade also needed protection, especially when operating abroad, and increasingly only the state could supply this. A symbiotic fiscal-military relationship grew up between states and dominant economic classes, cemented by constitutional forms enshrining the principles under which taxes could be extracted and wars undertaken. Paradoxically, every time they struggled over this, and whether or not the outcome of the struggle was despotism or constitutionalism, they cemented the universal, monopolistic, territorial, and national character of the state. This can be seen clearly in the changing nature of economic expansion itself. What had started out in the twelfth century as a highly trans-national economy, in which long-distance trade travelled virtually regardless of state boundaries, became increasingly *inter-national*, bounded and regulated by states. By the early nineteenth century the emerging economy of industrial capitalism was largely a segmented series of national economies, each one largely confined to the territory, the colonial dependencies and the client-states of the major powers. Capitalism was not encouraging transnationalism – quite the reverse, for it was *hardening* state boundaries.

This meant that neither capitalism nor industrialism was inherently pacific. They adapted to, and reinforced, a multi-state system in which international economic advantage was assisted, as it always had been, by a mixture of diplomacy and war. In any particular period the probability was that one power would be rationally attracted to war. For as yet the *costs* of war were not particularly severe.

The industrial phase of capitalism brought those massive and familiar changes referred to already. First it mobilised the people and brought them into this international society. The rise of the masses or the classes (according to one's perspective) is the most familiar story of modern social and political science. But it is not so often recognised that it is virtually the *same* story as the rise of the nation. Class consciousness and national consciousness rose up together. The economy and polity that the bourgeoisie, proletariat and peasantry became integrated into had already been established as a national one by the interplay of monarchs, lords and merchants over several centuries. Their participation converted it into a nation-state. Militarism became popularly mobilised.

We can easily exaggerate the force of this new militarism, however. It did not become more ferocious. Rather, relatively rational diplomatic decisions percolated downwards to the people as a whole. The balance of advantage to be gained from war rather than peace is rarely tipped decisively. Thus in the late nineteenth century the British masses probably began to gain somewhat from the successful imperialism of their state. At the same time the German masses would gain somewhat if Germany could acquire access to the British sphere of interest. Life and death did not depend on either, however. In fact, the balance of advantage was probably not dissimilar to that of English and Dutch merchants and commercial farmers in the late seventeenth century (or English, Flemish and Burgundians in the fourteenth).

The decisive tipping factor is really whether the war could be won at relatively little cost. Here we must always remember that in most of history, and in the medieval and early modern history of Europe, the costs of war were relatively low. That is why it was a relatively rational policy. But now came the second contribution from industrialisation: the increase in kill ratios and in economic mobilisation. Wars became so costly that they became, finally and wholly, irrational. However, the devastation increased so rapidly that each successive escalation was unexpected. It is characteristic of the nineteenth and twentieth centuries that the actual calculations of costs made before wars have been proved later to be severe under-estimates. But it is also characteristic that once the masses have realised this, they have recalculated and either rejected militarism (as in 1870 in France, 1905 in Russia, 1917–1918 in several countries) or demanded reform as a price for it. The relatively rational 'diplomatic game' concerned the peoples as well as the state élites and it now took novel, radical paths.

Finally, however, all these novel contributions, though pio-

neered by capitalism, became the common property of industrialism. Capitalism did make the late twentieth century a
uniquely dangerous place. There is no hiding place from nuclear
devastation and we must thank the tremendous vitality and
dynamism of capitalism for the predicament we find ourselves in.
But the danger would be maintained by *any* form of society which
did not abandon the level of technology bequeathed to it by
capitalism and which remained militaristic. The Soviet Union is
one such case; China is another. A revolution in the United
States, or Britain, or France, which established 'socialism in one
country', or Fascism, or a democratic empire, or whatever –
would also maintain the danger. Whatever we do about capitalism, the danger would remain. The *techniques* of danger are the
common property of industrial society. The forms of organisation
of these techniques will obviously differ. In the West large-scale
capitalistic industries have emerged with a close relationship to
the military arm of the state: 'the military-industrial complex'.
In the Soviet Union, the economic-military co-ordination is
wholly within state organisations. These particular organisations
obviously have a vested interest in war (unless they can quickly
diversify their activities) and are specific, highly-militaristic
interest groups. But as E. P. Thompson has argued – against
writers like Sir Solly Zuckerman – these are not the *sources* of
'the logic of exterminism'.[19] That source is the more general
militarism of societies involved in a multi-state system in which
warfare has been historically relatively rational. It is the common
legacy of industrial society. The techniques have ended that
rationality – but some élites and mobilised peoples still need
convincing!

CONCLUSION

I anticipated these conclusions in the six points listed near the
end of my introductory section. There is really very little that
is peculiarly militaristic *or* pacific about capitalism. The only
necessary connection has lain in the peripheral expansion of
capitalism which has always required a high level of expropriation of non-capitalist property rights. This expropriation still
occurs in the Third World today, but it is not easy to evaluate its
significance. For it has become closely entwined with the conflict

of the super powers. This, I argued, has very little to do with the nature of capitalism (or socialism). By far the greatest contributor to militarism is the multi-state system in which warfare has been a normal, and often rational, element throughout recorded history. If it is no longer rational (and hopefully not normal either) that is because of capitalism's unique and historic technical contributions to the methods of warfare. But even these contributions have become part of the general property of industrial societies.

Politically speaking neither the capitalism of the West, nor the state socialism of the Soviet Union, are the key enemies of those who desire peace and survival today. The enemies are rather the common geopolitical pretensions of the super powers – the *same* pretensions as Greece and Persia, Rome and Carthage, possessed, now rendered more technically alarming to the world. More particularly, the weapons of war are now so lacking in political discrimination that they render inappropriate any political strategy based on class or modes of production. Nuclear weapons cannot distinguish between classes or modes of production. Indeed, they can barely distinguish any more between individual states. In Europe, for example, geopolitical solutions on a continental scale are required – as the European Nuclear Disarmament Movement clearly recognises.[20] Capitalism may be worth fighting on other grounds. But on the agenda concerning our survival it should barely figure.

NOTES

1. P. Anderson, *Lineages of the Absolute State* (London: New Left Books, 1974) pp. 31–33.
2. A review article of much of this material which faithfully reproduces the silence is R. Jessop, 'Recent theories of the capitalist state', *Cambridge Journal of Economics*, 1977.
3. E. P. Thompson, 'Notes on Exterminism, the Last Stage of Civilisation', *New Left Review*, 121 (1980) and 'Protest and Survive' in E. P. Thompson and D. Smith (eds), *Protest and Survive* (Harmondsworth: Penguin, 1980).
4. M. Shaw, 'The Theory of the State and Politics: a Central Paradox of Marxism', *Economy and Society*, 3, 4 (1974).
5. H. Kissinger, *A World Restored* (New York: Grosset & Dunlap, 1964).
6. K. F. Otterbein, *The Evolution of War, A Cross-Cultural Study* (New Haven: Human Relations Area Files Press, 1970).
7. See also T. Brock and J. Galtung, 'Belligerence among the Primitives: a

Reanalysis of Quincy Wright's Data', *Journal of Peace Research*, III (1966); W. T. Divale and M. Harris, 'Population, Warfare and the Male Supremacist Complex', *American Anthropologist*, 78 (1976); B. Moore, *Reflections on the Causes of Human Misery* (Boston: Beacon Press, 1972).

8. M. Mann, 'State and Society 1130–1815: an Analysis of English State Finances', in M. Zeitlin (ed.), *Political Power and Social Theory*, Vol. 1 (Connecticut: Jai Press, 1980).

9. P. A. Sorokin, *Social and Cultural Dynamics*, Vol. III (New York: The Bedminster Press, 1962).

10. J. D. Singer and M. Small, *The Wages of War 1816–1965* (New York: Wiley, 1972); Q. Wright, *A Study of War* (University of Chicago Press, 1942); L. F. Richardson, *Statistics of Deadly Quarrels* (London: Stevens, 1960).

11. J. W. Spanier, *Games Nations Play* (London: Nelson, 1972).

12. J. P. Robinson, 'The Neutron Bomb and Mass-Destruction Conventional Weapons', *Bulletin of Peace Proposals*, 4 (1977).

13. R. Collins, 'Three Faces of Cruelty: Towards a Comparative Sociology of Violence', *Theory and Society*, 1 (1974).

14. S. Andreski, *Military Organisation and Society* (Berkeley/Los Angeles: University of California Press, 1971).

15. All these figures are only rough orders of magnitude. There are no accurate figures for GNP until the nineteenth century and since then there have existed several alternative ways of measuring state disbursement. See Mann, op. cit., and *The Sources of Social Power* (London: Tavistock, forthcoming) for details.

16. See K. Hopkins, *Conquerors and Slaves* (Cambridge University Press, 1978) and Mann, *The Sources of Social Power*, ch. 9, for details.

17. I. Wallerstein, *The Modern World System* (New York: Academic Press, 1974) and *The Capitalist World Economy* (Cambridge University Press, 1979).

18. Mann, 'State and Society 1130–1815'; see also several contributors to C. Tilly (ed.), *The Formation of National States in Western Europe* (Princeton University Press, 1975).

19. Thompson, 'Notes on exterminism'.

20. I discuss the implication of these remarks for the defence policy of the British Labour Party in 'Nationalism and Internationalism in Economic and Defence Issues' in J. A. G. Griffiths (ed.), *Socialism in a Cold Climate* (London: Allen and Unwin, 1983).

2 War, Imperialism and the State System: a Critique of Orthodox Marxism for the 1980s

MARTIN SHAW

We have lived through a transition at the beginning of the 1980s which has all the signs of being more fundamental than any since 1945. The start of the new decade coincided almost exactly with the Western decisions about theatre nuclear weapons and the Soviet action in Afghanistan. 1980–81, unlike previous crises in a twelve year cycle which goes back through 1968 and 1956 to 1944–45, has been overhung by the fear of war, even of the nuclear holocaust. The 'greatest international crisis' since the Second World War has threatened to swallow up the optimism generated in these previous years of change. True, there have been moments of hope to offset the more dangerous and damaging shifts in the international situation – in the rise of Polish Solidarity and the peace movement itself. But if long waves work in political history, the early 1980s threaten to mark a reversal of much that has been achieved throughout the post-war years.

This is an appropriate point at which to take stock of socialist theory. The desperate international conjuncture of the 1930s – fascism, Stalinism and world war – buried alive the classical Marxist tradition. Only slowly, in the years of the Cold War, was it possible to revive independent socialist thought. After 1956, the seeds of genuine new developments were sown. After 1968 the new tradition of socialist theory really blossomed, coinciding with the height of détente and the apparent evaporation of the Cold

47

War. The new Marxism, alert to the socio-economic contradictions of capital and the state, was based on the premise of
social revolt within advanced industrial states. It appeared to
come into its own as the post-war boom tailed off, and capitalism
headed into old-fashioned economic crisis, albeit with new twists
from state expenditure and oil prices.

The thinkers of the new Marxism shared – despite many
differences between them – the preoccupation with contradictions 'internal' to national societies and states. Although
naturally they saw the causes as arising from the nature of
capitalism itself, in its present phase, the manifestations were
primarily interior to specific societies. Nicos Poulantzas, in one of
his last works, produced an involved formulation which reflected
(if it did not clearly articulate) this common conception:

> It is, on the one hand, evident that the current crisis concerns
> the whole of capitalism-imperialism; this means that 'external
> factors', in the sense of external contradictions, intervene at the
> centre of the various social formations, where the reproduction
> of capitalism and the existence of the imperialist chain actually
> occur.

'But', he concluded,

> in the economic crisis, and more particularly in the political
> crisis, where the economic crisis is translated into political
> crisis, *the internal contradictions take primacy over the
> external factors, and this is also true for the crisis of the nation-
> state in the social formations where one finds such crisis.*[1]

It is difficult after the international events of the early 1980s to
assert this formulation with any confidence. As the Cold War
revives with a vengeance, arms spending spirals again and
'defence' becomes the cornerstone of many a state's budget, it
becomes clear that we are in a period where once more 'internal'
social contradictions can be overriden by 'external' political and
military crises. The two world wars and the period of cold war
may now appear not as gigantic exceptions to the 'normal' state of
capitalism, but rather as periods of high or active tension in a
world *generally* dominated by international conflicts. The new
international crisis raises questions as to how far the entire 'new'

Marxism has been premised on a systematic underestimation of international politics, warfare and the 'external' aspect of the state. Indeed, since most recent Marxist writing has rested on its appropriation of the classical tradition, it raises questions of this nature for Marxism as a whole.[2]

There are some indications of concern with this problem in recent work. Perry Anderson has criticised Marx for failing to register 'the great shift in the international state system' that accompanied the economic dynamism of capitalism.

> Marx assumed that capitalism would progressively mitigate and annul nationality in a new universalism: in fact, its development summoned and reinforced nationalism. ...A central theoretical silence on the character of nations and nationalisms was left, with very damaging consequences, to later generations of socialists.[3]

The question, 'What is the function and future of the nation-state?' is for Anderson one of the most insistent on the agenda of socialism.[4] He leaves it separate, however, from the pertinent questions in the Marxist theory of 'the state'. Tom Nairn, who has done more than anyone to remind us that the British State has a national character, and a contradictory one at that, puts matters more sharply:

> The main abstraction which has dogged analysis here is the idea that the functioning of British society and State can be explained wholly (or even mainly) in terms of the industrial economy and its 'relations of production' (the class struggle).

'There is', he goes on, 'a theoretical error at work here', and he then presents a brief formula which summarises the problem:

> All state-forms are the product of some specific historical balance between these internal factors and the external relations imposed by the world-system of capitalism.[5]

These nuggets, the value of which can be seen in Nairn's book,[6] are however buried in a footnote and not fully developed as a position.

Another direction from which the issue of the 'internal' and 'external' has been raised is in the work of the German 'state derivation' theorists and their British commentators. The central project of these writers is to 'derive' the capitalist state from the logic of the 'capital relation' itself. This is seen by John Holloway and Sol Picciotto as a materialist method, fundamentally superior to the assumption of the 'autonomy' of the state and politics made equally by Poulantzas and Ralph Miliband in their debate.[7] The emphasis on the 'logic of capital' is heavily derivative of Marx himself, and so in general produces little recognition of the special national character of state forms. When, however, the world market – the relations of which Marx deliberately excluded from *Capital* – is brought in, this method has allowed relevant questions to be posed. Claudia von Braunmühl, in an article which effectively undermines much of the rest of this school, raises the economic basis for 'derivation' to the level of the world market, and argues that

> The world market must be seen as an international state-organized and specifically structured, all-encompassing international context of competition, within which statehood arises and consolidates itself and states form their characteristic economic, social and political structure.[8]

The reference to 'state-organization' of the world market indicates, however, that states do not simply derive from, but also shape, the market. But when we move beyond such features as colonialism and protection, to consider inter-state competition as a whole, especially in its more extreme manifestations such as militarism and war, this qualification seems far too weak. Can we really derive the arms race from the world market? Does not the autonomy of the state, denied by the 'derivatists' in the context of internal class struggle, re-emerge with a vengeance in the logic of inter-state competition?

Von Braunmühl's position has been developed further in two articles by Colin Barker, who has carried out a small one-man crusade to attack Marx's assertion that:

> The executive of the modern state is but a committee for managing the common affairs of the whole bourgeoisie.

Barker insists that

The simple fact is that the bourgeoisie is a *world* class, an *international* class of exploiters and parasites that runs a *world* system of production. Capitalism, from its beginning, presupposed a world market. But the state form within the capitalist mode of production is decidedly not a world state, but a system of national states whose relations with each other are antagonistic. The *whole* bourgeoisie does not have, cannot have a state...When we talk of the capitalist state, we always mean the nation state, or rather the nation-state system.[9]

This polemic, apart from proposing that the Marxist theory of 'the state' should be replaced by a theory of 'states', has a serious merit in recognising the reality of the 'nation-state system'. Instead of von Braunmühl's derivation of states directly from the world market, Barker seems to allow space for the logic of inter-state relations to themselves shape the nature of states. (He blurs this position, however, in pursuit of another polemic against 'state derivatists' such as Holloway and Picciotto, Altvater and Offe, who have argued that the state of its nature can never act as a capitalist.[10] Barker is not content to rest with a legitimate objection to a rigid, *a priori* division between the categories of capital and state. Following the current tendency of the school associated with *International Socialism*, he argues for a concept of 'the state as capital'. Despite his disagreements with the 'logic-of-capital' school and some careful qualifications of the 'state-capitalist' argument, Barker ends up sharing the reduction of the state to capital which is now common to the two schools on which he draws.[11])

To recognise the reality of the system of nation-states, and its role in shaping the individual states within it, is surely to accept at least an initial autonomy of this system. If then we posit, as Barker does, a historical tendency of capital and states to 'fuse' in national units, in the course of international competition, it cannot be assumed that it is states which are conforming more and more closely to the general concept of capital. On the contrary, it may be that capital accumulation and the world market are becoming increasingly subordinate to the political and military necessities generated in the nation-state system. The historically overriding nature of strategic and military interests, and their often indirect relation to economic interests and market relations, is surely difficult to dispute. In short, instead of 'the state as capital' we might inscribe on our theoretical banners 'capital as state', as a more accurate and dialectical account of current trends in the world system.

This residual economic reductionism, even in those writings which alert us to the importance of the state-system, is reminiscent of so much else in Marxism. Indeed, it is particularly general in Marxist explanations of international relations which have been crippled by a conception of world economy in which states are reduced to a subordinate role. This inevitably takes us into Marxist discussions of imperialism, and to Lenin's work which, while much criticised, has succeeded in imparting its deepest deficiencies to its critics, as well as its admirers.

THE ARCHAISM OF LENIN

The most simple question to ask of Lenin's theoretical production in 1916–17 is this: why did he write two separate pamphlets, *Imperialism* and *The State and Revolution*? Both were written under the impact of war, as their characterisations of the capitalist economy and state bear witness, and yet the two subjects are treated entirely separately, with the links between them systematically suppressed. All sorts of contingent reasons for the separation may be adduced, but the anomaly remains striking: all the more so as it has been communicated to most subsequent Marxist writing on both subjects.

Lenin's *Imperialism* is widely understood today as a model and an explanation of the relations between advanced capitalism and the backward regions of the world. This was indeed a part of its purpose, but like most of Lenin's writings it served much more immediate ends. When Lenin came, in his uncensored prefaces of 1917 and 1920, to underline the political purpose of the work, it was the explanation of World War I which he brought to the fore:

> It is proved in the pamphlet that the war of 1914–18 was imperialist (that is, an annexationist, predatory, war of plunder) on the part of both sides; it was a war for the division of the world, for the partition and repartition of colonies and spheres of influence of finance capital, etc.[12]

It also served a particular function as a 'criticism of Kautskyism', which Lenin saw as an 'international ideological trend' of social-democratic and petty-bourgeois pacifism.[13] In the light of these political aims, there is a strikingly anachronistic logic to the theoretical purpose of *Imperialism*:

> to present, on the basis of the summarised returns of irrefutable bourgeois statistics, and the admissions of bourgeois scholars, a *composite* picture of the world capitalist system in its international relationships at the beginning of the twentieth century – on the eve of the first world imperialist war.[14]

In one sense, the aim is unimpeachable: to show the historical roots of the armed conflict of states in the competitive struggle of monopoly capital *before* 1914. In another, it was already, at the very time of its writing, a preoccupation with the problems of the past. The world war was changing capitalism so rapidly that a picture of the system at the beginning of the century, on the eve of the war, could not possibly be adequate as a picture of the capitalist world during the war – let alone as an indication of the post-war future.

Time and again, Lenin's attempt to link the pre-war world of classical imperialism and finance capital, the world of Hobson and Hilferding, with the world of the war, comes up against the limitations of the data and analysis he is using. 'Capitalism in its imperialist stage', he writes, 'leads directly to the most comprehensive socialisation of production';[15] but the most radical form of this socialisation, state ownership and control, is hardly broached in this analysis. 'Monopoly!' he exclaims. 'This is the last word in the "latest phase of capitalist development"'.[16] One would hardly guess that this 'last word' had already been superseded during the war, in which states in all the belligerent countries had taken huge powers of control over national economies. The world of state-regulated national capitalisms loomed, and imperialist war was the essential lever for its creation. But Lenin was still wholly preoccupied with the growth of monopoly out of free competition: a process which according to his own authorities went back to the 1860s, and was *definitely* accomplished at 'the beginning of the twentieth century'.[17]

Lenin laboriously investigates the links of industrial capitalists and banks: he does not refer to state finance, which the war had brought dramatically into view. He presents a portrait of the 'financial oligarchy', but wholly fails to investigate its links with the state and military. He presents his crucial evidence of the export of capital without indicating how the war had distorted the capital-accumulation process, leading particularly to the expansion of 'militarism as a province of accumulation' (already analysed by Rosa Luxemburg before the war).[18] Only when Lenin considers the 'division of the world among capitalist associations' does he finally mention in passing 'how private and state monopolies are interwoven in the epoch of finance capital'; but this only in the context of private profit 'at the expense of the state'.[19] Lenin's account of the 'division of the world among the great powers' begins with the argument, obviously essential to his whole purpose of explaining the war, that 'the colonial policy of the capitalist countries has *completed* the seizure of the unoccupied territories on our planet. . . . so that in the future *only* redivision is possible'.[20] But instead of proceeding to analyse the form of the struggle for redivision, he reverts immediately to an account of classical colonial expansion. Although he stresses imperialism as a system of contending powers fighting for the redivision of colonies and spheres of influence (this is the point of his polemic against Kautsky), Lenin gives hardly any attention to the consequences of this for the economic and political structure of capitalism.

The popular 'Leninist' account: imperialism = monopoly + export of capital + colonialism, follows therefore fairly closely from the logic of Lenin's own presentation in the main text. Only if we take sharp notice of his prefatory remarks on the censorship, of the polemic against Kautsky, of the goal of proving the 'annexationist, predatory plundering' character of the 1914–18 war, can we see the more contemporary problems which Lenin raises – but fails to answer. *Imperialism* is about a system driven to war; it leaves out of consideration not only the processes of war, but the state machines which fight it. It is about the economic structure of war-crazy capitalism; it leaves out the economic role of the state. Its argument was anachronistic in 1916, and is all the more so today.

The missing dimension of *Imperialism* is formally provided by *The State and Revolution*. But the complementarity is largely superficial: the later work only confirms the archaic division in Lenin's thinking between the economic and the political. If the state has only a walk-on role as coloniser in *Imperialism*, so imperialism and war are only the haziest of backgrounds to *The State and Revolution*. Lenin's first work is a *Hamlet* without the

Prince, his second gives us the Prince without the State of Denmark.

Once again, Lenin's preface is sharper than the text itself. The preface opens with a dramatic characterisation of the merger of state and capital, a theme almost absent from the main texts of both his pamphlets:

> The question of the state is now acquiring particular practical importance both in theory and in practical politics. The imperialist war has immensely accelerated and intensified the process of transformation of monopoly capitalism into state-monopoly capitalism. The monstrous oppression of the working people by the state which is merging more and more with the all-powerful capitalist associations, is becoming increasingly monstrous. The advanced countries – we mean their hinterland – are becoming military convict prisons for the workers.[21]

The political context, too, is clear: the imperialist war, and the 'miserable bankruptcy' of the opportunists in it, above all Kautsky.

There is no doubt that this context provides the most powerful impetus to Lenin's substantive argument that the state machine must be 'smashed and destroyed'. More than once he refers to the 'extraordinary strengthening' of the state machine in the epoch of imperialism, and to 'an unprecedented growth in its bureaucratic and military apparatus'.[22] Lenin is certainly aware of the gigantic march of the state since Marx's day, and he uses this argument to deal with the thorny problem of the latter's suggestions about 'peaceful' transitions in countries such as England and the United States. Marx had restricted the 'smashing' of the state to the Continent:

> Today, in 1917, [Lenin writes] at the time of the first great imperialist war, this restriction made by Marx is no longer valid. Both Britain and America, the biggest and the last representatives – in the whole world – of Anglo-Saxon 'liberty', in the sense that they had no militarist cliques and bureaucracy, have completely sunk into the all-European filthy, bloody mass of bureaucratic-military institutions which

subordinate everything to themselves, and suppress everything. Today, in Britain and America, too, 'the precondition for every real people's revolution' is the *smashing*, the *destruction* of the 'ready-made state machinery' (made and brought up to 'European', general imperialist, perfection in those countries in the years 1914–17).[23]

The term 'bureaucratic-military state' appears regularly in Lenin's pamphlet as a *description* of the modern state. Analytically, however, militarism is relegated to a subordinate place in Lenin's account. So concerned is he to base his theory closely on Marx and Engels themselves, that Lenin derives the existence of a special public power, the 'special bodies of armed men', entirely from 'the irreconcilability of class antagonisms'. Not once does he give specific, independent weight to the conflicts among national ruling classes, as a cause of the growth of the state. If Lenin had allowed himself to analyse this growth in the period of the war directly, he could not possibly have avoided the conclusion that the *main* reason for the growth of the state, of the 'special bodies of armed men', was the inter-imperialist conflict. But looking at it through the prism of Marx' and Engels' writing, he gave the overwhelming weight to internal class struggle. Militarism was introduced not as a cause of the state's expansion in general, but in its consequences for class struggle in particular – 'in connection with the intensification of repressive measures against the proletariat both in the monarchical and in the freest, republican countries'.[24]

The political rationale for *The State and Revolution* was radical, in relation to contemporary Marxism in general and even to Lenin's own previous thinking.[25] The proposition that the Marxist theory led to the conclusion of smashing the state broke with the generally-held view. But the theoretical method by which this conclusion was reached – essentially no more than an extended exposition and commentary on the views of Marx and Engels developed many decades earlier – was profoundly limited. Despite the descriptive incorporation of some changes in the state, Lenin's basic conservatism is clear. He does not place the changes where they belonged, at the centre of an analysis of the modern state. The state is not treated specifically as an instrument of imperialism and war. The role of the state within the national economy – the 'state intervention' which the 1914–18 war brought clearly into focus – is never tackled. There is more descriptive integration of the themes of imperialism and the state than is to be found in *Imperialism*, but the theoretical integration is just as absent.

BUKHARIN'S LOST LEGACY

Part of the archaism and conservatism of Lenin's work can be explained – as can most things in Lenin's works – by direct reference to the political situation in which he was writing. On the one hand there were the external constraints: the censorship, for example, which limited Lenin's comments on the predatory, annexationist tendencies of the main powers – and especially Tsarist Russia itself – in the war. Even more important were the limitations of Lenin's own purposes: the attack on Kautsky, the erstwhile champion of Marxist orthodoxy, partly dictated the appeal to the founding fathers in the pamphlet on the state. But crucial as these political reasons undoubtedly were, they cannot explain away the weaknesses which we have outlined.

The theoretical character of Lenin's work is all the more striking when we consider that he was in direct contact, before writing both his pamphlets, with the much more radical ideas of Nikolai Bukharin. Indeed, Bukharin – with whom Lenin at first violently disagreed – did influence Lenin towards the conclusion of smashing the state.[26] But Bukharin had achieved, in his book *Imperialism and World Economy*, published the year before Lenin's, and in his article 'Towards a Theory of the Imperialist State', also completed in the year prior to Lenin's parallel work, a theoretical integration of the themes of imperialism and the state.[27] This Lenin did not match.

Bukharin's work had the great advantage of dealing directly with the changes in world capitalism evident during the 1914–18 war. Its difficulties are very much the opposite of Lenin's: where he underestimated the transformation, Bukharin has inclined to draw too absolute conclusions from the war situation. Bukharin started, as did Lenin, from Hilferding's analysis of 'finance capital'; he concluded, as Lenin was also to do, that world competition between monopoly capitalists led logically to imperialism and war. But where Lenin, as we have seen, was largely to accept, unchanged, Hilferding's model of national capitalism, Bukharin developed a striking new one. National economies were being transformed, he argued, into 'state capitalist trusts', in which industrial and financial capital were merged with the state. The war was the lever for this structural transformation, but the effects would be permanent: the future belonged to 'state capitalism', in the sense of a system of competing state-directed and state-organised national economies.[28] Bukharin depicted this decisive shift sometimes as a tendency, sometimes as accomplished fact. In the first case there can be little doubt as to the accuracy of his concept in anticipating a major direction of twentieth-century capitalism; in the second, the argument is open to attack on the grounds of exaggeration and over-generalisation.

For Bukharin, modern imperialism was inherently state-dominated, and inter-imperialist competition was inherently economic, political and military at the same time. The corollary of this is that the state is to be analysed specifically as the *imperialist state*, its tendency to external expansion and war-making being a decisive part of its nature.[29] Bukharin saw the modern state as a predatory, even piratical, institution on the international level, and at the same time a means of total domination in the national society. He expressed, more clearly than anyone else, the logical outcome of the belief of most revolutionary socialists, that the war was undermining any basis for bourgeois democracy and leading to the creation of the 'monstrously oppressive', 'military convict prisons', which Lenin described. As Stephen Cohen puts it, 'Bukharin foresaw, however idiomatically, the advent of what came to be called the "totalitarian" state'[30] – in his terms 'militaristic state capitalism', the 'barracks society'.

The anarchy of capitalist production was now, according to Bukharin, transposed to the international level. Crisis was the expression, not of cyclical trends within national economies, but of conflicts between them. War was the ultimate form of this crisis, and the context within which proletarian revolution developed. Bukharin developed these notions in an even starker way in a work written at the height of the civil war in Russia: his *Economics and Politics of the Transformation Period* (1920).[31] In this book he not only saw war between imperialist states as the harbinger of proletarian revolution, but advocated 'socialist war' by the revolutionary state against capitalist states, as the decisive method for extending the socialist revolution.

In the context of the civil war, the dangers of the simplification involved in Bukharin's particular formulations became very clear. Although as Cohen shows, Lenin shared Bukharin's profoundly mistaken euphoria about 'war communism',[32] in Bukharin's own case the over-generalisation of the transition in capitalism was the logical pre-condition for this conclusion. By presenting the capitalist system and states as wholly militaristic, Bukharin laid the basis for casting the socialist alternative in the same mould.[33]

Sixty-five years later, despite a second world war and several decades of preparation for a third, we can see the highly contradictory character of the tendency towards state capitalism depicted by Bukharin. The gigantic growth of the activities of the state, the specific weight of these activities, the coordinating and manipulative role of the state within national economies, the strong economic, political and military rivalries between nation-states: all these can hardly be gainsaid. But the trend towards the internationalisation of capital (originally highlighted by Bukharin in his *Imperialism*) also remains, manifested particularly in the growth of multinational firms; the international integration of economic activity continues apace, undermining even the deepest of political-military divisions between states (such as the East-West conflict); the degree of unification of national economies is highly variable, and of state regulation even more so; the extent of state control over the national economy remains highly controversial, not only between classes but also within national ruling classes. The potential for military conflicts of many kinds (even, Mary Kaldor has argued, among the powers of 'the West' themselves)[34] is still strong, and is a most powerful lever for state economic control: but it is far from having produced a simple militarisation of economy and society on a world scale. Our overall judgement must be that what Bukharin produced was a powerful indicative analysis of an emerging set of relations, and in this sense his work remains a far better starting point than Lenin's. But the complexity of the system, the existence of counter-tendencies, the resilience of older economic and political structures, not to mention the manifold changes since his day, all require a careful development and qualification of his insights.

THE DISINTEGRATED CRITIQUES OF LENIN

The displacement of Bukharin's theses on imperialism by Lenin's

– which testifies to the influence of Stalinism on Marxist debate – has been almost total in the subsequent literature. In general surveys and collections such as Tom Kemp's *Theories of Imperialism* (London, 1967) or Roger Owen and Bob Sutcliffe's *Studies in the Theory of Imperialism* (London, 1972), Bukharin is lucky to receive a fleeting mention or bibliographical note. Only one previous writer has given his ideas their proper place: Lelio Basso who commented that 'it is odd that Bukharin is the only one among the three major Marxist students of imperialism we are considering who amply, and correctly, points up the importance of the role the State plays...' and who sees Bukharin's book as 'richer than Lenin's, although less vigorous'.[35]

Few writers have escaped the limitations of Lenin as a basic reference point. A major English-language work which comes close to doing so is Paul M. Sweezy's authoritative *Theory of Capitalist Development*, written in the early stages of World War II. Sweezy's starting point is Marx, and the greater part of his book assumes 'a closed and freely competitive system', which he acknowledges does not exist in modern capitalism. His initial treatment of the state is in this context. His discussion of imperialism, however, develops the connection between militarism and imperialism, and deals – if not in any great depth or detail – with the effects on the state. So far as these are concerned, Sweezy observes

> on the one hand a vast expansion in the power and functions of the state, and on the other hand the decline of parliamentarism. These are not two separate movements but rather two aspects of one and the same development which is connected in the closest way with the economic and social characteristics of imperialism in general.[36]

After Sweezy it becomes more common to find coherent criticisms of Lenin on either imperialism or the state, considered in isolation, but rare to find any discussion which clearly links the two topics. The underlying aim of both Lenin's and Bukharin's *Imperialisms*, to understand the modern capitalist system as a whole, including its political and military phenomena, no longer finds such an echo. Much of the interest in imperialism arose directly from the concern with 'underdevelopment' and the struggles for national independence in the colonial and semicolonial countries. It arose in a period in which capitalism was expanding economically, and political and military rivalries between Western nations were subsumed in the global conflict of East and West. The discussion of the state was even slower to revive, coming to fruition only in the 1970s when 'détente' had made even the East-West conflict of less immediate importance. These circumstances may help to explain why critics of Lenin have not only failed to challenge, but have even exacerbated, his artificial theoretical division of imperialism and the state.

A very large part of the literature on imperialism has been concerned almost exclusively with the mechanisms of the economic relationships between advanced capitalism and the backward countries. Lenin's theory has been treated mainly as an explanation of these relations. Thus Arghiri Emmanuel has redefined imperialism in terms of 'unequal exchange', not export of capital.[37] Samir Amin has analysed the 'unequal development' of capitalism in the 'centre' and 'periphery'.[38] While Bill Warren has put forward the view that 'underdevelopment' is not a logical consequence of imperialism: according to his very radical account, reminiscent of Marx's writing on nineteenth century India, the export of capital, trade and internationalisation of capital in general only lead to economic growth on a world scale.[39]

What these diverse critiques, with their sharply different conclusions, have in common is a reduction of imperialism to its economic consequences for the colonial (now ex-colonial) countries. None of them is centrally concerned with the structure of imperialist capitalism itself, or with the competition and conflict between imperialists. Nor are they concerned with the role of the state, except insofar as a discussion of colonialism itself inevitably reflects on state policy, or where Warren gives credence to the positive economic effects of political independence in the ex-colonial countries.[40]

The strength of economism in the general approach to imperialism is demonstrated by a critique from a very different direction. Michael Kidron manifestly was concerned with the structure and dynamic of capitalism in the metropolitan countries; his theory of the 'arms economy' focused on the economic consequences of the central inter-state conflict of the post-war world, the rivalry of East and West. But Kidron, too, was preoccupied with the economic mechanisms in isolation. For him, arms expenditure was a substitute for the export of capital, the magic 'leak' from the closed system of capital reproduction which offset the tendency of the rate of profit to fall and so staved off economic crisis.[41] Because he identified imperialism in general with the export of capital, he argued that imperialism itself had been displaced.[42] There was something highly paradoxical here: the arms spending which Kidron recognised as economic fact was in reality an expression of the dominance of political-military conflict in the world system. Obviously the East-West arms race reflected a change in the particular character and ideological colouring of such rivalry since Bukharin's day: but in other respects it corresponded closely to the model of fused economic-political-military competition which he saw as the essence of modern imperialism. Kidron, while borrowing the language of universal 'state capitalism' from Bukharin, gives little autonomy to the 'state' aspect of the system.[43]

Closely complementing the economism of Marxist critiques of Lenin on imperialism, we find a definite 'politicism' in the discussion of the state. From pioneering texts such as Ralph Miliband's *State in Capitalist Society* (London 1969) and Nicos Poulantzas' *Political Power and Social Classes* (London 1973), to most of the subsequent debate, there is a preoccupation with the processes of bourgeois rule rather than with the actual machinery of the state. Criticisms tend to dwell on dimensions of bourgeois democracy neglected by classical or recent authorities – as for example in Leo Panitch's recent discussion of the articulation of trade unions with the political system. Much of this discussion does not necessarily conflict with the underlying logic of Lenin: it can be seen, as Panitch puts it, as an attempt 'to move beyond the abstract formalism and level of generality that tended to characterise earlier work'.[44]

The nub of the discussion is, however, the extent to which the 'democratisation' of the capitalist state renders Lenin's conclusion of the need to 'smash' the state invalid. Parliamentary democracy has been consolidated, as Therborn documents,[45] in a larger number of capitalist states. A major part of the activity of states has become concerned with securing the 'welfare' of the population: the bureaucracies of the 'welfare state' have consumed a large proportion of state expenditure.[46] It has therefore been suggested by Eurocommunists such as Carillo that it is no longer possible, necessary or desirable to 'smash' the state.[47] A range of other writers, including both Miliband and Poulantzas, who still believe that parliamentary change is insufficient for the achievement of socialism, argue that the parliamentary framework is very deep-rooted. Socialism can be achieved by a combination of a parliamentary movement and extra-parliamentary mass institutions, which will themselves represent a modification of the state.[48]

What such analyses have underestimated – apart from the parallel growth of the traditional repressive apparatuses of police and prisons (the 'strong state') – is the expansion of the military functions of states. We are all familiar enough with the enormous proportions which world military expenditures have assumed in the period of 'peace' since 1945. Two processes are involved: the maintenance of permanently high levels of military preparedness by the super powers and their allies, and the emergence of new states which greatly increased the numbers of centres of military power. For a long time, in the 1960s and 1970s, the significance of these phenomena was largely hidden from socialist analysis. 'Détente', together with a relative reduction in military expenditure in the major powers (as a proportion of total state spending or GNP),[49] combined with the emergence of major social and economic contradictions to mask the continuing importance of militarism in the advanced North. The political face of 'Third World' militarism, the spread of military dictatorships, enabled us to limit militarism in the South to the context of internal social revolt. Despite the proliferation of local and regional wars in the last 35 years,[50] despite the evidence of enormous military build-ups in major 'Third World' states,[51] Marxist analysis has been unprepared for the logical conclusion of this process. Fixated on an 'imperialism/underdevelopment' analysis, it has no obvious explanations for increasingly active 'intra-Third World' militarism, let alone for its potentially nuclear form.

The Marxist debate about the state, far from developing the connection between capitalist expansion and the militarism of states which even Lenin suggests, or bringing it up to date, has largely remained within a highly one-sided reading of Lenin. The arguments have centred around the concept of 'smashing' the state, understood overwhelmingly as a conclusion from the 'internal' class struggle. The possibility that the 'external' context might have a crucial bearing even on this argument, has hardly been imported into the discussion.

CONCLUSIONS

The Marxism of the 1980s must be developed in a radically different context from that of the whole of the period from 1945. Economically, socially, politically, the situation has altered very drastically, and theory must respond to these changes. One of the most important, perhaps the most crucial of all of these, is the change in the world situation which has brought militarism to the fore again. We need to criticise the 'Marxism of the seventies' (of the period after 1968), and its particular reconstruction of important problems within the Marxist tradition. We need to re-evaluate not only the arguments about the imperialism and the state, between Lenin and Bukharin, but also the arguments about war, particularly between Lenin and Luxemburg, as I have suggested in a previous article.[52]

It is not possible to put forward developed analyses of all the problems broached in this article, but some basic theses may be advanced, in order to clarify some of the arguments and stimulate further discussion.

1. We need to recognise theoretically the existence of a world system of states, as an analytically separable level within an understanding of world society as a whole. This system of states pre-exists capitalism, indeed it was in part the framework within which capitalism developed, although it has also been transformed by it. The competition of states, with war as the ultimate means of resolution of conflicts, is integral to this system. This competition also pre-existed, therefore, and is not reducible to, the competition of capitals. However, as both capitalist and inter-state competition have developed to higher levels, there has been a tendency for the competitions of states and capitals to fuse, and for individual states to become more integrated with the capitals within their territories. This tendency to integration certainly entails, as Marxist analyses generally lead one to expect, that states will take account of the interests of their 'national capital', as well as being limited by the economic resources of those capitals. At the same time, however, this integration strengthens states within national societies, and given the monopolies of states on legitimate violence, together with the many other levers available exclusively to them, enhances their ability to impose their definitions of national interest on capitals. Hence the

competition of states has a tendency to dominate, and even to override, the competition of capitals in the strict sense. This tendency becomes extremely manifest in war, but it exerts a powerful influence at all times.

2. This recognition of the state-system has implications for our conceptions of world economy. This aspect has been least explored in this article, but we may suggest some points relevant to models generally employed by Marxists. Insofar as a world economy exists, in the sense of a world market, with world trade, internationalisation of capital, etc., this has never been anything like a pure market economy, as implied at least by the more abstract models which Marxists have used. It has always been, and remains very much, fragmented by the state-system: a state-segmented world economy. This point, in fact, was implicit in all the classical conceptions of imperialism. The economic significance of colonialism was not that it was undertaken, in each and every case, to secure particular investment possibilities, but that it created large state-protected segments of the world economy within which particular national capitals could operate freely. The end of colonialism has in fact increased the segmentation, as the number of states has grown dramatically. Although some of these new states are extremely weak and prone to continuing political and economic domination, all the signs are that a large number are using their power to some degree to control economic relations within their segments.[53]

   This model leads us to suggest that it was theoretically false to suggest, as many accounts of Communist and 'Third World' countries' economic prospects have done, that the choice is between submersion in or withdrawal from 'the world market'. This does not exist, in any strict sense, since patterns of trade, investment, etc. are mediated everywhere by the state system. Even between economies which are formally (even ideologically self-consciously) 'market economies', international economic relations are always partially relations between states. States can only ever be concerned with the degrees of openness of 'their' economies to capitals based in other states.

3. 'The state', as others have pointed out, does not exist: what we are concerned with are nation-states within the context of a system of states. The individual nation-state is indeed the product of the totality of 'external' and 'internal' relations in

which it is involved. Formally, as a territorial unit, as well as substantively, in the complex of economic, political, diplomatic and military relations, each state is largely determined by its role within the state-system. At the same time, it is determined by the economy, class relations, political system, culture and ideology of the national society within which it is based. This national economy, and the individual capitals within it, are of course themselves directly affected by competition with other national capitals; and indeed national politics, class struggle, culture and ideology are embroiled in further international relations. This points us towards the concept of a highly complex totality of a nationally-segmented world society in which both capitalism and the state-system are only two levels. The individual nation-state is the product of many relations within this.

This concept of the nation-state does not lead us to a one-dimensional 'militarist' concept of the state, as in Bukharin's 'imperialist pirate state' or even Lenin's 'military-bureaucratic' description. It is consistent, up to a point, with the emphasis of much recent analysis on the state as itself a complex of apparatuses (repressive, ideological, etc.). The point of our critique of theories of the Western democratic state is precisely how elements of formal and even substantive 'democratisation' have coexisted with powerful militarist tendencies. The complex determination of the nation-state implies varied, even contradictory, institutional forms within each state. A crucial issue is how, when and why particular imperatives and institutions become dominant for and within a particular state. To say that military imperatives have a greater inherent capacity to override others, still leaves us with many precise questions about the occasions on which this happens. The combination of increased military spending and welfare cuts in Western states such as the USA and Britain raises these issues sharply at the present time.

4. The competition of states within the state-system has always given rise to the tendency of states to dominate other states, or to control people and territory outside the given scope of existing states. The forms of such domination, both in previous historical periods and in the epoch of capitalism, have varied very greatly. The tendency has, however, always been associated with the very existence of states.

To approach the question in this way has very radical implications for Marxist concepts of imperialism. 'Imperialism' can, of course, be restricted as a term to particular forms of domination, by defining it as a tendency of mature capitalism. It can even be denied, by definition, that it is fundamentally a matter of political relations at all: imperialism may be seen simply as a process of economic exploitation (however that is defined) of 'backward' by 'advanced'. Classical Marxism, however, saw it as a complex of political and economic relations: even Lenin's definition, if it underplayed the role of the state, nevertheless insisted that the territorial division of the world was a basic component. At times Marxist accounts can be seen as differing from non-Marxist ones not so much about the nature of imperialist domination (colonialism, territorial redivision) as about its causes in a particular period (monopoly capital, capital export).

Marxists have, in any case, used the term 'imperialism' far more widely than would be justified by this particular economic context or explanation. Lenin himself consistently referred to Tsarist Russia's annexationist tendencies as 'imperialism',[54] although clearly Russia was a net importer of capital from the advanced Western capitalist economies. Tony Cliff has suggested that Japanese imperialism in the 1930s was actually based on the import of capital.[55] More recently, Fred Halliday has analysed Iran under the Shah as a form of 'sub-imperialism', because it was building up its armed forces in order to dominate its immediate region in alliance with the global power of US imperialism.[56]

These examples show imperialisms – and it seems mistaken to quibble about the label – developing in a variety of socio-economic contexts within modern capitalism, just as forms of imperial domination have existed in other socio-economic periods. It makes more sense to define imperialism as a general tendency of states, the particular forms of which are partially determined by the economic relations within which states exist, than to try to restrict the term to particular economically-conditioned relations. This approach does not divorce politics from economics, or state from mode of production, since at its most basic states only have the capacity to dominate militarily or politically when they can mobilise sufficient economic resources. Tsarist Russia, indeed, is an example of a state with a large but backward economy which attempted to dominate smaller but economically more advanced countries, and compete with other economically more powerful states. In the end, by 1917, the contradiction was too great.

The analytical importance of breaking the narrow mould of Marxist theorising about imperialism is not just to survey it on a wider historical scale, or even to be able to compare US and Soviet forms of domination. Above all, at the present time, its relevance is that indicated by Halliday's case of Iran. We are seeing an unprecedented competition between states on a continental, regional and local scale throughout the world, with the rise of many ambitious new military powers. Marxists cannot afford to write as though a handful of advanced Western states still controlled the world, or as though the only opposition to them were revolutionary, when the expansion of capitalism and the state-system has created a much more complex system of national ruling classes among whom the most intense rivalries are now developing.

NOTES

1. Nicos Poulantzas, 'The Political Crisis and the Crisis of the State', in J. W. Freiberg (ed.), *Critical Sociology* (New York: Livington, 1979).
2. For a more direct exploration of these themes in relation to the politics of war, see my *Socialism and Militarism* (Nottingham: Spokesman, 1981).
3. Perry Anderson, *Considerations on Western Marxism* (London: New Left Books, 1976) p. 115.
4. Ibid., p. 121.
5. Tom Nairn, 'The Future of Britain's Crisis', *New Left Review*, 113–114 (Jan.-Apr. 1979) p. 52n.
6. Tom Nairn, *The Break-Up of Britain* (London: New Left Books, 1977).
7. John Holloway and Sol Picciotto, 'Introduction: Towards a Materialist Theory of the State', in Holloway and Picciotto (eds), *State and Capital: A Marxist Debate* (London: Edward Arnold, 1978).
8. Claudia von Braunmühl, 'On the Analysis of the Bourgeois Nation-State within the World Market Context', in Holloway and Picciotto, op. cit., p. 167.
9. Colin Barker, 'The State as Capital', *International Socialism* (new series), 1 (July 1978) p. 19.
10. Colin Barker, 'A Note on the Theory of Capitalist States', *Capital and Class* 4 (Spring 1978) pp. 120–124.
11. When the 'state capitalist' analysis of Russia was first developed in Tony Cliff, *Russia: A Marxist Analysis* (London: International Socialism, 1963) a

great deal of emphasis was laid on the extreme and exceptional character of 'bureaucratic state capitalism' in relation to capitalism in general. It is now frequently argued for by 'proving' that Russia is 'capitalist', and any 'exceptionalism' is specifically rejected (see Peter Binns and Mike Haynes, 'New theories of Eastern European class societies', *International Socialism*, 7 (Winter 1980)).

12. V. I. Lenin, *Imperialism: highest stage of capitalism* (Moscow: Progress Publishers, 1966) pp. 7–8.

13. Ibid., p. 10.

14. Ibid., p. 7, emphasis in original.

15. Ibid., p. 23.

16. Ibid., p. 27.

17. Ibid., p. 18.

18. Rosa Luxemburg, *The Accumulation of Capital* (London: Routledge & Kegan Paul, 1963) pp. 454–467.

19. Lenin, op. cit., p. 67.

20. Ibid., p. 71.

21. Lenin, *The State and Revolution* (Moscow: Progress Publishers, 1965) p. 5.

22. Ibid., p. 31.

23. Ibid., p. 36.

24. Ibid., p. 31.

25. See Marian Sawyer, 'The Genesis of *State and Revolution*', *Socialist Register*, 1977, pp. 209–227.

26. Ibid.; also Stephen Cohen, *Bukharin and the Bolshevik Revolution* (London: Wildwood House, 1974) pp. 34–43.

27. Nikolai Bukharin, *Imperialism and World Economy* (London, 1972) and article summarised in Cohen, op. cit., pp. 28–31.

28. 'State capitalism' in this sense is obviously to be distinguished from 'state capitalism' in the sense of a totally state-owned economy, as analysed by Cliff, op. cit.

29. In an earlier article, 'The theory of the state and politics', *Economy and Society*, 3, 4 (1974) pp. 429–450, I pointed out one implication of Bukharin's theory of imperialism for the theory of the state, namely the fusion of state and organised ruling class. Like others, I was then unaware of his direct characterisation of the state as 'imperialist'.

30. Cohen, op. cit., p. 31.

31. Reprinted in Bukharin, in K. J. Tarbuck (ed.), *The Politics and Economics of the Transformation Period* (London: Routledge & Kegan Paul, 1979).

32. Cohen, op. cit., pp. 96–97.

33. For a critique, see my *Socialism and Militarism*.

34. Mary Kaldor, *The Disintegrating West* (Harmondsworth: Penguin, 1978).

35. Lelio Basso, 'An Analysis of Classical Theories of Imperialism', in Bertrand Russell Centenary Symposium, *Spheres of Influence in the Age of Imperialism* (Nottingham: Spokesman, 1972) pp. 122, 125.

36. Paul M. Sweezy, *The Theory of Capitalist Development* (London: Monthly Review Press, 1968) pp. 319–320.

37. Arghiri Emmanuel, *Unequal Exchange* (London: New Left Books, 1972).

38. Samir Amin, *Unequal Development* (Hassocks: Harvester, 1976).

39. Bill Warren, *Imperialism: Pioneer of Capitalism* (London: Verso, 1980).

40. Ibid. pp. 184–185.

41. Michael Kidron, *Western Capitalism since the War* (London: Weidenfeld & Nicolson, 1968).

42. Kidron, 'Imperialism: highest stage but one', in *Capitalism and Theory* (London: Pluto, 1974).

43. Kidron, 'Two insights don't make a theory', *International Socialism*, 100 (July 1977).

44. Leo Panitch, 'Trade Unions and the Capitalist State', *New Left Review*, 125 (Jan.-Feb. 1981) p. 21.

45. Göran Therborn, 'The Rule of Capital and the Rise of Democracy', *New Left Review*, 103 (May-June 1977).

46. Ian Gough, 'State Expenditure in Advanced Capitalism', *New Left Review*, 92 (July-Aug. 1975) p. 61.

47. Santiago Carillo, *Eurocommunism and the State* (London: Lawrence & Wishart, 1977).

48. Ralph Miliband, *Marxism and Politics* (Oxford University Press, 1977) pp. 154–190; Nicos Poulantzas, *State, Power, Socialism* (London: New Left Books, 1978), pp. 251–265; Geoff Hodgson, *Socialism and Parliamentary Democracy* (Nottingham: Spokesman, 1977).

49. Gough, op. cit., pp. 61–62.

50. For a list of wars see Appendix to Istvan Kende, 'Local Wars 1945–76', in Asbjørn Eide and Marek Thee (eds), *Problems of Contemporary Militarism* (London: Croom Helm, 1980).

51. For the striking case of Iran under the Shah, see Fred Halliday, *Iran: Dictatorship and Development* (Harmondsworth: Penguin, 1979).

52. Shaw, op. cit., pp. 27–30.

53. As indicated above, this is one of the secondary themes of Warren, op. cit.

54. Notably in the preface to *Imperialism*, op. cit.

55. Cliff, op. cit., pp. 178–180.

56. Halliday, op. cit.

3 Raymond Aron's Sociology of States, or the Non-Relative Autonomy of Inter-State Behaviour

JOHN HALL

WHY WRITE ABOUT ARON?

Personal impressions are notoriously tricky and untrustworthy, and often reveal more about the viewer than the object perceived. Nevertheless, the best way that occurs to me of highlighting the aims of this chapter is to record my own impressions of two taken-for-granted assumptions that lie at the back of the renewed interest in war, state and society. The first such piece of un-questioned background consensus is that the received canon of classical social theory, that is social theory excluding, for example, Clausewitz, has not deeply concerned itself with war and the military. Put so bluntly, this first assumption is of course quite wrong. Roughly speaking, in most of human history mili-tary activity, from raiding to organised warfare, has been the most obviously sensible and rational form of behaviour given the prevalence of poverty, disaster and famine. Many classical social theorists – above all Saint-Simon, Comte, Spencer and, more recently, Veblen and Schumpeter – knew this well; indeed this becomes obvious once we recall that their thought centres on the belief that industrialism creates sufficient to allow the businessman to replace the warrior, and peace to take the place of war. So it is only in a more specific meaning that we can make sense of the assumption noted: classical social theory tended to ignore war and its agents in the modern world since it felt that

71

the bandwagon of history had left such matters behind it. It is easy to understand why social theory took this character. Between 1815 and 1914, the European theatre *was not* excessively troubled by war; instead the drama of the age *was* that of industrialisation, and Gladstonian hopes for 'peace, retrenchment and reform' were quite amazingly generalised. The failure of 'post-classical' social theory to concern itself extensively with war is, however, deeply reprehensible, and tells much about the academicisation of the social sciences, that is, our ability to work within the confines of received paradigms rather than trying to confront historical experience more directly. And this brings me to the second background assumption.

The very fact that the poverty of social theory concerned with war is noted indicates the desire to improve matters. What sort of character is social theory concerning itself with war and its agents going to take? Now it is both honourable and a sign of continuing intellectual vitality that Marxists or those heavily influenced by Marxism have played the biggest role in pointing to the paucity of social theory concerning war. My second impression is that the demands and character of Marxism are coming to shape social theory now interesting itself in war. As is well known, modern Marxists are refined, academic and far removed from earlier entirely comprehensible but 'Stalinist' versions of Marxism. This distancing from the founding fathers is often regrettable; but it makes sense as far as the subject matter of this chapter is concerned, for Marx himself, albeit Engels went some way beyond him,[1] was very much a nineteenth century man, offering only occasional comments on relationships between war, state and society in the modern world. But Marxists have never been deterred by this and have sought to argue that the development of Marx's conceptual apparatus will, in the last instance, allow us to understand such matters. Lenin and Rosa Luxemburg are, of course, hailed above all others in this respect, but attention is now being accorded to Bukharin, Liebknecht, Trotsky and C. Wright Mills.[2] The 'last instance' of a fully developed Marxist theory concerned with war and the military has not yet arrived, and the adding of warfare to an already inflated list of relative autonomies looks at first sight worrying for the whole enterprise. But the ultimate aim of the approach remains the same: the occurrence and character of warfare can only finally be explained in terms of the needs of economic systems based on class. This is a powerful claim, as is its implicit corollary that socialism will be pacific, and it deserves to be considered in the open.

Nothing in what follows hinges on the correctness or falsity of my impressions which, as noted, seek to highlight the aims of the chapter. The first point to stress is that while recent mainstream social theory has ignored war, Aron has not done so. Bluntly, the circumstances of his life did not allow him to retreat to academic comfort: he encountered the rise of Nazism in Weimar Germany first hand, witnessed the collapse of France in 1940 (itself in part the consequence of the effect of the First World War), and spent most of World War II in London, commenting on the encounter of the 'two revolutions' as a key member of the editorial team of the Free French review *La France Libre*. Since 1945 Aron has had a second career as political commentator for, in turn, *Combat*, *Le Figaro* and *L'Express*, and in this role he has written and been forced to define his views on virtually every major diplomatic and strategic crisis in the post-war world, perhaps most famously in 1957 when his *La tragédie algérienne* caused a furore by advocating an independent Algeria. It is impossible to exaggerate the quality of Aron's uncollected analyses, although some impression of his capacity as educator can be gained from his critical dissection of American nuclear strategy, *The Great Debate*, and from his analytic history of post-war American foreign policy, *Imperial Republic*. But Aron's most significant contribution for our purposes results from his assessment of classical social theory in the light of twentieth century history. This is most obvious in his celebrated *War and Industrial Society*, the conclusions of which Aron has recently reviewed,[3] which bluntly dismisses the pacific hopes of the prophets of industrialism – even though Aron himself has a separate reputation as the foremost exponent in our period of the industrial society thesis. More important, however, are his two treatises, the very size of which makes it extraordinary that his contribution has been ignored. *Peace and War* was avowedly written in order to spell out the theoretical principles that lay behind his political commentaries, whilst his more recent *Penser la guerre, Clausewitz* is a labour of love seeking both to understand the character of a conceptual system and to demonstrate that its central tools retain their validity in the nuclear age. Now the central theme of these books is the second point which I wish to highlight in this essay. Aron's whole intellectual career has been an attempt to come to terms with Marxism, and his work on state behaviour is one of the key elements in his critique of Marxism. His central message is simple: economic systems do not explain the origins of warfare which is instead the result of completely autonomous political factors which Aron wishes to outline.

The minimum claim to be made about Aron's sociology of states is that it is high-powered and worthy of general consideration. But in fact I would assert more than this, namely that Aron's basic conceptual position and the consequent critique of Marx are in fact correct. Now Quentin Skinner and John Dunn have recently demonstrated how much confusion can result when endorsement merges with description to produce a mish-mash that is neither proper intellectual history nor sustained abstract critical discussion.[4] It is certainly the case that Aron's thought needs to be historically located, notably in his experience in Weimar Germany and in the stance he took on his return to Paris towards the Soviet Union: but this is not the place to situate Aron's thought in any detail.[5] I shall try and remain faithful to Aron's intentions here: most immediately by separating description and assessment, and more importantly by remaining as aware as possible of the danger of conflation.

THE ASOCIAL SOCIETY OF STATES

A paradox lies at the heart of Aron's work in international relations. It is very clear that Aron is a descendant of Machiavelli, Hobbes and Kant in believing that the crucial characteristic of the inter-state arena is that it takes place in a state of nature under no higher law. It is not surprising to find Hobbes being quoted approvingly:

> . . . . yet in all time Kings, and Persons of Soveraign authority, because of their independency, are in continuable jealousies, and in the state and posture of Gladiators; having their weapons pointing, and their eyes fixed on one another; that is, their Forts, Garrisons, and Guns, upon the Frontiers of their Kingdoms; and continuable spyes upon their neighbours; which is a posture of war . . .[6]

States, in other words, jealously guard their independence and traditionally regard the resort to war as a natural option always open to them. It is, of course, the case that many thinkers – Hobbes, Sartre, Pareto – have claimed that violence dominates *every* sphere of life, or, more precisely, characterises the inside of states quite as much as their external behaviour. Aron is deeply opposed to this idea. A society is something which at best can allow a community to participate in some conception of the good life; socialisation into such an entity is to be profoundly welcomed since it represents, simply, the chance of civilisation. Aron has made this point very forcefully recently in a criticism of the theory of Pierre Bourdieu that socialisation itself is a form of 'symbolic violence':

> A curious vocabulary because it no longer enables one to distinguish between different modes of socialisation: on the one hand, the inevitable and diffuse *influence* on individuals of the social group which tends to reproduce resistance, whether conscious or not, on the part of those who feel the pressure of social milieu and authority. Violence only retains a specific meaning when it designates a relationship between men which comprises the use of physical force or the threat to use physical force.[7]

This is a very typical passage and shows Aron's high valuation of the duties due to the societies which give them their very humanity. The absence of this common socialisation defines the character of international relations.

The basic argument of the book, then, sees war as a normal recourse given the independence of separate states. Thus it is very paradoxical indeed that Aron chooses as a legend to his book the observation of Montesquieu that:

> International law is based by nature upon this principle: that the various nations ought to do, in peace, the most good to each other, and, in war, the least harm possible, without detriment to their genuine interests.[8]

In order to understand this paradox we can do no better than to note Aron's summary of what he considers the key to Clausewitz's system, namely the final, trinitarian notion of war:

> War, considered in its concrete totality, is composed of a

strange trinity: the *original violence* of its element, the hatred
and hostility that must be considered as a blind natural
tendency; *the play of probabilities and chance* which make it a
free activity of the soul; and the subordinate nature of a
political instrument by which it belongs to the *understanding*.
The first of these terms is related to the people; the second, to
the military commander (*Feldherr*) and the third, to the
government.[9]

Aron considers that Clausewitz's final definition of war was
leading him to a rejection of the Napoleonic absolute war to
extremes which had earlier so impressed him, and towards something like an appreciation of Montesquieu's maxim. For in a
balanced system of competing states the extension of war to the
extreme cannot but be self-defeating since it will result in
countervailing alliances capable of eventually whittling down the
most brilliant of victories. Thus Aron suggests that by the end of
his life Clausewitz was beginning to reassess his two heroes,
Napoleon and Frederick II, since he had come to realise that the
limited wars of Frederick had in fact achieved far more in the
long run than had all Napoleon's revolutionary glory.[10]

This paradox is so important as to merit further illustration,
and these lie easily at hand since Aron's own interpretation of the
crucial conflicts of the twentieth century stress the disasters
consequent on allowing war to run to extremes, beyond the
control of politicians. The war that began in 1914 is seen by
Aron, in common with virtually all serious historians, as the result
of traditional state rivalries, rather than, as Marxists claim, the
result of imperial rivalries displaced into the European theatre.
But if the outbreak of war was the result of normal state rivalries,
its 'total' nature was altogether new, and Aron explains the
'escalation to extremes' in two ways.[11] Firstly, the character of
the war resulted from it being the first extended conflict in the
European theatre in which the means of warfare were supplied by
industrialism. This 'technical surprise' led almost inevitably to
total war; the changed character of warfare was perhaps best
symbolised by the emergence of Lloyd George from the Ministry
of Munitions to the Premiership in 1916. Secondly, however, Aron
stresses the important consequences of the involvement of the
people on the social and political stage – an involvement
symbolised in the introduction of conscription in preparation for

or under pressure of war. Conscription in itself increased the size of conflicts through the sheer size of the armies involved, but its greatest impact was more subtle. The classic European wars of the eighteenth century had been fought over dynastic claims of one sort or another, and had often been resolved by the ceding of a minor piece of territory. Bismarck's wars had been of essentially the same, limited type, but popular pressure began to change this. Thus, there was anger at the restrained treatment Bismarck showed in dealing with defeated France in 1870. The fact that a nation had to be mobilised meant that the aims of war became generalised in terms acceptable to the people. How quickly the war to defend little Belgium became a 'war for democracy' or a 'war to end all wars'! But although Aron so clearly understands why politicians allowed themselves to become little more than appendages to the war effort, he nevertheless judges them very severely. Bluntly, they failed in their duty of keeping the aims of war in clear view – in part because they themselves often succumbed to a false doctrine whereby peace could only be conceived as a result of destruction. In particular, the Allied politicians in 1917 refused to take the risk of opening peace negotiations at a time when the advent of America should have made them aware that victory would eventually be theirs. And the consequences of 'total victory' are judged by Aron to have been very great. Most immediately, the Russian Revolution was made inevitable by internal pressures resulting from defeat in war. More immediately disastrous, however, was the effect of the Versailles Treaty upon Germany. This treaty made the terrible mistake of alienating Germany when it should have been realised that a strong Germany was necessary if a European balance of power was to be maintained. This alienation was effected by making Germany own to a war guilt she did not feel. In this way was Hitler given the cards whereby he could construct an ideological and imperial regime that precipitated another world war. And Aron is just as harsh on the misjudgements made by Allied politicians. In a magisterial chapter critically analysing the origins of the Cold War, Aron judges especially severely Roosevelt's combination of suspicion about Western European colonies and idealism as to Russian intentions.[12] The details of his account do not concern us. But the import of his argument is clear: the war, and in particular the way in which it was conducted, was responsible for the spread of socialism in Eastern

Europe. There was, in other words, no inevitable logic to history whereby this could have been predicted, and Aron is very suspicious of those who write about Eastern Europe without a sufficient sense of the historical process whereby 'actually existing socialism' was established.

On the basis of this general standpoint, Aron addresses three sets of problems: the nature of explanation possible in international affairs, the exact nature of the contemporary world scene, and reflections on the courses of action, the praxeology, open to us. Something needs to be said about his views in each of these areas.

Aron insists that international relations cannot produce anything like a closed field of study and that, consequently, it is foolish to expect finality from anything that is dubbed theoretical. This is true to some extent in economics where no theory can legislate whether we should maximise at the moment or restrain ourselves in favour of future generations. But Aron argues that the area of uncertainty is very much smaller in economics as a result of the very considerable sway that a single objective, the maximisation of economic resources has over behaviour. International relations theory cannot be anything like as closed as this because no single aim can be ascribed to state behaviour. This essential equivocacy in reality is illustrated by Aron in pointing out the weaknesses in two theories that falsely ascribe to inter-state behaviour a single aim. The first of these theories suggests that states act in the national interest. The weakness of this theory is its vacuousness as national interest can be defined in different ways:

> ... whatever the diplomacy of a state may be, nothing prevents one from asserting after the fact that it was dictated by considerations of 'national interest', as long as 'national interest' has not been strictly defined.

> Indeed, the so-called theory of 'national interest' either suggests an idea as undeniable as it is vague – that each actor thinks first of itself – or else tries to oppose itself to other pseudo-theories, for example that the foreign policy of States is dictated by political ideology or moral principles. Each of these pseudo-theories means something only in connection with the other. To say that the Soviet Union conducts its foreign affairs on the basis of its 'national interest' means that it is not guided by ideological consideration, by its ambition to spread Com-

munism. Such a proposition is undeniable, but to conclude from it that the rulers of a non-Communist Russia would have had the same diplomatic policy between 1917 and 1967 is simply absurd. The purpose of the empirical study of international relations consists precisely in determining the historical perceptions that control the behaviour of collective actors and the decisions of the rulers of these actors.[13]

The second pseudo-theory that Aron himself has remorselessly criticised, is related to this in that it argues that states are concerned to maximise only one end, namely, their power. Aron's initial objection to this is simply that power is a means, which may or may not be embraced, towards different objectives which can include a simple search for independent glory, for empire or for the sway of an ideology. The second objection to this pseudo-theory is that it leads to a false praxis which fails to take account of historical specifity. The failure on the part of American strategic thinking over Vietnam is illustrated below, but it can be stressed immediately that Aron objects on the general grounds that the falsely rationalist definition of 'the search for power' tends to suggest, against Clausewitz, that peace is but an interruption to wars and not the aim and end of war.

The purpose of Aron's approach now becomes obvious. The fact that certainty is impossible does not mean that we cannot have the conceptual tools necessary to 'think war' in all its diversity. This Kantian search for the proper conceptual apparatus was most fully undertaken by Clausewitz, the freshness of whose *On War* can be seen in part with the aid of Aron's own recent commentary; Aron's own conceptual tools in *Peace and War* might well have been sharper if he had at that time known Clausewitz better. This is especially the case in the definition of war; *Peace and War* would have attained greater impact had Aron realised earlier the conceptual clarity of Clausewitz's trinitarian definition of war. As it is, Aron bases his concepts around the simpler definition of war as a 'continuation of politics by other means'. This allows him to introduce the figures of strategist and diplomatist, and to characterise force as a means of foreign policy. To this he adds that international systems can be bipolar, as today, or multipolar, as in the eighteenth century; and this variable must be considered in relationship with another, namely that of the heterogeneity or homogeneity of culture of the states involved. All these factors lead to a certain 'rapport of forces' between the contending states. This in itself would lead to re-emphasising that the management of strategic relations is more of an art than a science (something in which Aron has come to follow Clausewitz closely). Since the number of factors involved in a duel between opponents means that rigid calculation is beyond scientific powers, as in chess, judgement alone can be taught (and this remains capable of beating chess computers).[14] But Aron attempts his own demonstrations of the essential uncertainty involved in international affairs when discussing the goals of foreign politics. Here, Aron shows that states can choose goals that go beyond mere security and, characteristically, he chooses to emphasise that such choices, given the international state of anarchy, are felt to be, and often indeed are, sensible and rational. A clear example of the dangers of mere security was one that Aron himself experienced, namely the refusal of France to consider military action against Hitler at the time he occupied the Rhineland; here the search for security at all costs proved self-defeating.[15] And Aron goes further in adding an essential indeterminacy, namely that states sometimes choose to participate in power for its own sake, and so prefer to take risks rather than to lead a secure and peaceful life:

> Even the desire for revenge is not more irrational than the will to power. Political units are in competition: the satisfactions of amour-propre, victory or prestige, are no less real than the so-called material satisfactions, such as the gain of a province or a population.

> Not only are the historical objectives of political units not deducible from the relation of forces, but the ultimate objectives of such units are legitimately equivocal. Security, power, glory, idea are essentially heterogeneous objectives which can be reduced to a single term only by distorting the human meaning of diplomatic-strategic action. If the rivalry of states is comparable to a game, what is 'at stake' cannot be designated by a single concept, valid for all civilisations at all periods. Diplomacy is a game in which the players sometimes risk losing their lives, sometimes prefer victory itself to the advantages that would result from it.[16]

One apposite example of this has been offered by Aron very

recently. Where Western nations abandoned their colonies when they become more expensive than they are worth, Aron insists that Russia retains her interest in Eastern Europe although in the process she thereby damages her own standard of living.[17]

The conceptual tools offered by Aron help us to 'think' war in any society. But they will scarcely carry conviction unless he is able to undermine the view, held by Marxists and classical sociology, that social conditions can account for warfare. Now we have already seen Aron arguing that the social conditions of 'democracy' and industry change the character of war. But he remains insistent that society conditions rather than determines war. He has no difficulty in dismissing two material factors often considered as determinants of wars.[18] The first suggests that the search for space, or the character of space possessed, exercises a profound causative effect on war. This theory is perhaps a peculiarly French one, and it is perhaps treated so kindly out of respect for Montesquieu. But Aron's conclusion is characteristic; space provides a circumstance to which men must react, but there is no certainty that they will react in the same manner. Poor soil can depress, but can also encourage trade; and the hills around the Mediterranean Basin have produced dissimilar cultures. The second supposed social determinant is population. Whilst Aron is quick to note that overpopulation can provide an all too rational reason for war, he nevertheless insists that not all wars are due to population factors. The French Empire, for example, was gained at a time when the population was actually falling.

Such social causes are relatively easy to reject, and Aron devotes much more attention to the thesis that wars can be explained in economic terms. Aron has analysed most closely the Marxist view of imperialism. Such theories explain the imperialism of late nineteenth century Europe or twentieth century America as necessitated either by the search for new markets (Lenin's position), or the need for new areas in which to invest capital (Rosa Luxemburg's position).

Aron does not dispute that arguments over empire had occurred, and notes that the rules of the European state system had been covertly broken in the case of Morocco in that Germany's position as a great power had not been duly recognised in tangible rewards.[19] Aron also recognises many of the realities noted by Lenin and Rosa Luxemburg, especially the increase in industrial monopolies and the fact that war, once declared, partly became defined in terms of economic objectives. But the war is not for all this considered as made inevitable by the problems of capitalism. Very much to the contrary, Aron presents a series of banal but forceful arguments designed to refute the Marxist position. Most obviously, Marxism fails to pay account to a great deal of data that does not fit its theory. The excess capital of France in the late nineteenth century, for example, found outlets in South America and Russia with ease, and was generally unwilling to invest in North Africa – not surprisingly, given the generally poor rate of return. And an explanation is offered for the claims made by politicians that colonies *would* produce profits:

> Marxist historians have a tendency to believe that all statesmen choose to dazzle their listeners with visions of power and glory, whilst all the time, in reality, they are motivated by an unavowable passion for economic gain. In this particular instance, I suspect that the contrary is true: the statesmen of the time were exploiting an economic argument – frigid, passionless, but rationally acceptable to their contemporaries – in order to disguise their dreams of political grandeur – dreams which found their expression in the sight of the banners of France floating proudly over Saigon or Rabat.[20]

More importantly, Aron knows enough economics to disagree profoundly on simple Keynesian grounds with the Marxist insistence that capitalism suffers from over-production necessitating imperialism. He insists that there is no reason whatever in principle why capitalism cannot prosper by almost indefinitely expanding the home market, and rightly observes that, with a few significant exceptions, the West has done precisely this since 1945. And Aron adds an important corollary to this. If it were the case that advanced capitalism's overproduction crisis necessitated colonies, how is it in any way possible to explain the miracle of Western post-war economic growth *in conjunction with* decolonisation? The nub of Aron's case for an independent Algeria was that the colonial market was small and that productive factors are anyway not fixed but capable of being redirected elsewhere and that any reform policy seeking to raise the standard of living of local inhabitants would cost far in excess of any possible return. This general line of argument is also seen at work in his careful analyses of American economic imperialism. Characteristically, he seeks to distinguish different phases and areas of such imperialism. In careful and considered argument he disentangles economic from political aims of American foreign policy in Europe, and concludes that certain economic favours granted to America are probably best explained as the result of its providing troops for European defence.[21] However, Aron believes that the presence of American multinationals in Europe has probably helped rather than hindered European economies, and has thus counterbalanced the great stocks of non-convertible dollars. On the other hand, Aron does argue that it is quite appropriate to talk of economic exploitation in other parts of the world where multinationals repatriate all their profits.[22] But here too his case is balanced. With very few exceptions, such exploitation is not strictly necessary (and in the case of South East Asia thus certainly cannot explain American involvement in Vietnam) since Western countries have basically prospered since 1945 by trading *with each other*; thus he dismisses the notion that the West depends on the exploitation of the Third World, fearing, to the contrary, that the greater long-term danger might well be complete lack of interest by the developed world in what happens outside its own confines.

If imperialism is not an economic phenomenon, how are we to explain it? Aron provides us with a political theory of imperialism designed to take the place of flawed Marxist notions. In a world in which states rival each other, it can be perfectly sensible to pursue glory and prestige, and states certainly act in this belief. This explains why France, afraid of losing its status as the result of Germany's rise, took the scramble for Africa so seriously *despite* objective facts such as slothful industrialisation and population decline which in the abstract might have encouraged passivity. And this general view has served Aron well in his recent interpretation of the American involvement in Vietnam.[23] Aron rejects the Marxisant notions of American 'revisionist' critics asserting that the needs of the American economy dictated involvement as highly implausible. Instead, Aron sees the American involvement as the traditional phenomenon of a great power, acting perhaps arrogantly and certainly not, especially from its own point of view, intelligently, seeking to uphold alliances at any cost. Remembering the hopes of Comte and Spencer, Aron notes firmly that the aims and character of the war were determined by civilians, indeed largely by intellectuals; this as much as the events of the twentieth century belie the belief that only warriors would be 'militant'. Similarly, Aron was by no means surprised that the triumph of socialism in South East Asia did not, *pace* Marx, lead to peace. The war between Hanoi and Peking merely goes to show the autonomy of inter-state rivalry.

Two final social determinants of war are considered more briefly by Aron, namely the quality of regime and the very existence of national states. His thought constantly oscillates on the matter of the importance to give to the type of regime in certain circumstances. There is no doubt in his mind but that the shared faith of Russia and China made the split between them especially venomous; but the fact of the split does not surprise him given the natural rivalry between states. Similarly, Aron is prepared to admit that the conflict between Russia and America is exacerbated by heterogeneity but he seems increasingly drawn to the view that the more fundamental cause of the conflict is again the sheer fact of rivalry.[24] Aron's position in regard to nationalism is much more tolerant, as we might expect given his high valuation of a national society as the potential bearer of a specific way of life. He is well aware that nationalism proceeds hand in hand with industrialism, and he specifically points out that an educated native minority will try to wage anti-colonial wars:

> It is an irony of history, but an intelligible one, that Algerians who had received a French education headed the nationalist movement, just as it was those about to become French who were the ones who wished most to remain Algerian. This is readily explained; they understood that they were the victims of an inferior status imposed upon them by the French minority, and they had everything to gain by establishing a state in which they would become part of the ruling group by virtue of the removal of French competitors with comparable training.[25]

The national principle will, Aron adds, very likely lead to further wars designed to keep together states artificially drawn up by colonisers. But he does not consider that the fact of increased numbers of states is itself responsible for burgeoning hatred and war. The First World War was not inevitable, while the Second World War had an imperialist and ideological character rather than a nationalist one. Moreover, he argues, as we shall see, that

the course of realism is to learn to deal with national states as he
sees no evidence that national collectivities are losing their hold
over loyalties of their citizens.

It is now obvious why Aron's theory of state behaviour is not a
general or closed theory: the *activity* of states does not allow this.
Thus the most we can hope for when thinking of, say, the First
World War and its consequences is to understand what
happened, rather than to impute to events a false determinism.
Such a position naturally pays close attention to historical
decisions, and the balance of diplomatic-strategic forces at any
one time. Something has already been said as to Aron's own interpretation of late nineteenth century Europe and of the two world
wars, and this must be complemented by a brief appreciation of
his analysis of the balance of forces in the contemporary world,
both between the super powers and between the developed and
Third World.

At the end of the war, Aron quickly became convinced that the
size and industrial strength of America and Russia would give
them the status of super powers, a fact quickly confirmed by the
ability of only these powers to support a full nuclear arsenal, i.e.
first *and* second strike capacity and so on. In *The Great Debate*
he chronicled and analysed the change in American strategic
thinking from 'massive reprisals' to 'limited steps only at the last
resort leading to nuclear war'. Aron certainly believes that all the
lessons Clausewitz taught concerning the intentions of one's
opponent have lost none of their validity even though war is no
longer a recourse naturally open to nuclear powers, and for this
reason amongst others he favoured thinking about the possibility
of war once Korea proved that the mere presence of nuclear
weapons would not place a taboo on all military activity.

Despite the great subtlety of American theory, Aron has always
had reservations about it – or, at least, he has been aware of
paradoxes within such theory. Most obviously there is an
irremediable contradiction between a taboo on nuclear war
and the expectation that war will act as a deterrent; nothing is
ever likely to detract from this. Secondly, Aron is absolutely clear
that strategic theory makes it perhaps worse than useless for
France and England to have incomplete nuclear systems, only
utilisable in a first strike capacity and therefore inviting a pre-
emptive first strike themselves. Nevertheless he recognises the
presence of a sort of nuclear illusion whereby possession of such

weapons translates itself into prestige – a factor Aron is not prepared to consider insignificant in international politics. Thirdly, he has now come to believe that some of the claims recently made for the doctrine of limited response have been exaggerated. Thus, he no longer accepts that the subtleties of this doctrine were demonstrated in the Cuban Missile Crisis; indeed, one of the greatest unknowns of the whole equation remains Western uncertainty that Russian strategic doctrine even recognises the same realities. Instead he thinks that Soviet action was curtailed on that occasion because of the overwhelming superiority of American conventional forces at the scene.[26] Fourthly, he has always been aware of the fear recently generalised by the siting of Cruise missiles in Europe, namely that Europe would be the theatre for war the ravages of which America would escape. Recently, Aron has expressed fears about the relations of forces in both central and theatre systems. As we shall see, he does not think that the disarmament of Europe can be achieved, but neither, interestingly, does he in fact believe that the presence of Cruise missiles, so long as Europe has so many American 'hostage' soldiers and the renewed possibility of first strike effectiveness, is in itself likely to lead to war. His fears come from the typically Aronien tactic of trying to put himself in the shoes of political leaders. He suggests that such leaders may be swayed, as has happened in his lifetime, by the moral weight gained by a state prepared to arm to the teeth. Increased Russian strength may be insufficient to upset pure theories but Aron is not prepared to rule out completely the political impact, in Europe and elsewhere.[27]

One of the most curious facts about the creation of super powers is that the very size of the means of destruction has made it difficult to control the developing world. This can be seen in the case of, say, Egypt which has been prepared to bargain with both major powers for maximum national advantage. And this inability to control allies can be further seen in America's inability to prevent India fighting Pakistan and so establishing the new nation of Bangladash. This war is judged by Aron to have been a classical one in that it was waged with all available means; it was thus unlike Korea where America felt unable to use all its means and came to realise that the preservation of the status quo was an appropriate political aim. Aron has considerable praise for Mrs Gandhi's handling of the war; he argues moreover that the war probably prevented greater killing and that an accurate calculation was made between forces available and the goal to be achieved. His views in this matter contrast strongly with his sad analysis of the Middle East situation. In 1967 Aron instantly realised that the classical victory of Israeli arms meant little:

> Israel could have lost the shooting war, she cannot win it. She has won *a* military victory, but not *the* victory. A state of two and a half million inhabitants has not got the wherewithal to force the Arab countries as a whole to capitulate. She has destroyed two armies, but she has not destroyed either the States or the populations against which she was fighting.
>
> This lack of symmetry partly explains the course of events; it also contains lessons for the future. Whether in the short or the long term, the only true victory for Israel would be peace.[28]

Another element of Aron's understanding of relationships with the developing world can be seen in the first of two points to be made about his conception of praxeology. In the last fifteen years he has become a harsh critic of the mechanical and consequently false conception of theory that guided American practice, archetypically in Vietnam. His highly impressive analysis of the Vietnam débâcle stresses that the Americans made the fearful mistake of trying to treat the Vietnamese situation under the aegis of a strategic theory designed to deal with a super power. But no theory can take the place of examining local geographical and physical conditions; the failure to do so in this case led to the sending of the wrong sort of army, and, crucially, to a lack of awareness that the 'stake' involved was not perceived in similar terms on both sides. The ability of the Vietcong to endure bombing attacks has led many to declare that America had to lose the war as it was in its essence a war of liberation. Aron refuses such outright conclusions and prefers to think that the war was lost basically through mistakes. The Vietcong were 'partisans of a regime' rather than 'national liberators', and the Americans, had they been wise, might have been able to create national feeling in South Vietnam as they did in South Korea. The guerila wars of this century do not, contrary to popular opinion, tell us of inevitability of victory for guerilas. Indeed in an interesting recent aside, Aron has argued that the Cuban revolution is very much the exception to the rule in South America, and that no inevitable link between revolutionaries and peasants exists.[29]

The second point that needs to be stressed about Aron's conception of praxeology is its firmly statist character. Two related points are important. Firstly, Aron clearly places his hopes on political leaders becoming sufficiently wise, or, rather, sufficiently well-versed in Clausewitzian principles, to act as 'the personified intelligence of the state'.[30] This is not, of course, to say that he believes that political leaders always do act in this way, and he has recently been particularly critical of the tendency of American foreign policy to veer between widely differing alternatives.[31] But although he is perhaps open to the criticism of not considering sufficiently the control of foreign policy, his characterisation of the nuclear situation as a 'wager upon reason' makes a formidable case for the education of the political élite. Secondly, Aron considers directly the question of the continuation of states themselves. In an exceptionally lucid and striking analysis of the Marxist (especially Maoist) hope that a transnational struggle between classes will take the place of inter-state rivalry, Aron makes clear his belief that nation-states in fact offer us the greatest chance of peace. He rejects the Marxist position since he believes that it would encourage an endless war of partisans. Similarly he refuses, after long and careful deliberation, to place his hopes in the emergence of any new world organisation capable of outlawing war. The impracticality of such organisations strikes him forcefully, but ultimately he does not embrace this position because his own experience has overwhelmingly convinced him that wars can still be just:

> Tomorrow, other men will live by different passions. French, of Jewish origin, how could I forget that France owes her liberation to the strength of her allies, Israel her existence to her arms, a chance of survival to her resolve, and to the resolve of the Americans to fight, if need be.
> Before feeling guilty, I will wait until a tribunal decides who, between the Israelis and the Palestinians, has the proper claim to the land which is holy for the three religions of the Book.[32]

CONCLUSIONS

When a full-scale intellectual history of the post-war world comes to be written, I believe that it will judge Aron's real originality to have been the concepts he created to understand Eastern and Western political variants of the common 'mode of production' of industrialism. His work in international relations, in contrast, though obviously high-powered and wide ranging, is best seen as one contribution to the revival of a neo-Clausewitzian approach pioneered elsewhere by thinkers such as Bernard Brodie, Alastair Buchan and Peter Paret. But rather than untangle the exact contribution of Aron to the neo-Clausewitzian school as a whole, we can here conclude with three more general points.

To begin with, is the anti-Marxist insistence on the autonomy of state behaviour so strongly stressed by all neo-Clausewitzians in fact correct? Whilst some arguments of Aron are probably wrong, and others open to question, his general approach has much to recommend it. No serious historian believes that the First World War was the result of displaced imperial rivalries, and unless Marxism is capable of producing an alternative explanation of that event it must be judged deeply deficient – for Aron is quite correct in arguing that the ramifications of that war have made the world we now inhabit. Perhaps the most convincing way in which to support Aron's general argument about imperialism is to recall the examination of the Marxisant 'revisionist' case concerning American involvement in Vietnam made by Barrington Moore – since he, unlike Aron, is a thinker of impeccably left-wing, albeit empiricist, credentials. Moore's examination of the evidence leads to almost exactly similar conclusions to Aron's: American capitalism did not call for nor require involvement, which can only be explained in terms of power politics.[33] And interestingly, Moore's pupil, Theda Skocpol, has recently implicitly confirmed Aron's viewpoint in general and interpretation of the Russian Revolution in particular, in her *States and Social Revolutions*.[34] The thesis of this much praised book is that revolutions can only be understood when an analysis of international pressures, i.e. of the strength or weakness of competing states, is added to traditional Marxist categories concerned with peasants, workers, capitalists and landlords. And this point can be generalised: Marxism cannot be expanded so as to include warfare; on the contrary, it must be complemented by proper and independent understanding of political factors operating in their own right. And it is worthwhile spelling out why this is so. Mary Kaldor has argued that the vision of Marxism may only be attainable when states cease to exist.[35] Now this is highly intelligent in at least admitting that state behaviour interferes with Marxist expectations, but it is open to the crushing objection that it does not seem to be in the cards currently offered us by history — surely a worrying matter for a Marxisant thinker. In other words, we must take seriously Aron's view that twentieth century history records the spread of nation-states throughout the world. It is not enough to bemoan the fact that nation is a factor in social life at least as strong as class, as Miliband so often does.[36] It is necessary to follow Aron in trying to theorise about its effect.

One weakness of Aron's anti-Marxist approach is that at times it is content with the rather easy victory (over crude Marxism rather than Marx himself, as Aron well knows) gained by pointing out that men, and states, have ends other than the purely economic. Another way of putting this is to say that Aron does not extend his generalisations quite as far as he might. The second conclusion is that Aron's work best serves us if it is used as a building block. And it is possible to suggest which sort of generalisations we need. Michael Mann's work-in-progress on types of social power has already demonstrated convincingly the creative and productive role that warfare played in history by integrating imperial systems, above all the Chinese, Roman and Persian.[37] Mann was also intimated that he will seek to prove that military, as well as geopolitical, factors have an autonomy of their own. I am less sure of this given that the Chinese Empire, free from the pressure of organised state competition, refused to adopt the military revolution implied by the invention of gunpowder.[38] This is to imply that as a primary matter we need to explain why it was that Europe developed a multi-state system in the first place.[39] But once given a system of competing states, Mann is indeed right to stress the crucial impact of changes in military organisation. As Max Weber, Otto Hintze and Samuel Finer have argued, such changes in military organisation necessitate the rationalisation of states.[40] The fact that such rationalisation was forced upon European states has a great deal to do with the rise of the West: the first transition to the modern world was not just from feudalism, but from feudal, multipolar and Christian Europe.[41] Once again, the possibility of explaining very large issues depends upon our developing theories of the political and the military capable of complementing Marxist analysis of the economy. But this need to develop Aron's thought is not to imply that his thought is wrong in all respects. In particular, he has a strong case when arguing – and here his views are opposed to those of Mann[42] – that any theory of inter-state behaviour must be limited in character; as noted, if the First World War was the result of traditional diplomatic rivalries there was nothing inevitable or logical about its actual occurrence.

Finally, it is worth stressing that Aron has always been a very European thinker. This is clear to those aware of his high valuation of the tradition of European liberalism, but it is something that marks his views on defence. Although Aron sometimes suggests that the two world wars have debilitated Europe as much as the Peloponnesian War did Greece, his deepest hope is that Europe can continue to play some part in the world scene. In order to do so, Aron has always insisted, Europe must possess what he continues to regard, even in the age of economic inter-dependence, as the key characteristic of sovereignty, namely its own defence policy. Aron wrote a distinguished analytic history of the failure of the European Defence Community in the early 1950s in which he pointed to two longer-term factors, i.e. factors other than the then current fear of German rearmament, that made any such policy difficult to achieve.[43] The first factor is the continuing power of nations to generate support for their own interests – something which Aron sees as responsible for defeating transnational hopes placed in the European Community. However, Aron regards this as less important than the second factor. In a brilliant, sceptical essay, he has recently argued that Western European societies are not becoming militarised; on the contrary, civilian styles and demands are pressuring the military.[44] More importantly, he insists that it is historically very strange, but not unique, that an extremely rich area depends for its defence on an ally overseas; he regards this as almost a type of degeneracy, and has never been surprised that Europeans have had to put up with strategic theories that they might well not choose for themselves. Recently Aron has allowed himself to hope that a withdrawal of American troops from Europe might shock European states sufficiently to generate a common political, and hence defence, policy.[45] This is a very complex matter, and it seems to me that America's interest in Europe remains strong enough to prevent this from happening. But Aron nevertheless seems to me quite right in arguing that Europe cannot have independence without defence, i.e. without any cost at all.[46] And it is of course entirely typical of the thinker that his analyses suggest that his hopes will probably not be fulfilled, and that Europe will not choose an independent course. This refusal to write his own hopes into history seems to me admirable and rare; Aron, in other words, seeks to make us think rather than to believe.

NOTES

1. On Marx and Engels, see Bryce Gallie's excellent *Philosophers of War and Peace* (Cambridge University Press, 1978).
2. For an account of such thinkers see, for example, Martin Shaw's chapter in this volume.
3. Raymond Aron, 'War and Industrial Society: A Reappraisal', *Millenium*, 7 (1978/9).
4. The clearest statement of their objections probably remains Q. Skinner's 'Meaning and Understanding in the History of Ideas', *History and Theory*, 8 (1969).
5. For a fuller treatment see my forthcoming *Raymond Aron: An Intellectual Biography* (Harlow: Longman, 1984).
6. Hobbes, *Leviathan*, Part 1, ch. 13, cited by Aron in 'La Guerre est une caméléon', *Contrepoint*, 15 (1974).
7. Aron, *Penser la guerre, Clausewitz*, Vol. 2 (Paris: Gallimard, 1976), p. 225 (my translation).
8. Montesquieu, *L'Esprit des Lois*, Part 1, ch. 3 cited by Aron in *Peace and War* (London: Weidenfeld and Nicolson, 1966) p. vii.
9. Aron, 'Reason, Passion and Power in the Thought of Clausewitz', *Social Research*, 39 (1972) pp. 607–8.
10. Ibid. pp. 618–21.
11. Aron's interpretation is available in several places. Perhaps the fullest account is that of *The Century of Total War*, Part 1 (London: Derek Verschoyle, 1954), but the most critical analysis of the failure of the politicians is perhaps *Penser la guerre, Clausewitz*, Vol. 2, op cit., ch. 1.
12. Aron, *The Imperial Republic* (London: Weidenfeld and Nicolson, 1974) ch. 1.
13. Aron, 'What is a Theory of International Relations', in M. B. Conant (ed.), *History and Politics* (New York: The Free Press, 1978) p. 174.
14. Aron, *Penser la guerre, Clausewitz*, Vol. 1, op. cit., ch. 5.
15. Aron has made this point on many occasions, for example *Peace and War*, op. cit., p. 41.
16. Ibid., p. 91.
17. Aron, 'War and Industrial Society: A Reappraisal', op. cit., p. 200.
18. Aron, *Peace and War*, op. cit., chs. 7–9.
19. Aron has written about imperialism on many occasions. Perhaps the most striking are 'Imperialism and Colonialism' (Montague Burton Lecture, Leeds University Press, 1959), *War and Industrial Society* (Oxford University Press, 1958), *Peace and War*, op. cit., especially ch. 9, *La tragédie*

algérienne (Paris: Plon, 1957), *The Imperial Republic*, op. cit., especially Part II, and *Plaidoyer pour l'Europe Décadente* (Paris: Robert Laffont) especially ch. 6.

20. Aron, 'Imperialism and colonialism', op. cit., p. 6.
21. Aron, *The Imperial Republic*, op. cit., Part 2, ch. 2.
22. Ibid., Part 2, ch. 3.
23. Aron's account is in two places: *The Imperial Republic*, op. cit., Part I, ch. 3 and *passim* and *Penser la guerre, Clausewitz*, Vol. 2, ch. 5, section 3.
24. A careful reading shows a change in tone in his interpretation of the Russian/American rivalry as between *Peace and War* and *Penser la guerre, Clausewitz*, Vol. 2.
25. Aron, *Progress and Disillusion* (Harmondsworth: Penguin, 1972) p. 86.
26. Aron, *The Imperial Republic*, op. cit., Part 1, ch. 3, especially pp. 108–9.
27. Aron, 'De l'impérialisme américain à la hégémonisme soviétique', *Commentaire*, 5 (Spring, 1979).
28. Aron, *De Gaulle, Israel and the Jews* (London: Andre Deutsch, 1969) p. 86.
29. Aron, *Penser la guerre, Clausewitz*, Vol. 2, op. cit.
30. Aron, *Penser la guerre, Clausewitz*, Vol. 2, op. cit., ch. 6.
31. This is in effect the central theme of *The Imperial Republic*.
32. Aron, *Penser la guerre, Clausewitz*, Vol. 2, op. cit., p. 286 (my translation).
33. B. Moore, *Reflections on the Causes of Human Misery* (Boston: Beacon Press, 1972) ch. 5.
34. T. Skocpol, *States and Social Revolutions* (Cambridge University Press, 1979).
35. Mary Kaldor, 'The theory of warfare and capitalism', paper to Hull conference, 1981; version in E. P. Thompson *et al*, *Exterminism and Cold War*, (London: New Left Books, 1982).
36. See especially, R. Miliband, *Parliamentary Socialism*, 2nd edition (London: Merlin Press, 1973) *passim* but perhaps especially the postcript.
37. M. Mann, 'States, Ancient and Modern', *European Journal of Sociology*, 17 (1977).
38. This point is made strikingly by M. Elvin in his *The Pattern of the Chinese Past* (California: Stanford University Press, 1973) ch. 8 and Part 1 as a whole.
39. See my 'The Role of a Multi-State System in the Transition to Industrialism', in E. Gellner (ed.), *The Emergence of Ideas and Institutions*, forthcoming.
40. Max Weber, *The Religion of China* (New York: The Free Press, 1951), ch. 2; Otto Hintze, 'Military Organisation and the Organisation of the State', in F. Gilbert (ed.), *The Historical Essays of Otto Hintze* (New York: Oxford University Press, 1977); and S. Finer, 'State and Nation-Building in Europe: The Role of the Military' in C. Tilly (ed.), *The Formation of National States in Western Europe* (Princeton University Press, 1975).
41. See my 'The Role of a Multi-State System in the Transition to Industrialism', op. cit.
42. Or at least to the views M. Mann expressed in a paper entitled 'A Sociological Critique of Historical Materialism' given to the 1980 session of the British Sociological Association.

43. Aron and D. Lerner (eds), *La Querelle de la C.E.D.* (Paris: Colin, 1956).
44. Aron, 'Remarks on Lasswell's *Garrison State*', *Armed Forces and Society*, 5 (1979).
45. Aron, *The Imperial Republic*, op. cit., postcript.
46. I have learnt a great deal in this general area from Michael Mann, 'Nationalism and Internationalism in Economic and Defence Policies', in J.A.G. Griffiths (ed.), *Socialism in a Cold Climate* (London: Allen and Unwin, 1983). Mann argues very much the same case as Aron, but I think I detect one difference, *viz* that Mann believes that European nuclear disarmament plus conventional rearmament would not increase defence spending in the long run; Aron regards such an increase as inevitable.

4 War Resistance, State and Society

NIGEL YOUNG

This paper deals with the state, war and militarism as viewed from the perspective of the study of social movements.

Re-developing a sociology of the state and perhaps creating a developed sociology of war is, or should be in the view expressed here, an exercise in demystification. In particular, we have inhabited the nation-state framework long enough for it to appear, like militarism, part of the order of things. The role of war or conquest in the origins of the state, the role of military force in the creation of the first modern states or the states we inhabit, the role of militarism in nation-state building and expansion in more recent times – including the developments of revolutionary states – has been receiving attention again, and this volume of papers is symptomatic of that re-focusing and potential demystification. What tends to be omitted from this rediscovery is the role of popular resistance to war.

The revived interest in work of classical sociologists who paid attention to war and the state: Weber, Spencer, Otto Hintze and Franz Oppenheimer; the work of those more recent anthropologists tending to confirm conquest theories of state origins, like Robert Carneiro; and the work of peace researchers and historians on war and militarism and of sociologists and political scientists on transnational non-state actors and relationships, can be seen as a dimension of that same demystification process.[1] What has become clearer is that war, though it almost certainly preceded the state's formation, has, since the latter's emergence, always been intimately intertwined with its development so that there are continuities in state coercion over the 4–5000 years of its history even if we have entered a qualitatively new phase in its development during the twentieth century.[2]

Part of my argument here will be that just as significant in the demystification process have been the societal challenges to that growing monopoly of violence; that as a social category, war resisters have represented potential, if not always actual, demystifiers in terms of their opposition. War resisters are not necessarily aware of a process of demystification through action, but they tend inevitably to hasten a relativisation of state and national frameworks and also provide crucial evidence for the professional demystifiers amongst social theorists and others.

This paper's starting point is a descriptive model of the state's modern growth which tries to give historical flesh to a sociological (Weberian) definition of the state which emphasises territoriality, legitimacy and the monopoly of violence (militarism).[3] It then looks at actual and theoretical challenges to that institution as a limiting definition of social and political life in terms of groups of people who have for a diversity of reasons challenged that monopoly and even limited the claims of state authority in relation to military service.[4]

There is a tendency to perceive the state, war and militarism as detached from other aspects of society, especially from those communities, cultures and relationships that are directly or indirectly destroyed by war or by the rise of the state (or by both); or as unrelated to the movements of social opposition and revolutionary challenge which as a result confronted this destructive process. Yet, it is in this context that the action of challenging the state's monopoly of violence by war resisters has indicated both the limitations and the innovations of state activity in a given period; both new forms of coercion and of legitimation; and it is these elements in Weber's definition of the state that need to be related to such oppositional action and to the concept of national territoriality.

The significance of war resistance thus lies partly in its indication of the actual or potential limits to a state's political growth, increasing militarisation, and state claims in an era when these have been seen to be almost limitless.[5] But in addition they also may indicate possible routes of historical reversal. Of course the study of war resistance reveals many new impositions, not least conscription, in different societies at different times and generally highlights the ongoing relation between militarism and social structure.

But the conditions under which the challenges of war resisters are sustained also throw considerable light on areas of social autonomy, conditions of social resistance and change, and thus possibly even scenarios of global restructuring in the longer term which may spring from these conditions and autonomies.

I would argue that by studying the social context and reinforcement of the rather drastic step of resisting compulsory military service, sometimes at risk of death, one can conceivably discover clues, not only to the state's rise, but to the potential role of social autonomies or political detachments in its transcendence – hints of a transformation of society, that imply the possibility of taming both war and the state. For any wider demystification must in the end be linked to such social autonomy and detachment, challenge and change. The social reinforcement of resistance can not only reveal how pockets of social resistance have occurred in the past. It can also indicate actual scenarios in a period of state collapse, which are linked to regeneration of communal or sub-state relationships, and transnational or extra-state relationships, both of which it can be argued empirically are now on the increase. The challenge to the monopoly of violence is thus relevant to both internal *and* external change – as I will contend the evidence of the draft resistance movement and the Vietnam War opposition indicated.

In surveying a number of other case studies[6] of war resistance – socialist, religious, pacifist, peasant, or nationalist – it became clear that the parameter of the state as a nationally defined and legal unit was crucial in determining action and resistance; yet that often the most highly conscious groups were the least likely to be able to sustain resistance. The war resistance of significant minorities – the dying wail of some social groups and birth screams of others – was often based on social distance and in that sense a *lack* of social consciousness.

For strategic reasons the key moment around which much of my research has centred is the introduction of universal compulsory military service, the major moment when war resistance, however briefly, became a mass popular phenomenon. Nevertheless, the much smaller groups of conscientious objectors and absolutist resisters – who rarely run into tens of thousands – have their own special significance, as do resisters (deserters, mutineers, non-co-operators) within the armed forces themselves. There may be an implicit voluntarist assumption in all this that people in opposition to developments of statism and militarisation can 'make a difference' in the long term and I make no apology for that. In what follows, I will deal first with the issue of the state and coercion; then look at war resistance in relation to the state, at some case studies of war resisters, and then return briefly to the state and its future.

THE STATE

The nation-state has become a 'norm of modern political organisation as ubiquitous as it is recent'.[7] Its key empirical functions have been those of control, socialisation, domination, co-ordination and mobilisation. Of its mobilising functions, not the least is 'defence', that is the monopolisation, deployment and legitimation of the violence at its disposal both against internal opposition (law and order) and external threats or rivals. Though the state has ebbed and flowed in its legitimation of violence, centralisation and monopolistic and unitary character over the past two thousand or more years (the mediaeval period was a period of state weakness, dispersal and the plurality of sovereignties), the nation-state system has in the past 200 years become a comprehensive and continuous one. All societies are now more or less organised into a global pattern of territorially similar and contingent entities.

War mobilisation highlights this control of society by the state and its logic in the twentieth century has been towards totalism (and not only in the so-called totalitarian states). Conscription on a universal, compulsory basis into that hierarchy of organised, collective violence is a key dimension of that development and is characteristic of all but a handful of modern states.[8] Women are now being drawn into this process, especially in the newly created states. The atomisation of society and the mobilisation of individuals into large bureaucratic organisations such as armies is symbolised by this relation of the state to the individual.

Other elements in the modern state's growth (taxation systems, welfarism, state intervention in the economy, educaton and comprehensive legal systems) are complementary and parallel developments.[9] But it is arguable that the warmaking and violence-deploying aspects are more central and more critical given the history of the state's development and the prevalent (conquest) theories of the state's growth. Weber's definition, despite its static quality, does make this factor central and links it to legitimation (ideology) on the one hand and territoriality (national boundaries) on the other. The legitimation of armed domination by a ruling group in a given territorial area was the crucial moment in the founding of all states. War, mobilisation, conscription, the loyalty of the armed forces remain the most crucial test of sovereignty (i.e. loyalty, legitimacy and effectiveness). The mythologies of contract, popular (including socialist and republican) sovereignty, citizenship, constitutionalism and legality, do not change the actual authority relations and the potential of centralised state power. These mythologies – liberal, socialist and conservative – have tended to shun the model of the state's growth used here since it legitimates opposition, radical pluralism and resistance. The fact that the monopoly of coercion – by force or fraud, by conquest and by persuasion – has been at the basis of the development of the other more benevolent aspects of state power is an uncomfortable and embarrassing one for the idealist theorists; only the crudest realists and pragmatists can shrug off or justify this history. The boundary-definition and sovereignty-accumulating process has been achieved by the bloody and treacherous elimination of social rivals – including communities and whole peoples. The value of Oppenheimer's thesis is that it sets out a plausible scenario of how the 'bodies of armed men' first dominated, then incorporated, peoples into the legitimate murder of others especially those who stood outside the perimeters of the state.[10] As he points out, the 'first strong states were formed as territorial states'. The irrational dimension of modern nationalism has synthesised, through ruling ideology, the coercive domination of the state with popular identification with national units (however inexact). Its effect on socialism and liberalism, through twentieth-century wars and collective repressions, has proved catastrophic. In the context of the nuclear arms race, it may prove terminal.

The acceptance of war, and then military service on an increasingly widespread and legitimated basis, in the past three hundred years is a significant complement to the contract theory of the state. The right of 'defence' and 'law and order' is exchanged for the state monopoly of murder and the duty of military service to murder others in the state's name, internally or externally. War crystallises the nature of the state more than any other activity, though, despite Bourne's dictum it is not always healthy for it in the longer term.[11] It helps repress opposition and unify sovereignty, it mobilises and legitimates the monopoly of violence, it may integrate society by incorporating (or pacifying) socially emergent groups (workers, women, ethnic minorities), it justifies greater centralisation and gives an occasion for nationalist excess. The state's emphasis on the defence or expansion of boundaries of the 'nation' or an empire reinforces the focus on territoriality, as does its destruction of supranational authority and the loyalties and ties that transcend the state. Whilst human inhibitions about intra-species killing pre-date the state, the systematisation of law, and the successful claim to monopolise killing by the state, go some way to 'out-law' individual murder, and is part of its legitimation (thus arises one dimension of the 'contract' myth). But though the right of individuals, families, groups and communities to kill each other is regulated, the ambivalence about killing, even when ordered by the state, remains and this doubt represents a minority tendency within most major religions. The general norm of inviolability of persons from violent attack, is qualified by legality and territoriality – the protection of people involves legal violence against those who violate the state's sovereignty from within or outside its borders.

Treason, desertion and mutiny become capital crimes, crimes against sovereignty and territoriality. War resistance can be portrayed as close to these.

WAR RESISTANCE IN THE CONTEXT OF STATE BUILDING

In appraising war resistance it is crucial to place it in the context of the relation between inter-state and intra-state relations. The contest between state and local community continued over hundreds of years; whenever the peasant community retained some autonomy the military and monopolistic character of the territorial state were potentially challenged.[12] Popular war resistance as a political phenomenon thus parallels almost exactly the intrusion and breaking, by the state, of the hold of the local community on people's lives and loyalties. Even the revolutionary organisers of the last fifty years have found the peasant village obdurate and independent and unwilling to make more than tactical sacrifices unless terrorised.[13] The secularisation of the new state, bourgeois or revolutionary, nationalist or Leninist, also sharpened the religious bases of opposition. The capitalist expansion as the basis of war and economic domination brought socialist and anti-colonial resistance to the war-making state. In each of these ways the social transformation of the past few centuries has engendered pockets of resistance to war and conscription; communities of opposition, alienated social minorities.[14] The changing character of war parallels the evolving character of the state – it eliminates rivals, and defines boundaries. The mercenary army and feudal host are replaced by the professionals and the conscripts; both are deployed to mop up resistance in the countryside. Peasants are conscripted or killed. Communities are incorporated or destroyed. Armies become one of the key bureaucratic institutions of the centralised modern state; society is secularised and modernised and made 'national'. Armed violence smashes opposition – the possibilities of war resistance or social non-co-operation appear nullified. The new forces of mobilisation are unleashed in imperial expansion. The consolidation of the market and central control, and colonial and interstate wars, justify the permanent war economy. Fascism takes this process to its ideologically extreme form, mobilising the whole of society on behalf of state purposes. In so far as war can be turned inside physically and ideologically as well as outside a state boundary, the question of rights and duties – the right of defence and the duty of military service – becomes a universal reciprocal exchange in all modern states.[15] The constitutions of Eastern bloc countries, and the rhetoric of Western liberalism say much the same thing; citizenship implies conscription and military service.

The ideologisation of war represents itself as the democratisation of war – the peoples' war, the citizenry in arms, the socialist war of 'national' liberation or defence;[16] conscription as the expression of an apparent collective will to fight. Yet each such claim contains the seeds of its own challenge and subversion. The nature of the state, or the decision to make war; the legitimacy of the ruling groups, their profit from war and control or expansion of society; the legitimacy of the national unit and the counter-claims of minorities (or of internationalism); the justification of war, monopoly and violence – inside or outside the national boundaries – all these questions are raised acutely. They are raised in the face of claims made, not only by socialists, Marxists, anarchists, pacifists, but also by various more traditional groups and communities and individuals brought face to face with the state in its most acute imposition, its demand that people fight, kill and if necessary die, for the nation.

As the state becomes apparently more classless, more neutral and more remote, defence and policing gain widespread acceptability in the abstract, where popular sovereignty is invoked. But the state's sole right to make war, to execute, and to order others to kill on its behalf still depends on acceptance of both its legitimacy as a territorial authority – and of the right to kill in certain circumstances.

In some countries, conscientious objection is a minor right, but an exception that still confirms the universal responsibility. The formal incorporation of dissidence in this way ensures the legitimation of the larger duty. For a war resister to accept CO status may signify acceptance of citizenship and legality – the state; only the small minorities of absolutist resisters have realised that and acted accordingly.[17]

Of course the development of the bureaucratic military state has not always been smooth or unilinear. Its legitimation has often been frail with the decline of traditional supports. The ambiguity of the plebiscitarian justifications which accompany the *levée en masse* is that they stress rights as well as duties. In an era of unprecedented mobilisation, collective violence and militarisation, consciousness of militarism, potential non-co-operation and some systematic claims against certain states by war resisters, also begin to grow.

Where doubts about war and the state reinforce one another, pockets of resistance remain. Mutiny, desertion, refusal of military service, evasion of conscription, emigration, armed revolt and unarmed non-co-operation – even treason – characterise this continuing tension over many centuries of the state's growth, and continue in the newly formed states. Some of the challenges to state legitimation have been closely aligned to the social roots of war resistance. The nationalism of minorities and emigrants has often produced crises in the civic framework; rights and duties only apply to those formally within the territorial unitary frame.[18] There has been a crisis in the extent of control implied by conscription. How far can the principle of the absolute disposal of citizens' lives be taken by a state? For how long? How monopolistic can the state become? How political can a society be? The contradiction of rights and duties became most acute for the very middle classes who helped foster the modern state's growth, yet found their protector turning against their liberties and the lives of themselves and their sons.

There is of course an overlap, which will be returned to later, between all these strands of opposition: the demand for peasant autonomies, the demand for civil rights, the demand for religious toleration, the demand for socialist control of production, the demand for ethnic recognition. All these are intertwined in war resistance as a tradition, and particularly in resistance to the logic of totalism implicit in modern statebuilding, of which compulsory universal military service is one key dimension in most states of the world. In its most advanced forms it challenges too the territorial basis of legitimation and emphasises local community, global society and transnational linkages and networks.

STUDYING WAR RESISTERS

War resistance became a mass phenomenon only with the introduction of universal compulsory systems of military service – from the *levée en masse* of 1793, through the spread of such systems throughout Europe, Russia and the Americas during the following hundred years, and the spread to the rest of the earth since.[19] Its mass character has been expressed by massive emigration (Russia, the Balkans, Italy), mass anti-militarist campaigns (France pre-1914), strikes (France, Spain), mutinies, often of revolutionary implication (Germany, France, Russia), mass desertions (Russia, Germany, Vietnam), draft evasion (UAR, Spain, USA), going to jail (USA, Australia, UK), and mass application for conscientious objector status (USA and West Germany in the late 1960s and 1970s). Throughout the nineteenth century, mass avoidance was possible. But in the twentieth century with Stalinism, the Third Reich and the spread of bureaucratic centralised autocracies, war resistance became much more dangerous. In a few liberal democracies however the loophole of conscientious objection, although partial, was widened.

Had a sociology of conscription and militarism developed in this period, the social relationship of the individual actor to the modern state in the context of compulsion and war mobilisation would perhaps have been better analysed and understood. As it is, one has to draw from a wide range of historical and biographical sources, in order to situate the relationship comparatively in relation to the development of war, nationalism and the state. It is to such studies that I will now turn.

The analysis of war resistance clearly overlaps with the study of anti-militarist and anti-conscriptionist movements in peace time, with pacifist conscientious objection, with nationalist and socialist resistance and ethnic and religious withdrawal from a given state, and indeed with revolutionary opposition. In the West, one of the key roots of such resistance was Protestant non-conformity with its radical, critical and democratic strands. Such strands were in deep tension with centralised state building. As was suggested in the last section, war resistance is in part a phenomenon of the great transformation, of cultural disruption. It can be deduced from this that studying war resisters is in part the study of bizarre congeries of anarchists and religious deviants, of peasant and ethnic movements in remote areas, of nomadic and tribal minorities, of unincorporated workers and immigrants of economically doomed or marginal groups, of the excluded and excommunicated, the 'unconscious' non-co-operators with the tides of history.[20] But there is nevertheless a continuity with the emergent consciousnesses of rationalist political nonconformity, radical secular pacifism, socialist internationalism and anti-militarism.

In some cases, as with syndicalism in France and elsewhere, war resistance begins to touch and organise the great battalions of the urban areas, the railway workers or miners.[21] At this juncture, the synchronisation of the spontaneous and the planned becomes historically plausible: that was the glimpse that the visionaries caught of potential global transformation in pluralist socialist scenarios. But it was submerged in the tide of war and statism, of nationalism and imperialism.

The abstract theoretical character of socialist internationalism was superimposed on movements which whilst not clamouring for civic status were nationally organised for economic and political advance within given national frameworks. There was no true transnationalism, i.e. the linkage of community to community, producer to producer, across political and military frontiers. The internationals were dominated by the leaders of national parties and unions working within distinct pyramids of power. Linkages between the grass-roots of each labour movement were inevitably minimal. This is why it was difficult to talk about – let alone implement – a concrete practical strategy of war prevention or counter-mobilisation.[22] Narrow national interests had not been fully challenged, there was no objection amongst most socialists to the state in principle (merely to its class character), class solidarities were often narrowly economistic within the national frame (a by-product of imperial expansion); there were few links with foreign movements and no link directly from community to community except through emigrant, kinship linkages. The statist and oligarchic tendencies of labour organisations further undermined the potentiality of a pluralist socialism, communal control and extra-parliamentary resistance.

Of course war resistance and the tradition of pacifism overlap, but they are nevertheless distinct. The history of pacifism appears much older, and only occasionally manifested itself in war resistance (e.g. Christians in the Roman Empire before Constantine).[23] As has been seen, war resistance is often based not on a principled pacifism, but on a refusal to engage in war, for a whole variety of political, social, cultural and economic reasons. It has become predominantly a secular phenomenon, whilst pacifism, until the early years of this century, was predominantly a religious one. War resistance may oppose a specific war rather than war in general (or 'internal' war). Whilst most modern pacifists support war resistance in principle, only a minority of them actively engage in it. But what all war resisters have in common is in withdrawing individually – and sometimes collectively – increments of the state's monopoly of violence.

Pacifism, religious or secular, radical or liberal, arrives at the realities of the state by a different route: through the struggle for autonomy, tolerance and detachment; through cosmopolitan humanism or spirituality; through emigration, voluntary or enforced; through persecution and imprisonment; through the creation of alternative communities and institutions. Even movements which in their essence are retreatist or millennial are forced into confrontation with the state, and into recognising the reality of the conflict between national coercion and social freedoms.

War resistance in this tradition, unlike socialist anti-militarist resistance, starts from a position of quiescent passivity and attempts conformist respectability. It is often rejected and discovers painfully that to take on the state in its role as monopoliser of violence it is not just taking on a distinct and partial dimension, but one that is integral. As a result, liberal and religious pacifists who sustain their war resistance often become converts to political radicalism, socialism or anarchism, as the classic biography of A. J. Muste in the USA illustrates so clearly.[24]

The *levée en masse* achieves a synthesis of popular sovereignty and territorial identity which affirms the co-optation and incorporation of dissent, or justifies its repression or conscription. In general, war mobilisation tended to rupture the movements and created a counter force that helped erode the bases of opposition and counter-mobilisation – the classic case being August 1914. War resistance in wartime is thus only partly continuous with these peacetime traditions, and in part reflects a spontaneous reaction to the inner structure and injustice of the wartime situation (the trenches of 1915–16 created a new mood and consciousness). Much the same can be seen in recent Third World conflicts.

Studies of World War I suggest how informal organisation grew up in the armies and then between armies or units in different sectors.[25] The specific factors of trench warfare (proximity of trenches, separation from officers, especially staff HQs, the sharp class distinctions in the army, the careless expenditure of lives, and the recognition of common interests) made this perhaps a special case sociologically. Nevertheless the reciprocal limitations of killing, the ritualisation of war ('fire when fired upon'), the internal controls of some units, the live-and-let-live principle, leading in some cases to fraternisation, in others to mutiny, have a more general significance. Casualties and war weariness often lead to a decline in state legitimacy: a questioning of war aims and strategy, an alienation from leadership groups or classes. In World War I, the 'we' and 'they' began to change, orders to fire were refused, so were orders to advance. Fear and reciprocity forced a change of orientation. After 1917, the French army ceased to be an offensive military instrument. The primary combat groups had become a means of subverting and transcending the war aims of military élites. The community of the trenches was the basis of the transnationalisation of feeling and action.

Within the armed forces, a corporate identity has often been identified at the primary group level where the loyalty is to the team, be it related to an organisational or technical rationale (i.e.

a weapons system). But this can be inverted; the camaraderies of the trenches could run against the officer class and its sponsors; rank and file could fraternise and identify across the caricatures of national military frontiers – the muddy no-man's land of the Western Front, for example. This line of argument suggests that though the state apparently successfully destroys autonomous centres of traditional power, it recreates new ones at least in potentiality. The complex dialectic of nationalism and internationalism, of acquiescence and resistance, can thus be related to the revolutionary collapse of strong states and powerful armies. The grip of nationalist ideas in ostensibly internationalist movements is real, but partial and superficial; in crisis it can evaporate.

War resistance raises sharply the problem of transnational concepts of social change. War may transform a liberal into a revolutionary or a revolutionary into a recruiting sergeant for the state. In part, individual biography sheds some light here, but what is of more significance is the degree to which a movement or constituency has become embedded in state functions, rhetoric and boundedness. The national polity and economy that captured the German Social Democrats or later the Russian revolutionaries – politically but physically and conceptually as well – was just emerging in Britain in the two decades before 1914 as a counterpart to the implicit populist syndicalism emergent in the working class movement.[26] The result was that the leadership in the main was neither communally rooted nor transnationalist. Socialist pluralism and libertarian anti-militarism was already losing out to statist progressivism; Marxist, social democratic or Fabian.[27] The lateral linkages between communities of producers were difficult if not impossible to sustain, and thus the anti-militarism of the international could have no strategy and no contingency plan; only three years of war put it back on the agenda.

What the First World War and the Indo-China War both did (and these are the two examples I have concentrated on here) was to raise the issue of what Boulding called the terms of trade between the individual and the state-rights and duties.[28] Yet even where those terms were seen to be disadvantageous it is my argument that without either a strong subcultural basis, or a cross-frontier linkage or identification (and possibly both) counter-mobilisation and resistance is unlikely to take place except on an isolated individual basis. For the war resistance tradition, even where it is intertwined with 'bourgeois' individualism, is closely related to collective opposition by village, church, occupational group, political sect or ethnic community. The ability of the state to cut cross-national ties, to break supra-national loyalties, and to isolate and penetrate the local community thus remains crucial in breaking down war resistance.

In 1914 and again after 1918, the moment had been lost, the alliances dismembered, the cross-national linkages were ruptured. But the vision remained. The decentralist anti-authoritarian communalist dream was not entirely divorced from the globalist, transnationalist impulse. In consciousness and in practice that synthesis and relation emerged again with the threat of nuclear war, and the internationalisation of issues like Indo-China or civil rights. The New Left tentatively hinted that such a revival might coincide with new emergent social forces.[29] The challenge to the coercive state was once again linked not only to the immediate problems of war (nuclear or colonial), but to strategies of social change; the internal and external linkage of state violence were illustrated by movements which were unaligned and relatively autonomous. The critical social theorists of the 1960s tentatively aired new scenarios and alliances albeit of a limited kind.[30]

The internationalisation of the opposition to the war in Indo-China still represents a crucial test case where solidarity between war resisters in two contexts becomes politically salient. Yet there were ambiguities in the degree to which a movement detached from nation-states initially, later began to align with national protagonists, that is an emergent revolutionary or conquest state. Because of what Galtung described as the 'asymmetry' of the Indo-China war before 1968, it was difficult to achieve a true alliance between oppositional groups; it became for many a choice of military élites.[31] Those who resisted war as such in Vietnam (and they represented a massive proportion of the population eligible for conscription by both sides in the South) found themselves at odds with the drift of the Western peace movement;[32] in the end state triumphed over community and society in each country. There was in the ultimate analysis no true transnationalism of war resistance – it became an international, as much as transnational, movement but one that often identified with a more 'progressive' nation-state.[33]

The contrary tendencies to accept or reject national frameworks are thus reinforced, weakened and reinforced again in a cyclical fashion. Those groups that sustain continuity are of most significance and it is they who affirm the thesis that communal and transnational linkages and frameworks of understanding are a key to explaining potential transcendence and subversion of the nation-state in arms. In the 1960s those who were able to sustain the detachment necessary to maintain resistance were those groups whose social base reinforced autonomous values and lifestyles (urban and rural communities, counter-cultural enclaves, ghettos). The limitations of this new communalism and the superficiality of the transnational linkages in many cases explain the minority and transient character of US draft resistance between 1965 and 1972.[34] Nevertheless the emergent minorities had in common either an inherited or manufactured detachment that contained this potentiality for both subversion and transcendence of national military loyalty. Women, Black groups, student subcultures, other ethnic and disadvantaged subcultures provided separate identifications, which were to a degree synthesised in the transnational concern with the Indo-China war, the linkages of the peace movement across national boundaries and the concrete acts of resistance within the armed forces and by inductees.

Where these elements are overlain and given a social basis of detachment, insulation and autonomy, then both normatively and physically resistance is more likely to be sustained. On the whole, the stronger bases are the traditional and communal, which are detached from nation-states to a degree, but lack any sophisticated transnational consciousness – even when involved in emigration. The more contemporary examples are strong on transnational consciousness and linkages, but weaker in communal bases of detachment. The former are vulnerable politically, culturally and militarily; the latter are vulnerable ideologically and economically – they lack economic autonomies. During the 1960s a romantic streak in the radical movements of the West began to perceive and to actualise relationships between themselves and the other communities of resistance: of the poor and Blacks in the USA, of the peasant villages of South East Asia. Symbolism began to transform itself into practical alliances in Europe and America and to some degree – in fragile and superficial fashion – with the oppressed of the developing world. The war resistance of the New Left was in this sense forward looking:

it was strengthened by its sense of identity with a global movement of change. This leads one to a general conclusion about communally-based resistance: that it can become isolated, introverted and retreatist unless it can link and communicate with similar communities even on a largely symbolic basis. Subcultures and movements (like Feminism) which cross national boundaries have potentiality in the way the labour movements of 1900 had. The difference now is that the plurality of such constituencies and transnational agencies has multiplied.

The question is raised whether the self-conscious recreation of a synthesis (of these relatively accidental syntheses in the past) can become the basis of a more sustained anti-militarism of the future. It also raises the question of continuity between the persisting detachment of subcultures which separate members from national and military norms and socialisation and the new emergent subcultures of newly self-conscious minorities. Both have shown themselves to be significantly associated with the phenomenon of war resistance. The reasons, as I have shown, become sociologically obvious.

The further question, and one which may exercise national states, is whether these syntheses go beyond war resistance to the dismantling of the violence-monopoly not just for war or war preparation but for centralised political-legal control as such. Thus even liberal or socialist societies have traditionally been ambivalent about the rights of war resisters, who are defined as treasonable and even punishable by death. This can be seen in terms of the logic of the challenge to the state, in which there is the potential foundation of a new global polity. Despite Bolshevik ambivalence, many Russian war resisters were shot, both in 1917 and during the Civil War.[35]

If one is to summarise the evidence for war resistance and war resisters, it is that they cannot be separated from the character and history of given societies; war resisters have been drawn especially from groups that have cross-national affiliations whether ideological or ethnic, from groups which have migrated from country to country or community to community, from those who are on the move from town to town, village to city; subcultural and transnational orientations are often found together and are overrepresented as social dimensions of those who have resisted war. Strong subgroups have insulated their members from the impact of national mobilisations, something which mass

socialist parties have not been able to acquire. In fact, mass parliamentary socialism has drawn people on to the framework of
potential recruitment and willing conscription.

The actual evidence that I have summarily generalised about
here, concerns relatively small groups of people in a numerical
sense, but it is arguable that we are talking about strategic
minorities which are in certain contexts – as Marxists and
Weberians have both shown in their work – world-historical
actors. Their variety and isolation and successive defeats should
not disguise what they have had in common, and the fact that
they have occasionally acted in rough unison. The 'natural'
peasant anarchist[36] who is a member of both an ethnic minority
and a millennial or pacifist religious sect, who moves across
political frontiers, who deserts from at least one army, and who
becomes a first generation industrial immigrant socialist and
anti-militarist in an urban village is an invention – a conceptual
archetype, yet one which illustrates the patterns that exist at a
certain point of state growth. We may be nearing a point where a
similar archetype emerges as that process begins to reverse: the
difference being sixty or eighty or a hundred years of historical
consciousness, a new starting point, new states, new communities,
new non-state actors, new transnational relations and new non-
governmental groups, and – not least – the threat of a new kind of
war and militarism. The incremental withdrawal of violence from
the nuclear monopoly is a different act from that of classical war
resistance, though in terms of modern state violence, the latter
remains highly relevant. The transnational orientation of a
nuclear-free community is a symbolic restatement of that
connection.[37]

CONCLUSION: FROM RESISTANCE TO GLOBAL COMMUNITY

On the one hand the logic of the twentieth century state is
towards totalism, with the potentiality of intensifying each
dimension of Weber's definition: a more comprehensive
monopoly of power and violence, and a greater territorial
definition and legitimation, and an increased capacity for
violence at all levels, and paradoxically potentially and often
actually greater political legitimation.[38] Moreover, we have seen

this as a global export so that the past two decades have seen the completion of a universal process of nation-state demarcation and with it increased militarisation, military regimes and armed repression, the spread of conscription to almost every state, the spread of arms trading throughout the world, and the extension of a nuclear threat to every human society, through proliferation and potential irradiation on a world scale.

On the other hand, we can judge the nation-state to be obsolescent in dealing with the very problems it has been part of and which it has helped create. The key human possibilities and solutions lie outside the nation-state system. That system is an obstacle to progress. As against intensified nationalism and territoriality there is a new global consciousness and sense of species identity especially amongst specific transnational minorities and categories. Moreover, there is a resurgence of the local and regional community from the street to the village to the province to the suppressed national minority, evidence of the renewed defence of communities under threat from war and state-building. Moreover, in the 1960s a new ideological impulse (the New Left) attempted to synthesise these elements and pit them against the military industrial monoliths – especially during the Vietnam War. The transnational character of war resistance in this period was a key factor in its effectiveness.[39] Then, and since, there have been some signs of a loss of control – or at least of nerve – by that nation-state system and the military-industrial élites that use it.

It is in this context that the components of the state, as Weber defined it, are brought into question; the monopoly of killing (war), the territorial basis of coercion and legitimation, the extent and success of the claims made by the 'bodies of armed men' who control it.

In the examples I have used, the three elements in Weber's definition – the monopoly of violence (war resistance), legitimacy (delegitimation of authority), and territoriality (transnational linkages of communities and non-governmental groups), find their historic counterparts. But what is crucial is that the alternative to state organisation is multiple: communal *and* transnational. The evidence suggests that both as means and ends, subversion *and* transcendence of given polities are necessary.

In the twentieth century, through bureaucratic administration of millions, and technological innovations, war becomes distanced and depersonalised – from the trenches of World War I, to Dresden and Hiroshima, and then on to the computerised long-distance attacks on Indo-China (or the potential launching of nuclear missiles across hemispheres) – society has seen an evolution of great rapidity linked to the harnessing of science by the state.

The elements of hatred, of aggression, of ideological motivation in so far as they were ever a dominant factor in getting people to kill (and even in the world wars they proved transient and partial enough) are gradually drained away from the armies (or military machines) of the great industrial states. With the nuclear threat, the life and death risks of the conscript are spread more evenly over the whole society; the combat soldier may be marginally safer than the civilian, in part because he is functionally more important.

Not only do most individuals, consciously or not, suspend their morality of the inviolability of human beings on an individual basis: now such suspension is on a societal or species basis ('Thou shall not destroy whole peoples' is the new commandment to be broken). The territorial monopoly of coercion has reached its genocidal zenith in this capacity to destroy all, including itself, either by nuclear war or the breakup of the state-system, or both.

In closing, one may perhaps indulge in a Utopian futurology built on these paradoxical tendencies. Transnational non-governmental initiatives, extra-parliamentary communal based alternatives, did not die, even with the collapse of the radicalism of the sixties. Based in new constituencies a non-aligned internationalism, that which connects global issues with community life and is detached from the interests of both monoliths East and West (and of the northern hemisphere itself) is coming into an alliance with those activists who resist militarism and the overblown nation-state. They thus can link human rights and anti-militarism (Amnesty with CND and END) and see the strategies that build on the historic social realities revealed by generations of heroic war resisters as a potential synthesis that can perhaps provide a strategy to reverse the race towards nuclear barbarism.

NOTES

1. I deal with this at greater length in my *War Resistance and the Nation State* (Berkeley: University of California Press, forthcoming). For a summary of the recent revival of interest in the state see C. Hamilton, Introduction to France Oppenheimer, *The State* (New York: Free Life Editions, 1974) and Robert Carneiro's important article, 'Theory of the Origin of the State', *Science*, CLXIX (Aug. 1970).

2. On these developments see H. Lubasz, *The Development of the Modern State* (New York: Macmillan, 1964) especially the excerpt by Hintze. Hintze is also included in the anthology, Reinhard Bendix (ed.), *State and Society* (Boston: Little Brown, 1968).

3. Weber's definition varies from text to text, but see for one of them, *Theory of Social and Economic Organisation* (Glencoe: Free Press, 1964).

4. Peter Brock's work provides some of the most comprehensive historical evidence, e.g. his *Pacifism in Europe to 1914* (Princeton University Press, 1972). I have assembled more in my own work, op. cit., fn. 1.

5. This theme was followed up by political sociologists in the 1950s: Hannah Arendt in her *Origins of Totalitarianism* (London: Allen & Unwin, 1967), as well as Robert Nisbet, *Community and Power* (New York: OUP, 1962) and C. Wright Mills, *The Power Elite* (New York: OUP, 1956).

6. These as specific case studies are few in number, and have to be reconstructed from other historical sources and sociological evidence.

7. See Geoffrey Ostergaard, 'Resisting the Nation State: the Pacifist and Anarchist Traditions' in L. Tivey (ed.), *The Nation State* (Oxford: Robertson, 1981). See also April Carter's *Political Theory of Anarchism* (London: Routledge & Kegan Paul, 1971) and A. D. Smith, *Theories of Nationalism* (London: Harper Row, 1971).

8. See the stimulating essay by V. Kiernan, 'Conscription and Society in Europe before the War of 1914–18' in M. Foot (ed.), *War and Society* (London: Elek, 1973), and also D. Prasad and T. Smythe, *Conscription, A World Survey* (London: WRI, 1968).

9. Ernest Barker, 'The Rise of Conscription in Western Europe' in *Development of Public Services in Western Europe* (New York: OUP, 1944).

10. See Oppenheimer, op. cit., but also Kropotkin's essay, 'The State, Its Historic Role' (London: Freedom Press, 1969).

11. Randolph Bourne, *War and the Intellectuals* (New York: Harper & Row, 1964).

12. E. Wolf, 'Peasants and Revolutionary War, unpublished paper (some of his ideas are contained in the conclusion of his *Peasant Wars of the Twentieth Century* (London: Faber, 1970).

13. Wolf, ibid. and my '*On War, National Liberation and the State*' (London, Christian Action, 1972, to be republished).

14. See my *War Resistance and the National State* op. cit.; Brock, *Pacifism in Europe to 1914*, op. cit., and his *Pacifism in the Twentieth Century* (New York: van Nostrand, 1972).

15. These ideas of T. H Marshall, *Citizenship and Social Class* (Cambridge

University Press, 1960), were developed by Reinhard Bendix, e.g. in his *Nationbuilding and Citizenship* (New York: Wiley, 1964), and are paralleled by Barker's works, op. cit.

16. See M. Shaw, *Socialism and Militarism* (Nottingham: Spokesman pamphlet, 1980), and my response in *Peace News*, 10 July 1981.

17. L. Schlissel, *Conscience in America* (New York: Dutton, 1968), and J. Rae, *Conscience in Politics* (London: OUP, 1970).

18. Arendt's point in *Origins*, op. cit.

19. Prasad and Smythe, op. cit.

20. The view of these groups expressed by Edward Thompson early in his book on *The Making of the English Working Class* (New York: Pantheon, 1966) evaluates their efforts differently from either an orthodox Marxist: E. J. Hobsbawm, *Primitive Rebels* (Manchester University Press, 1959) or a liberal historian: G. Rude, *The Crowd in History* (New York: Wiley, 1964).

21. See F. F. Ridley, *Revolutionary Syndicalism in France* (Cambridge University Press, 1970); G. D. H. Cole, *History of Socialist Thought* (Vol. 3) (London: Macmillan, 1963); and W. Kendall, *The Revolutionary Movement in Britain* (London: Weidenfeld & Nicolson, 1969).

22. The major accounts of this are in chronological order, G. D. H. Cole, op. cit.; Julius Braunthal, *History of the International* (London: Nelson, 1966–7); James Joll, *The Second International, 1889–1914* (New York: Harper, 1966); and Georges Haupt, *Socialism and the Great War* (Oxford: Clarendon Press, 1972).

23. G. Nuttall, *Christian Pacifism in History* (Berkeley: World Without War Council, 1971), and the work of Brock, op. cit.

24. A. J. Muste, *Essays* (New York: Touchstone Books, 1970); N. Hentoff, *Peace Agitator: The Story of A. J. Muste* (New York: Macmillan, 1963); Charles Chatfield, *For Peace and Justice* (University of Tennessee Press, 1971).

25. T. Ashworth, 'Sociology of Trench Warfare', *BJS*, 1968. Note also the *American Soldier* series, Stouffer and the work of M. Janowitz, *The New Military* (New York: Norton, 1969).

26. Kendall, op. cit. and Cole, op. cit.

27. Young, *War Resistance and the Nation State*, op. cit. and R. Miliband, *Parliamentary Socialism* (London: Merlin Press, 1964).

28. K. Boulding, 'The Impact of the Draft on the Legitimacy of the State' in Sol Tax (ed.), *The Draft* (University of Chicago Press, 1967).

29. See my *An Infantile Disorder? The Crisis and Decline of the New Left* (London: Routledge & Kegan Paul, 1977), and April Carter, *Direct Action in a Liberal Democracy* (London: Routledge & Kegan Paul, 1973).

30. Ibid. and H. Marcuse, *An Essay on Liberation* (London: Allen Lane, 1969).

31. J. Galtung, 'Violence and the International System', *JPR*, 1969.

32. Young, *Infantile Disorder?* op. cit.

33. Ibid.

34. M. Ferber and S. Lynd, *The Resistance* (Boston: Beacon Press, 1971); M. Teodori (ed.), *The New Left* (New York: Bobbs-Merrill, 1969).

35. P. Brock, *Twentieth Century*, op. cit.; and references in Shub, Carr, Avrich (*The Russian Anarchists*) and other accounts of post-1917 Russia.

36. Wolf, op. cit.

37. I have developed this in a British Association paper 'Averting Holocaust?'

published in F. Barnaby (ed.), *The Nuclear Arms Race* (London: F. Pinter, 1982). The literature on transnationalism has been proliferating recently.

38. On this legitimation see R. Miliband, *State in Capitalist Society* (London: Weidenfeld & Nicolson, 1969).

39. Young, *Infantile Disorder?* and *War Resistance and the Nation State*, op. cit. I have summarised this is an article 'Transnationalism and Communalism', *Gandhi Marq*, India, forthcoming.

Part II

The Cold War and Defence Policy

5 The Politics of Peace and War

RALPH MILIBAND

I am concerned here with the 'causes of World War III', to use the arresting (and, one hopes, over-pessimistic) title of a book which C. Wright Mills published in 1959.[1] More precisely, I am concerned with the reasons which render possible (some would say probable) a major confrontation between the United States and the Soviet Union, escalating into a full-scale 'nuclear exchange' between them, and leading to a nuclear holocaust of hundreds of millions of men, women and children, and to the lasting devastation of a large part of the planet. The gravity of the threat is sufficiently indicated by the fact that no one, whatever his or her opinion of its causes or remedies, can deny that its realisation is, at the least, within the realm of the possible.

Threats of lesser wars also abound. 'The smell of blood rises from the pages of history', Joseph de Maistre said in the aftermath of the French Revolution. But it is in the twentieth century that the stench of death in war has become overpowering. Some two hundred 'small' wars of a 'conventional' kind have been fought in many parts of the world since the end of World War II, at a cost, it has been estimated, of some 25 million lives. Such 'small' wars must be expected to go on as long as nation-states, or rather their governments, believe it to be in their interest to wage them, and are able to do so; and the ever-greater efficiency of the 'conventional' weapons with which such wars are fought guarantees that they will become steadily more murderous and destructive.

It must also be supposed that, as more and more countries acquire nuclear weapons, one or other of them, engaged in a 'small' war and facing defeat and disaster, may seek to retrieve the situation by using such weapons. The use of even low-capacity

119

nuclear weapons would cause vast casualties and great destruction: all the same, this would be much more modest (if one can use such a term in this context) than the death and devastation that would be produced by a 'nuclear exchange' between the United States and the Soviet Union. The effects of even a limited exchange between them would be tremendous – many times greater than what occurred at Hiroshima and Nagasaki[2] – and even those people who do believe that a limited exchange might not lead to an unlimited one cannot deny that it might. The very fact that so much death and destruction would be produced by a limited 'nuclear exchange' would itself create conditions in which escalation, far from being inhibited by the impact of such an exchange, would be made more probable as a result of it. The question is why the prospect of such a catastrophe should now threaten the human race; and what hope there is of preventing it.

Two related reasons have frequently been advanced in recent years for thinking that a 'nuclear exchange' between the super powers was possible or probable.

The first is that an accident is quite capable of occurring which would lead to nuclear war. On this 'scenario', military computers in the United States or the Soviet Union would indicate, mistakenly, that either country had launched a nuclear attack upon the other. Further mistaken signals would appear to confirm that an attack was on the way. The time available to decide whether to launch a counter-strike would be measured in minutes, or it might even be eliminated altogether by an automatic 'launch-on-warning' response. A nuclear war would then be on.

A number of computer misreadings have occurred in the United States, and led to alerts which were called off when the errors were discovered, well before (so it is said) matters were in any danger of getting out of hand. It may be assumed that computer misreadings have also occurred in the Soviet Union and produced more or less advanced stages of alert.

It clearly cannot be taken for granted that any such errors, which are bound to occur, will always and inevitably be rectified in good time. However improbable, a chain of errors, misreadings, mishaps and accidents is possible. Moreover, accidents and their consequences are not purely 'accidental'. What is made of accidents is not only a matter of objective and technical appraisal: much also depends on the international conjuncture in which accidents occur. In a period of relative quiescence, when the relations between the super powers are not particularly bad and there is no major international crisis, there would be a very strong urge to treat alarming signals with great caution and scepticism, to check again, and to delay to the utmost an irremediable nuclear response. This is what makes the notion of an automatic 'launch-on-warning' response so sinister. In a period of intense and prolonged international crisis, on the other hand, possibly with some limited military incident having already occurred (a ship sunk, planes shot down, some soldiers killed), there would exist a strong predisposition to find in erroneous signals a confirmation of expectations and fears that the other side had decided to strike, and there would be a greater willingness to initiate what would be believed to be a counter-strike. We are therefore driven back to ask what are the forces which shape the international conjuncture and which produce crises in which accidents are likely to turn into catastrophes.

The second reason often advanced for thinking nuclear war possible or probable is the arms race itself. 'The immediate cause of World War III', Mills wrote in the book referred to earlier, 'is the military preparation for it'.[3] On this view, the people in charge of affairs in the United States and the Soviet Union are governed by pressures and constraints which are driving their countries and the rest of the world towards nuclear war. Much the same view has been expressed more recently by E. P. Thompson, for instance in an article entitled 'The Logic of Exterminism', in the May-June 1981 issue of *New Left Review*.[4]

In that article, Thompson writes that 'to structure an analysis in a consecutive rational manner may be, at the same time, to impose a consequential rationality upon the object of analysis'. But what, he goes on to ask, 'if the object is *ir*rational? What if events are being willed by no single causative historical logic ...but are simply the product of a messy inertia?...Detonation might be triggered by accident, miscalculation, by the implacable upwards creep of weapons technology, or by a sudden hot flush of ideological passion'.[5] To the left's 'anthropomorphic interpretation of political, economic and military formations, to which are attributed intentions and goals', Thompson therefore counterposes 'the irrational outcome of colliding formations and wills'.[6]

It is easy to see why the view that the super powers are caught

up in an irrational process should have gained so much currency
For it *is* irrational to prepare so feverishly for death and
destruction on such an immense scale, and to devote enormous
efforts and resources to the production and improvement of
weapons of war; and it is all the more irrational when so much
needs to be done to make life more tolerable for hundreds of
millions of people who suffer chronically from hunger and want,
not to speak of all that needs to be done even in countries whose
inhabitants are not on the edge of starvation and death.

But to say that the arms race is irrational is not at all the same
as saying that it is itself a prime cause of war. It may well be
argued that the arms race creates conditions in which any
attempt to achieve a significant measure of disarmament is made
more difficult and problematic; that the ever greater sophistication of weapons technology constantly reduces and may
annul the time available to decide on responses to alerts, and
therefore make more 'accidents' potentially lethal; that the arms
race poisons further the climate of relations between the super
powers; and that it strengthens all the forces – and there are
many – which have an interest in opposing détente and disarmament. On any such count, the arms race must be reckoned to be
an important contributory cause of World War III.

Even so, there are dangers in placing the prime emphasis on
the arms race itself: for to do so obscures other and different
factors which are at the core of the antagonism between the super
powers and which serve as fuel to the arms race. The chances are
that, if nuclear war does occur, it will be as a result of an
escalation of a crisis originating in these factors. If *they* could be
made less explosive, the danger of a nuclear confrontation
between the United States and the Soviet Union would be greatly
reduced; and détente and disarmament would have a better
chance. This is why it is important to locate accurately the
reasons for the antagonism between the super powers.

In essence, the danger of armed conflict between the United
States and the Soviet Union stems from the proliferation of re-
volutionary movements which has occurred since the late fifties.
By then, an exceedingly difficult and partial process of ac-
commodation between the super powers had been achieved, with
the more or less reluctant acceptance by the United States of the
Communist bloc that had come into being following World War
II, and which included Eastern Europe and East Germany, North

Korea, China and North Vietnam. If all revolutionary strivings in the world had then been frozen, and stayed frozen, the Cold War might have been replaced by 'peaceful co-existence'; and even if the arms race had continued, it is quite likely that it would have continued with much less intensity, and there would have been less danger than there is now of accidents escalating into nuclear war.

But revolutionary strivings were not frozen, and could not be. The Cuban Revolution and Fidel Castro's entry in Havana in 1959 mark the beginning of a new historical phase, which amounts to permanent revolution, though not of the kind and in the style which Marx and Trotsky envisaged. Some revolutionary movements since then have been able to achieve power, for instance in Algeria, Angola, Mozambique, Ethiopia, South Yemen, Nicaragua and Iran. Others have been able to pose a major challenge to their regimes, for instance in El Salvador and Guatemala. Yet others are at an earlier stage of development and can still be contained, usually with American help. In some cases, revolutionary movements have been temporarily crushed, as in Indonesia.

These movements differ very greatly in their specific ideological and political orientations. Unlike earlier movements, they are not communist-led, though communists often do play a part in them. But however much they may differ in other respects, they do have in common a very strong *nationalist* consciousness. Whatever the extent to which they are social-revolutionary, they are certainly national-revolutionary; and this is as true for those movements which proclaim themselves to be Marxist-Leninist as for any other. They may seek Soviet support, but they do not want subordination. Earlier (communist) movements equated allegiance to the Soviet Union with allegiance to the cause of the revolution in general, and to the cause of revolution in their own countries in particular. These more recent movements do not.

Revolutionary movements do not only challenge the *status quo* in their own countries, but internationally as well. The regimes which they replace are usually closely allied to the United States. The victory of revolutionary movements, whatever their specific ideological orientation may be, signifies a rupturing of military, economic and political bonds with the United States and other Western powers; and it requires the forging of a new relationship with them, which is marked by suspicion and hostility on both sides, with the constant and well-grounded fear of the new regime that it stands in danger of 'de-stabilisation' by the United States and its allies. The revolution which overthrew the Shah in Iran shows well enough that the depth of suspicion and hostility on the revolutionary side is not simply a matter of how 'left wing' and 'communist' the new regime may be: what is at issue is the determination of the revolutionaries to establish a new set of conditions, one of whose main features is independence from the United States and the West in general.

The international *status quo* which revolutionary movements challenge and disturb was established in World War II and after and it was marked, most notably, by the predominant position which the United States was then able to assume in the world. That predominant position was sanctioned by the treaties, alliances, understandings and concessions which linked most countries outside the communist bloc to the United States. It found expression, in practical terms, in the economic access which the United States had to these countries, and in the military bases, facilities and arrangements which it was able to obtain from them. It is to all this that revolutionary movements, to a greater or lesser degree, pose a real threat.

Revolutionary or dissident movements of a different kind also pose a threat to the predominance which the Soviet Union was able to achieve in a number of countries in the post-war period: Hungary in 1956, Czechoslovakia in 1968, Afghanistan in 1979 and after, Poland in 1956, 1970 and 1981 provide the most visible and dramatic signs of this challenge. Yugoslavia provided another as early as 1948. But the area of Soviet predominance is very much smaller than that of the United States: in global terms, it is the United States and not the Soviet Union which is the 'conservative' power in the world. For it is the United States which is mainly concerned to maintain the *status quo* and which therefore opposes all the forces which seek to upset it – except of course in the area of Soviet predominance, where it is the Soviet Union which plays the 'conservative' role.

There is nothing particularly complicated about the reasons why the United States seeks to maintain the *status quo* in its area of predominance. One such reason is economic. The American Government seeks to defend American business interests anywhere in the world, and wants to keep the largest possible part of the world open to capitalist enterprise, notably to American capitalist enterprise. The coming to power of revolutionary movements is thought to pose a clear threat to such purposes: revolutionary governments have a bias towards nationalisation, often with the threat of actual expropriation of nationalised assets, or with offers of compensation to foreign interests which are not satisfactory. Moreover, such governments make more cumbersome and expensive the operation of foreign enterprises, where they allow them to operate at all. In any case, existing regimes are much more favourable to American and other capitalist interests than any revolutionary government is likely to be, and are much more easy to deal with. The fact that they may also be vicious tyrannies, which keep the vast majority of their people in conditions of extreme exploitation and poverty, is a matter of secondary importance. After all, such regimes can be relied on to be ruthless with the left and they also ensure that labour relations present no problem to the foreign interests in their country.

There are also important strategic considerations which affect American policy. As noted earlier, the coming to power of a revolutionary government brings into question existing military arrangements and threatens future ones. Moreover, it may open the way to a Soviet presence in the country, even possibly a Soviet base. To these strategic considerations may also be related the danger, from the American point of view, and from that of the West in general, that strategic minerals and oil supplies might come under the control of revolutionary governments, and be denied to the United States and its allies while being made available to the Soviet Union.

These would be grounds enough to explain American global interventionism against revolutionary movements. But how is this linked to the arms race and the conflict between the super powers? The answer is quite straightforward: in seeking to oppose and defeat the challenge posed by revolutionary movements, it is not only these movements which the United States encounters, but also the Soviet Union. Fred Halliday makes the point as follows:

. . . the new wave of Third World revolutions occasioned a substantial and visible exercise of Soviet military power in support of them. The USSR supplied the heavy military armour needed for victory in Vietnam; it provided the air-lift and strategic equipment for Cuban forces in Angola and Ethiopia; and it directly deployed Soviet forces themselves in Afghanistan. Even where there was no Soviet military involvement as such, states allied to the USSR or revolutionary movements in conflict with the West were in some measure protected by the fact that the new strategic potential of the USSR stayed the hands of US officials who might otherwise have envisaged direct intervention, as in Iran.[7]

The Soviet presence in the world may, in many instances, be quite undramatic. But it *is* a presence, and it does make the maintenance of American predominance in the world more difficult. For some policy-makers in Washington, Soviet help to revolutionary movements or states, whether it takes the form of economic or military aid, is proof enough of Soviet 'expansionism'. But even those policy-makers who take a more moderate view of Soviet purposes cannot but be aware of the Soviet Union as a hindrance to their own purposes – not necessarily insurmountable but real. They may know that revolutionary movements would exist, even if the Soviet Union did not. But it is a reasonable presumption that these movements would be easier to deal with if the Soviet Union did not exist. Cuba is the most obvious case in point. The Cuban Revolution owed nothing to the Soviet Union, but the survival of the Cuban regime would have been impossible without Soviet help, or at least exceedingly doubtful. The overwhelming chances are that it would have been strangled by blockade, even if it had not been destroyed by military means.

The reasons which impel the Soviet leaders to engage in their own global interventionism have nothing to do with a supposed irresistible craving for world domination. By far the most rational view of this Soviet interventionism is that it is produced by a primarily defensive concern for Soviet security. It is this above all which led Stalin to impose communist regimes in Eastern Europe and East Germany, since communist regimes seemed to him to be the only real guarantee that these contiguous territories would not turn into bases for the Soviet Union's enemies. It was the same concern which led to the invasion of Hungary in 1956, of Czechoslovakia in 1968 and of Afghanistan in 1979. The point is not that the calculation was correct: there is much to be said for the view that it is very short-sighted, in that it fails to take into account the fact that an imposed and illegitimate regime is not reliable in an emergency, and that there is a very large price to be paid, in international terms, for 'security' bought in this way. However this may be, it is security for the Soviet Union, as the Soviet leaders understand it, which best explains their international strategy.

It is this, rather than 'expansionism' or ideological proselytism which determines the degree and kind of support which the Soviet Union extends to revolutionary movements and states across the world. Such movements offer the hope of greater influence in the world for the Soviet Union; and they are also likely to be an embarrassment, great or small, to the United States. Here too, Cuba provides a good example of both points. It is similarly of some advantage to the Soviet Union that Nicaragua should be ruled by a left-wing regime rather than by a reactionary one, closely allied to the United States. Even revolutionary regimes which are opposed to the Soviet Union, like Iran's Islamic revolutionary regime, are better than reactionary ones, since they are also opposed to the United States.

Such perspectives do not make for 'ideological' politics and Soviet foreign policy has in fact been extremely 'pragmatic'; its one consistent thread being precisely the pursuit of security. This search, however, produces many Soviet actions and policies which help to confirm American policy-makers in the view that they are confronted by a country bent on aggrandisement and aggression. The search of Soviet leaders for security does lead to global interventionism in one form or another, and its motives matter less than its consequences. Not only does it confirm American policymakers in their view of the Soviet Union; even more important, it helps them to convince the American people that they face immense dangers from the Soviet Union. The latter's 'image' is in any case greatly damaged by the repressive nature of the regime: its interventionism abroad completes the picture of a country which only armed might can contain. The propaganda value of drawing an analogy, however false, between this situation and that of the thirties, is obvious. 'Appeasement' of the Nazis then meant war, not peace: we must therefore not make the same mistake again. Much of the arms race is based on such *non sequiturs*. The emphasis on Soviet 'expansionism', and on the need to contain and fight it, has many advantages; one of them is to obscure the fact that the containment which the United States is seeking to achieve is that of revolutionary movements throughout the world.

Even among those who most ardently believe in Soviet 'expansionism', there cannot be very many who hold the view that the Soviet leaders are only waiting for an opportunity to launch a nuclear war against the United States. In fact, there is probably a very general measure of agreement, even among people who otherwise differ fundamentally, that, accidents aside, a nuclear war would most probably be the result of an escalation of a local crisis which had got out of hand. Neither the United States nor the Soviet Union want anything from each other: there are no territorial, or other such bones of contention between them, as there are, for instance, between the Soviet Union and China. Their only real point of contact, in terms of conflict, is where revolutionary movements do threaten the *status quo*, either against the United States, as is usually the case, or against the Soviet Union. It is at these points of contact and conflict that lie buried the seeds of World War III.

For it is not difficult to imagine a set of circumstances in which a revolutionary movement is taken by the United States to threaten its vital interests, and in which it would therefore decide to intervene militarily, by sending units of its rapid-deployment forces to help a threatened regime. In doing so, it might well encounter the Soviet Union, or Cuba, or other forces allied to the Soviet Union. The chances of incidents of varying gravity would then be considerable; and so, in such circumstances, would be the chances of 'accidents' turning into catastrophes. How things would develop would depend in large part on the coolness and caution of the participants, and on their willingness or ability to compromise and even retreat, as happened in the Cuban missile crisis of 1962, when Nikita Khrushchev did retreat. It is an indication of the immense dangers that the human race now confronts that the possibility of escalation from crisis to full-scale nuclear war should depend on the responses of a few people on either side, who may or may not be cautious and cool under stress, and who may in any case be overwhelmed by events.

These dangers are all the greater in that revolutionary movements are not only likely, but certain to develop further in many parts of the world, including highly 'strategic' and 'sensitive' areas. It is not very rash to suggest, for instance, that revolutionary upheavals will occur in Saudi Arabia, or the Gulf states, or the Caribbean, or Guatemala, or Haiti, or the Philippines, or South Korea, and so on. The rise of such movements in the Third World has only just begun; and there would have to be very good prospects of a spectacular improvement in the conditions of poor countries, under their existing regimes, for revolutionary movements to subside, or to be permanently and effectively contained. There are no such prospects; the trend, for most such countries, is the other way.

Nor is it only in the area of American predominance that there exist potential points of conflict and crisis between the United States and the Soviet Union: they also exist in the area of predominance of the Soviet Union. In one or other country of this area, movements of contestation will seek to undo the *status quo* and the United States may be tempted to help in one way or another.

Most parts of the world, in fact, provide dangerous points of contact between the super powers. Unfortunately, 'crisis management' is not a sufficiently precise and assured craft to provide any sort of guarantee that it would necessarily be effective in all circumstances; the more reasonable assumption is that it could easily fail.

The conclusion is inescapable that, as revolutionary movements grow in the coming years, so too will the dangers of nuclear war. This is one of the great 'ironies of history', to use Isaac Deutscher's phrase. The rise of the 'wretched of the earth' against exploitation and subordination is the most remarkable and inspiring social phenomenon of the twentieth century; and its grandeur is not dimmed by the fact that it cannot achieve more, at best, than a small part of its aims. The irony consists in the fact that the endeavours of revolutionary movements also provide the occasions for crisis and escalation into nuclear war. The question is how such a consequence can be averted, and how the dangers of nuclear war, from whatever source, can at least be reduced.

To begin with, the fact has to be faced that no great reliance can be placed upon disarmament negotiations between the super powers. Given the view of Soviet purposes which has held the field among American policy-makers since World War II, there is no reason why the arms race should not go on for ever, or until nuclear war brings it to an ultimate conclusion. The American assumption of Soviet 'expansionism' robs disarmament negotiations of any real meaning. For if Soviet leaders are believed to be moved by an inflexible will towards expansion, it follows that they can only be deterred – if they can be deterred at all – by an American nuclear force so great as to turn Soviet nuclear blackmail in support of aggressive policies into an empty threat, since Soviet nuclear aggression would amount to certain national obliteration. (This also assumes, of course, that Soviet rulers irrational enough to seek world domination, and to threaten the use of nuclear weapons in pursuit of their aims, would be sufficiently rational to be deterred by any threat: it is a very large assumption.)

As for Soviet policy-makers, they too clearly believe that they must have the capacity to threaten the United States with assured nuclear devastation, if they are not to be vulnerable to pre-emptive attack or to nuclear blackmail; and they too therefore strive to possess the strongest possible nuclear arsenal, which also means the least vulnerable one.

Given this belief in 'deterrence', it is not surprising that the arms race has if anything accelerated while negotiations over disarmament have been proceeding. But even if progress *was* made, and a substantial reduction in the capacity for 'overkill' which both super powers now possess *were* to be achieved, this would still leave them with enough such capacity to make nuclear war between them possible, and on a scale perfectly adequate for total devastation. Whether both super powers have the capacity to destroy each other, and much of the rest of the world, a hundred times over, or fifty times over, is not a matter of huge significance. Richard Barnet has noted that

> even if the worst assumptions of American military planners prove correct and the Russians develop the capability in the nineteen-eighties to destroy ninety per cent of the American land-based missiles, the submarines, cruise missiles, and bombers would still be able to deliver far more than five hundred nuclear warheads to the Soviet Union.[8]

The point also applies to disarmament. The only sound principle in this field is 'no nuclear weapons, no nuclear war'. Anything else is a potentially lethal second best. This is not to say that partial disarmament should not be pressed as hard as possible: any such pressure, and any real gain, must be welcome in so far as it may help create a climate in which further gains can be made. But the prospects for really significant advances towards disarmament must be reckoned to be poor: not sufficient, at least, to offer real prospects that nuclear war between the super powers might actually become *impossible*. Yet, nothing less than this will do.

It is the acceleration of the arms race, and the proposals to introduce new 'theatre' weapons in Western Europe in 1983 which have led to the resurgence in recent years of disarmament movements in a number of West European countries, notably Germany, Britain and Holland, with proposals for a nuclear-free zone in Europe, 'from Poland to Portugal' (and from Iceland to Italy), with the elimination from European soil of all nuclear weapons, and of all bases for the launching of such weapons.[9]

This amounts in effect to *nuclear pacifism*, and it is the only reasonable response to the danger of nuclear war. There is *nothing* for which it is worth fighting a nuclear war. The slogan 'better dead than red' (or black or blue) still made sense, whether one agreed with it or not, *before* the advent of nuclear weapons. Any war that was then fought, however devastating, still left the survivors with a life to live; and however great the destruction, there was no doubt that the grass would grow again and that new generations would be able to treat what had happened as no more than history. Nuclear weapons have changed all that: it is now scarcely in dispute that nuclear war on any major scale must bring civilised life to an end over a large part of the planet if not over the whole of it. This is the new dimension of war, and it is this which makes any strategy based on the *possibility* of nuclear war the ultimate example of what Mills aptly called 'crackpot realism'.

As in the case of all proposals relating to disarmament, whatever specific and concrete gain can be made by the European peace movements is useful; and stopping the installation of Cruise and Pershing II missiles in Western Europe would be an important gain and a great encouragement to further endeavours.

Here too, however, it must be said that there are severe limitations on what the European peace movement can be expected to achieve, at least in the near future. For the purpose of achieving concrete results, 'Europe' means separate states and governments, all of which are opposed to the policies and purposes of the peace movement. The initiative would have to come from one country or perhaps two where a breakthrough had been achieved, and where a government had come to office determined to implement nuclear disarmament. No united European initiative, *at government level*, can be expected for a very long time to come, not least because the French left is not much less opposed than the French right to any policy that would appear to threaten France's *force de frappe*.

Moreover, the kind of disarmament proposals which the European peace movement quite rightly puts forward constitute a revolutionary project which must be attended by the same difficulties as any other revolutionary project. The traditional Marxist view has always been that a government of the left, seriously seeking to implement fundamental measures of social and economic change, must expect great and implacable opposition from many different sources, at home and abroad. But the same kind of opposition must also be expected if the attempt is made to effect a fundamental change in the strategic orientations and policies of countries like Britain and Germany. The minimum condition of success of such purposes is mass support, and the bringing to office of a government pledged to implement peace policies. Nothing of this can be achieved quickly.

A further point needs to be made about the contribution which Europe can make to the diminution and elimination of the chances of nuclear war. This is that Europe cannot itself be the decisive voice in regard to peace and war: it is not there that the crucial decisions will be made. This is why the real value of the European peace campaigns does not lie primarily in what they can actually accomplish, but in encouraging resistance to the nuclear arms race beyond Europe, and above all in the United States.

For it is above all in the United States that a major, fundamental change in policy is required if nuclear war is to be averted. It is the determination of the United States to maintain the *status quo* in the world which mainly threatens to furnish the occasions out of which nuclear war may derive. What the Soviet Union does, or does not do, is also of the utmost importance: the two super powers clearly react upon each other, and it is in this sense on both of them that the prevention of nuclear war depends. But it is in the United States that the major shift must occur, simply because it is mainly the United States which will, in the years to come, be confronted by major challenges and choices, produced by the occurrence of revolutionary upheavals in many different part of the world.

It is not required that the United States should actually welcome such upheavals – though this might have unexpectedly favourable results for it. It is only necessary that the United States should not seek to defeat revolutionary movements by military means and in ways which create occasions for heightened tension and conflict.

Quite obviously, there are very powerful forces in the United States which will always press for the development of military power, intervention, the need for more and better weapons: economic interests bound up with the armaments industry, military interests seeking their own aggrandisement, ideological interests pursuing their particular crusades, political interests seeking political advantage through chauvinist overbidding. This is a formidable combination of forces with vast resources and great influence in government, the media, the press, the universities, and throughout the country. Yet, the hope of averting nuclear war must to a large extent depend on the defeat of these forces.

This could only occur by way of an immense strengthening of counter-forces in the United States which would have to be drawn from the ranks of labour, professional and academic strata, ethnic minorities, the women's movement, religious groups, ecology groups, and the existing peace movement itself; these counter-forces would need to acquire sufficient political weight and influence to be heard with political effect and to be able to bring to power people who reject interventionist perspectives and who can stand up to great interventionist pressures.

To speak in this vein is to invite disbelief and derision, given the enormous disparity of power, influence and resources that exists between interventionist forces and their opponents. But much here depends on what is being sought. The point is not to bring to Washington a socialist president or Congress who would proceed to the creation of a socialist society in the United States. It may be assumed that this will not happen for some time to come. Similarly, it is obvious that all the difficulties which are present in the achievement of European nuclear disarmament are also present – and a hundred times greater – in the United States.

But even limited measures by the United States in the halting of the arms race, provided they were not just cosmetic and public relations exercises, would be progress. Nor, in any case, is disarmament the only issue on which progress needs to be made. For it is American global interventionism which makes it possible or likely that nuclear weapons will be used in confrontation with the Soviet Union; and it is a shift away from global interventionism that is required. Furthermore, disarmament itself is more likely to follow such a shift than to precede it. Far from being a condition of détente, disarmament of a significant kind may well be a consequence of it.

It would be foolish to deny that to achieve a shift of this nature in American foreign policy is itself a very large enterprise. But it is reasonable to hope that more and more Americans will come to see the direct linkage that exists between inflation, recession, unemployment and cuts in expenditure on health and other welfare services on the one hand, and the foreign and defence policies their country pursues on the other; and that, in seeking to find alternatives to reactionary policies at home, they may also come to reject global interventionism abroad. A modern version of the New Deal is one of the alternatives which may be produced by the economic and social pressures at work in the United States: such a New Deal would now be very likely to include a major reappraisal, not only of policies on arms, but also of the relations of the United States with the Third World and with the Soviet Union.

Of course, nothing of this may come to pass, in which case the danger of nuclear war will continue to grow. But the defeat of interventionist forces does not only depend on what happens in the United States: it also depends on what the Soviet Union does abroad and on what happens inside it as well. Any major Soviet intervention, anywhere in the world, even within its own area of predominance, inevitably brings about a heightening of tension, increases the chances of confrontation, and both strengthens interventionist forces in the United States and weakens the peace forces everywhere. It was not the Soviet invasion of Afghanistan which caused the failure of Salt II and which produced a further escalation in the arms race, but it nevertheless gave a vast amount of excellent ammunition to all those in the United States – and beyond – who have an economic, military, ideological or political stake in the perpetuation and exacerbation of the Cold War. The rulers of the Soviet Union can do a great deal to strengthen the peace forces in the United States. But they can only do so by showing convincingly, by what they do and do not do, and not merely by proclamations of good intentions, that they are seriously seeking détente.

This is not only a matter of what they do abroad or of their policies on disarmament: what happens in the Soviet Union itself is also a matter of the greatest importance. The repression of dissent and the denial of civic freedoms are not only internal Soviet issues; they also have a direct bearing on the question of war and peace. The more repressive the regime is, the easier it is also for all the interventionist forces in the United States and elsewhere to proclaim that 'communism' must be opposed in the name of freedom and democracy and that this requires more and better weapons and the deployment of military strength everywhere in the world. 'Liberalisation', on this score, is not only desirable in itself and for the peoples of the Soviet Union: it is also necessary to reduce the danger of nuclear war.

NOTES

1. C. Wright Mills, *The Causes of World War Three* (London: Secker and Warburg, 1959).
2. See e.g. John Cox, 'A "Limited" Nuclear War', in E. P. Thompson *et al*, *Exterminism and Cold War* (London: New Left Books/Verso, 1982). The author discusses the consequences of a 400 megaton attack on Europe which would, he writes, be 'quite a "small" limited nuclear war': apart from the extreme material devastation this would produce, 'the death toll is likely to exceed 150 million...', pp. 175, 179.
3. Mills, op. cit., p. 85.
4. The article is reprinted in Thompson *et al*, op. cit.
5. Ibid., p. 1.
6. Ibid., p. 2.
7. F. Halliday, 'The Sources of the New Cold War', in Thompson *et al*, op. cit. p. 299.
8. Richard J. Barnet, 'The Search for National Security', *The New Yorker*, 27 April 1981, p. 61.
9. See K. Coates, 'For a Nuclear-free Europe', in E. P. Thompson and D. Smith (eds), *Protest and Survive* (Harmondsworth: Penguin, 1980).

6 Western Capitalism and the Cold War System

MICHAEL COX

INTRODUCTION

In this paper I attempt to look at the structure of the Cold War system, the reasons why that system broke down in the 1960s, and to what degree the era of détente has given way – as many seem to imagine – to a new Cold War. The paper is divided into a number of related sections. The first briefly examines the world crisis in the period between 1917 and 1947, that is between the Russian Revolution and the Truman Doctrine, and argues that on the basis of the inter-war system it was quite impossible to establish any form of equilibrium in the world. It is also suggested that even after the USSR had renounced world revolution, its very existence further contributed to the general crisis in this era. The second part of the paper examines the different alternative positions which the USSR might have occupied in the post 1945 world system. The following three parts of the paper show how the Cold War system effectively eliminated the major sources of instability in the Western world and created, as a result, a new equilibrium – an equilibrium which had been absent since 1917. It is suggested however that far from the Soviet Union challenging that equilibrium, it contributed to it in several ways. The great 'threat', in other words, became indispensable for Western capitalism after 1947. The sixth and the seventh sections of the paper examine why the Cold War system broke down in the late sixties, suggesting that parallel crises, in both the capitalist and 'communist' worlds, forced a rapprochement between the two systems. I put forward the thesis that détente was the attempted means by which the West tried to reconstruct a new equilibrium, not around the exclusion of the communist world from the world system but by its inclusion, and hoped that, in the long term, détente would lead to its reintegration into the international division of labour. I then show why détente has entered a critical period, but argue that this does not mean the world is returning, or even could return, to a Cold War system. In the concluding section I suggest that the slogans of 'peace' and 'one Europe' can in no way solve the major problems of our time, and argue that only a genuine socialist renewal in Europe as a whole and the Soviet Union can bring real equilibrium to a divided continent.

WORLD CRISIS: 1917–1947

The Russian Revolution was both symptom and cause of a deep world crisis that emerged after the First World War and which was not to be resolved until after World War II thirty years later. Europe in effect never recovered from the political and economic consequences of the 1914–18 war. In turn the international system which emerged from the war made any stable equilibrium impossible. In historic terms the development and spread of industrial capitalism before 1914 shattered the old nineteenth century order, undermining the conditions necessary for stable relations both within and between the major capitalist states thereafter. Revolution followed war, and despite the temporary stabilisation of the 1920s – the result of American economic support for Europe – it was clear that there was no viable basis for stability in Europe. Once America withdrew her economic support and retreated into protectionism between 1929 and 1931, the inevitable result was the distintegration of the world economy, further political instability, and war.

Soviet Russia challenged the already disturbed world order in several ways. Its withdrawal from the world division of labour removed a large part of the international system from the domination of capital. In the process, the USSR renounced all foreign debts, an act which had a disturbing impact upon European financial arrangements in the immediate post-war period – particularly for France. Equally upsetting was the new regime's opposition to traditional international politics. Soviet attacks on bourgeois diplomacy did much to weaken the legitimacy of the inter-war international order, whilst its rejection of

normal power alliances removed the major counter to German
expansion in the East. Furthermore, albeit in a less direct way,
successful revolution in Russia reinforced the position (many
might argue, necessitated the establishment) of a myriad of small
unstable political entities in Eastern Europe whose main historic
role was to block the spread of communism to Western Europe –
especially Germany. Successful though the strategy of establishing a 'cordon sanitaire' may have been, what was created
in Eastern Europe was fundamentally unstable and destabilising
for the rest of Europe. Saving the West from communism carried
a very high price indeed and not just in Eastern Europe; in effect,
the attempt to contain Bolshevism through nationalism severely
disturbed the European equilibrium as a whole. Finally, the
establishment of Soviet power in Russia had a profound impact
upon the class struggle and ideological discourse in Western
Europe in the inter-war years. At first the Bolsheviks called and
directly organised for revolution abroad. Later, even after the
regime had abandoned world revolution, the very existence of the
USSR posed a challenge to a bourgeois order which, after 1930 in
particular, was palpably unable to solve either its own economic
or international problems. The nature of the communist threat
underwent a subtle but real metamorphosis in the inter-war
years: but even after Bolshevism had been abandoned, the fact
that an alternative existed, and appeared to work, providing full
employment and growth, could only further undermine
bourgeois security. Fascism and fellow travelling were very
different, but related, indices of a deep loss of confidence within
the West about the future of the market economy and democratic
political process. Not surprisingly, by the end of the 1930s, as
one contemporary observer noted, even 'the bourgeoisie itself
[had] in large measure lost confidence in its own ideologies'.[1]

The great inter-war crisis, the war which followed, and
Europe's post-war economic problems, however disturbing, led to
neither the collapse nor the overthrow of capitalism. The danger
(or the opportunity) passed. The crisis was deep, but the political
left posed no real threat. European social democracy remained
wedded to reformism; the communists to the defence of the Soviet
Union.[2] Further, the potential link between war and revolution
was broken in the 1940s by politically crucial promises of post-war
reform and full employment.[3] Finally, by drawing upon the
lessons of past dangers and failures, American planners guarded

against the revolutionary disintegration[4] of Europe by the provision of massive aid and food relief after 1944.[5] At one level the Second World War raised major problems for world capitalism. At another however it created the conditions necessary for international stability. In 1919 several major capitalist states vied for position and ultimate domination. In 1945 there was only one major capitalist power of any real importance – the United States.[6] The Second World War had not only led to a simplification of the world system, but equally important, to European and Japanese dependence upon the United States. This reshaped world system made possible the implementation of US plans for a liberal, open, and it was assumed, harmonious world economy.[7] Unlike the situation in 1919, the way was open in 1945 for the elimination of disturbing inter-capitalist conflicts, and the creation of a more stable inter-dependent world economy, led and underwritten by the United States' enormous economic and military power.[8]

THE SOVIET UNION AND THE POST-WAR ORDER

The specific position of the Soviet Union within the new world order remained problematic, although by no means a real danger to it as later Cold War apologists asserted. Militarily, economically, and strategically, the Soviet position was very fragile after 1945. Amongst other things, it was open to atomic attack, confronted great economic difficulties in its own reconstruction, and finally, was encountering massive problems of consolidation in Eastern Europe. Russia's main interests were at home, not abroad, and in general this was understood by those planning the post-war order in Europe and America. The 'intelligence' case against the Soviet threat was well-documented and compelling. Militarily the USSR was regarded as no danger;[9] politically, its opposition to Western reconstruction after 1947 was of little real consequence. Russia, in short, was not the major problem for America, Europe or capitalism in general. Real divisions of interest existed between the Soviet Union and the West; these however did not make the Soviet Union a threat.[10]

Between 1944 and 1947 it is possible to isolate three Western strategies towards the USSR. The first, advocated by Roosevelt and culminating with the Yalta agreements of early 1945, attempted to use the wartime alliance to create post-war cooperation between America and Russia. In essence, this New Deal incorporationist vision sought to exploit Soviet economic needs and America's economic strength to create a Russian dependency relationship upon America. By offering aid and recognising Soviet security (notably in Eastern Europe), Roosevelt envisaged both short and long-term gains for the West. First, Russia – whose weakness this approach presupposed – would reduce its dependence upon disturbance in the world system; in effect would not challenge the stability of the world, if America would help Soviet reconstruction.[11] Second, Roosevelt argued that Russia could not be pressured out of Eastern Europe, and therefore only by recognising Soviet interests there could one expect any Western influence to remain. The withdrawal of Russia from Eastern Europe would take time, and could only occur if the West reduced the Soviet Union's sense of insecurity which, it was argued, was its main reason for remaining in Eastern Europe.[12] Finally, in the longer term, Roosevelt sought to break down the isolation and undermine the closed character of the Soviet system. Only in this way, it was assumed, could evolution and liberalisation occur in the USSR. Again this presupposed reducing Western hostility towards the USSR; a hostility which had done more to legitimise the Soviet state than change its character. In time, as many of Roosevelt's political intimates later testified, the object of Roosevelt's policy was the reintegration of the USSR into the West or, as Stimson put it in 1944, to bring it back to the 'fold of christian civilization'.[13] The 'drop-out' of the world system had to be reclaimed, and could be, the New Dealers believed, if the West pursued a consistent détente with the Soviet system.[14]

The breadth of Roosevelt's strategy was as sweeping as its failure was inevitable: for the Soviet élite was not going to trade its political independence for economic aid, or permit forms of Western influence into Eastern Europe. Equally, it was not prepared to totally abandon its connection with the loyal international communist movement for a close relationship of subordinate dependence with the American bourgeoisie. Furthermore, deep though its economic problems were in 1945, it still had enough assets domestically (as well as within Eastern Europe) to avoid turning to the West. There was also truth in Churchill's famous comment that Western hostility was less difficult for the Soviet system than Western friendship.[15] The 'capitalist threat' after all, maintained discipline at home, and (as Roosevelt and Churchill understood), reinforced the isolation which was essential for the continuation of Soviet power. The vast problems the USSR faced at home and abroad after World War II, and the nature of the system itself made close relations and cooperation with the West unthinkable.[16] Détente, tempting though it was, carried too high a political price. Cold War isolation and Western antagonism were costly but safer for Russia. Finally, Roosevelt's grand strategy was undermined by developments in America and Western Europe after Yalta. At home, his domestic support was fast disappearing, with a powerful reactionary coalition successfully attacking his Russian policy as a means of undermining the New Deal and the Democratic party's broad social basis in America.[17] In Western Europe, the deepening economic crisis made Roosevelt's Russian policy irrelevant, as it was clear that the USSR had no interest in helping the West to overcome its difficulties. By 1946 the New Deal vision of 'one world' was dead.

The collapse of Roosevelt's strategy, buried in effect by an unholy coalition made up of the Soviet élite and Western conservatism, left two options open to the West in terms of its relationship with the USSR. The first of these accepted the impossibility of close post-war cooperation between the West and the Soviet Union, but reasoned that some form of relationship could be maintained. The 'realist' school – to be found mainly in Europe, within large sections of the British foreign policy establishment, and given support by influential figures like Kennan[18] and Lippmann in America – assumed that the major priority was European reconstruction and the Atlantic relationship, not the USSR or the presumed 'threat' of communism. Not surprisingly this loose group eschewed the 'ideological' interpretation of Soviet behaviour which became dominant after 1947.[19] In spite of their conservatism and detestation of the Soviet system, they saw it as weak not threatening; insecure rather than dangerous; defensive rather than expansionary. The West was strong: in every way the Soviet Union was by far the weaker party.[20] This school feared in particular that a total breakdown of East-West relations would inevitably reinforce the division of Europe. If it was not possible to deal with the USSR as a normal political and economic entity, it was still necessary to maintain diplomatic and economic intercourse with it so as not to freeze the European and Russian positions. In time it was hoped, indeed this was the basic premise of Kennan's analysis of the Soviet system[21], that the several problems of the USSR would bring about major change. When this occurred one could expect to see evolution within Soviet society and, by implication, in Eastern Europe as well. Pressure could not change the Soviet bloc; time and its inherent contradictions would. Obviously this approach neither offered nor promised any quick change, but it did maintain that a flexible, albeit firm Western policy could take advantage of developments when they did occur. Western inflexibility and hostility would hold up the process of change in the USSR and Eastern Europe, not hasten it. Cooperation along Roosevelt's line may have been impossible, but total separation from the USSR however would be counterproductive.

The premises of both Roosevelt's strategy and that of the realists were in effect quite similar in so far as they both assumed that the USSR was no major challenge to the West, and that the major aims of Western policy must be first, the long term withdrawal of the USSR from Eastern Europe and second, change within the Soviet system itself. In reality both approaches were jettisoned after 1946 and 1947 and replaced with a strategy which was entirely different in terms of its theoretical premises and practical implications. The collapse of Rooseveltianism, and the rejection of realism,[22] opened the way for the Cold War system. Through it, US policy planners sought to place American hegemony in the world system on a firm foundation. However, its logic led, as we shall see, to the acceptance of two world systems[23] and to the reinforcement of the new European status quo which the New Dealers and the 'pragmatists' had regarded as both illegitimate and avoidable. The reconstruction of a new world order, of a stable international capitalism, and the launching of a new American imperialism after 1947, although couched in violently anti-Soviet terms, tacitly came to accept Soviet power as necessary and possibly even desirable. The launching of the Truman Doctrine marked not only the beginning of America's leadership of world capitalism as a system, but of that paradoxical yet real interdependence which gradually emerged between American power, European division, and the existence of the Soviet Union. This was the essence of the Cold War system. Having failed to pull the USSR back into the Western 'club',[24] the

United States proceeded to reconstruct a new international equilibrium around the separate existence and opposition of the
system regarded as hostile to the West. What began as a realistic
but resigned acceptance of Soviet isolationism, the loss of Eastern
Europe, the division of Germany, and Soviet opposition to the
West, developed into a coherent system with its own necessary
logic. The unplanned outcome of the Second World War became
the foundation upon which the West was rebuilt after 1947.
Russia, which had been such an important factor in the inter-war
crisis – in some ways a cause of it – became an equally important
factor in post-war capitalist stability. We might argue that
whereas after 1917 Russia upset the world system, after 1947 it
facilitated its stabilisation.

THE RISE OF THE SOVIET THREAT

Between 1945 and 1947 two entirely separate developments were
deliberately linked by State Department planners: the deepening
economic crisis in Western Europe and throughout the world,
and the breakdown of East-West relations. America in effect
found a solution to the first by exploiting the extraordinary
propaganda potential inherent in the second. The emergence of
an 'enemy' proved fortuitous for the USA. America's very
immediate concrete goals, which would have been the same even
if the Soviet Union had not existed, and its broader global plans,
were in this way both obscured and legitimised by anti-
communism and anti-Soviet rhetoric. The Soviet Union, by no
means the author of the West's difficulties was, henceforth, identified as the sole cause of all Western problems. This device,
which was successful in ensuring the passage of the European
Recovery Programme in the United States,[25] was thereafter made
the focus for American policy. After 1947, American plans were
in effect posed in terms of 'containing' a Russian military threat
which was known not to exist, and a Soviet communist menace
which was regarded as minimal.[26]

   In the construction of the Cold War in America, an image of
Russia was projected which assumed its inherently expansionary
character and its implacably hostile nature. Driven outwards by
the logic of Marxism-Leninism, the official view of the USSR

accepted as its basic premise that 'the supreme aim of world revolution (was) the logical outcome of Stalin's theoretical position';[27] this being so, no compromise, co-operation or even relationship was possible with it.[28] As the system was totalitarian it was by definition a menace. In so far as it was unchangeable, there was little point pursuing policies (like those advocated by Roosevelt or Kennan) which assumed that change or evolution in any form was at all possible.[29] The only feasible policy which the West could pursue was to contain the system from without, not hope for any internal transformation. The 'enemy' was unscrupulous, therefore there was little point in negotiation. The Soviet Union only understood strength.[30] The West must unite, rearm, and launch an ideological crusade at home and abroad to warn the people of the constant and ever-present world-wide threat to civilisation.

The Soviet threat was not based upon a concrete analysis of the USSR. Indeed, its assumptions were rejected by America's leading Soviet expert.[31] The threat was, and was always understood to be, a strategic concept, a planning device, stated, as Acheson admitted, in terms which were somewhat 'clearer than the truth'[32] in order to have maximum domestic and international impact. America thus entered the world in 1947 carrying aloft the banner of anti-communism. Its strategy, it reasoned, was essentially defensive; its purpose, the disinterested guardianship of the 'free world' from Soviet imperialism. The threat was of course both military and ideological. The USSR worked through the Red Army; it also used its communist 'fifth column' to weaken the West in preparation for the final takeover. Divisions therefore, at home and abroad, could not help the USSR. There could be no neutrality, or neutralism, in the great global struggle between freedom and the dark forces of satanic communism.

The Cold War construction of Soviet reality and Russia's external drives did not alter much after their elevation to the level of official Western doctrine in 1947. Analysis which suggested Soviet weakness, the limits of its power, or indeed that its goals might be more defensive than offensive, was ignored or marginalised. The suggestion that Stalin might have rejected world revolution as an option with the defeat of the left opposition came to be regarded as scandalous, hopelessly naive, liberal (possibly Trotskyist!) nonsense. The whole American academic community, particularly the new branch of Kremlinology, was mobilised to prove the essential correctness of both the assumptions and ramifications of the doctrine of the Soviet 'threat'. An academic discipline blossomed after 1947, not just to study Soviet Russia, but to understand better how to fight it. American Sovietology became little more than a branch of the US state, worked for it, shared its view of the world and was dependent upon it for its very existence.

The image of the Soviet Union which was projected was repeated *ad nauseam* to the point where no alternative position could be stated and heard. In political terms the drive to prove the existence of the Soviet threat was a massive success. Made credible by the USSR's formal attachment to the rhetoric of Marxism, by its incorporation of Eastern Europe, and the Soviet Union's continued links with the communist movement (in fact by the awful nature of Stalinism as a system), the Soviet threat came to occupy a central role in American political and strategic planning throughout the Cold War. The precise timing of the emergence of the Soviet threat was itself significant. It is extremely important to be reminded of Russia's general position in 1947: to recall that America's struggle against the great 'threat' began at the same moment in history when Russia's post-war demobilisation had reduced its military budget by half[33] and its army strength to three and a half million (twenty five per cent of what it had been in 1945);[34] in the actual month when the Soviet economy, according to both the *Economist*[35] and later head of American intelligence, was passing through a profound crisis;[36] and when the newly formed CIA had just concluded 'that the Soviet Union would not, within the foreseeable future, risk a global war'.[37] Just two years after a war which (according to one State Department report)[38] had destroyed well over a quarter of Russia's national wealth, or something close to the economic equivalent of two Five Year plans, and at a time when its GNP (according to an OSS estimate) was only approximately thirty per cent of that of the United States,[39] the USSR was stated to be a major menace to the world. The Soviet threat in fact clearly emerged when Russia was particularly weak. The 'discovery' of the threat undoubtedly tells us more about America's intentions than Russia's; clearly less about Soviet foreign policy than that of its American adversary. Only by looking at the Soviet threat in this way, is it possible to explain the otherwise inexplicable fear of Russia[40] manufactured in powerful America in the post-war period.

The emergence of the Soviet threat coincided with the rise of

America to dominance in the world system and at that moment when America was embarking upon its great task of under-writing, both economically and militarily, stability in Europe and throughout the globe. In 1947 the United States and the world stood at the beginning of a new epoch. The struggle against the world-wide communist threat provided America therefore with the necessary ideological *raison d'être* to mobilise its people behind the great tasks which lay ahead, whilst legitimising its own imperialism abroad. By linking its own destiny and prosperity with anti-Stalinism, the United States effectively mobilised consent at home and provided itself with ideological validation for its new world role.[41] At home, anti-communism swept all before it.[42] Opposition to US foreign policy was destroyed (note the fate of the Wallace progressives in 1948).[43] Public indifference to foreign affairs, which was measurably high in 1946, was undermined.[44] The roots of traditional American isolationism, which had so constrained American imperialism in the past, were totally eliminated.[45] In the process, the United States was con-verted into the garrison state so feared by liberals like Lasswell[46] in the early 1940s – free of dissent, ideologically conformist, trau-matised by fear of attack from without and subversion within. As a result the left was defeated, the working class concussed, American society militarised and disciplined, its economy transformed.[47] Anti-communism also merged and became synonymous with a powerful American nationalism which iden-tified patriotism with anti-communism, thus producing that stifling conformity which became the hallmark of American culture.[48] One could not be neutral in America; it was essential to be loyal in a demonstrably positive way. To be American meant being anti-communist.[49] A panic[50] was induced which laid the seeds of repression which culminated in McCarthyism in the early 1950s. In the fight against the Soviet threat America was con-verted into the perfect base for American policy abroad: unquestioning, patriotic, safe.

The Soviet threat came to play a crucial role in the conduct of American policy after 1947. It is not insignificant that every major measure taken to further US foreign policy – rearmament, universal military training, foreign aid, the formation of NATO in 1949, the development of counter-insurgency in the 1960s – was justified in relation to the Soviet threat. In this way (as Acheson frankly admitted in his memoirs) the 'average man' was provided with a simple but effective explanation of what the state was doing in his name.[51] Furthermore, those who were called upon to administer, implement and defend American policies, had a ready-made justification for their role.[52] The Soviet threat was above all a mobilising and legitimising device. With this 'strong and dramatic message'[53] Congress was moved to support Truman in 1947, Marshall in 1948, and all subsequent American leaders – until the débâcle of Vietnam twenty years later. At several crucial points, Soviet actions (none of which particularly threatened the West) were utilised by policy planners in America. The Czech coup was thus used to hasten the passage of Marshall Aid in 1948.[54] The Berlin blockade helped to justify and legitimise NATO a year later.[55] Events in Korea in 1950 swept aside all opposition, conservative as well as liberal, to an already planned rearmament programme.[56] Not surprisingly, repression in the USSR, but more especially in Eastern Europe, was seized upon to confirm and validate America's world role, and to justify its own support for repression in other parts of the world. Equally important, communist opposition in and to the West only reinforced Western unity, invariably justified Western policies, and, more often than not, increased Western self-confidence.[57] The brutalities of the Soviet system, its often clumsy and counter-productive initiatives at home and abroad, its identity with international communism,[58] served America and Western capitalism well in the post-war period.

The Soviet threat emerged in 1947, became codified into the *idée fixe* of American foreign policy in 1950 during the crucial NSC–68 debates, and was to remain the central and unchallenged focus of American policy until the late 1960s when the 'crisis of the Cold War' began to undermine the credibility of the concept. Its advocates regarded the doctrine of the threat as functionally 'relevant' to America's requirements rather than necessarily based upon a 'rational', or concrete study of the Soviet Union's real capabilities or intentions. Acheson's attitude to the doctrine was indicative of the instrumental way in which it was regarded by policy planners. For instance when Kennan and Bohlen, during the NSC–68 discussions, pointed to the limits of Soviet power, its non-expansionary character, and to the enormous problems it faced at home as well as in Eastern Europe – where it was assumed that the USSR had become dangerously over-extended – Acheson made no attempt to counter their arguments empirically. As one important commentator on the NSC-68 directive has noted, Acheson's response to critics was 'what difference does it make (as though) the accuracy and internal consistency of the document were not important'. Significantly Paul Nitze argued that the threat should at all times be maximised in order to have greatest political effect. Simple empirical refutation of the threat missed the point. Those who defended the concept of the threat did not really base their judgement upon what the Soviet Union was, but what American foreign policy needs were. Kennan was not wrong – just irrelevant. The Soviet Union was too important, too useful to be left to the experts.[59] As Hammond has pointed out, after 1947 and by the time of the discussions in 1950, Acheson, the architect of American policy, was 'more interested in the polemic value' of the threat, than in studying the actual dynamics of Soviet society. Kennan, it should be recalled, was criticised not in terms of his faulty analysis of the Soviet Union, but because his views did not lead to the right political or strategic conclusions.[60]

The Soviet Union thus provided the United States with what James Forrestal had once regarded as essential; namely 'a pattern for world policy . . . a central objective in the long range course of conduct';[61] in other words, a specific and clear point of opposition around which to organise the free world. As the threat was enormous, the rest of the free world would inevitably have to gravitate towards the one force which could contain it – the United States. The Soviet threat thus reinforced the dependency of the rest of the world system, especially Europe, upon the United States. In so far as the threat exploited all divisions, it was essential for the West to remain united, to recognise that past differences must be subordinated to the greater goal of survival. The threat provided therefore the perfect ideological cement for inter-capitalist unity in the post-war period. Because the Soviet Union worked at several levels, often using others, even innocents, to further its goal of world domination, America and its allies were justified in using every means available to counter 'Soviet aggression': support for authoritarian rule in the Third World; the discrediting of opposition at home and abroad; covert actions where necessary. The Soviet threat resolved a whole series of moral and political dilemmas for if nothing was worse than communism anything and everything was justified in preventing its spread. Denazification could be halted in Germany, genuine nationalist leaders could be removed in the Third World, even fascism was preferable (shades of the 30s). Every measure which advanced American interests by definition blocked the spread of 'Soviet power'. All opposition to America, in fact any force for change, was equated with the Soviet threat, thereby legitimising its repression by one means or another.

The construction of the Soviet threat by American policy planners after 1947 was designed to unite the West behind America's economic and military leadership in the establishment of a new global order and equilibrium. Accompanied, as it was bound to be, by a crusading anti-communism which helped to defeat the left and divide the working class, it reinforced the political and ideological foundations, both within and between the advanced capitalist countries, of social stability and inter-capitalist harmony, thereby facilitating the new accumulation process world-wide. Without America, world capitalism clearly could not have recovered after World War II. Without the Soviet Union, and the threat it was supposed to represent, the conditions essential for that recovery could not have been created. The Soviet threat, and the real and justified fear of Stalinism, played a crucial role for Western capitalism in and after 1947. America was thus furnished with the perfect crusading morality with which to police the globe, for was it not inevitable that all those who were repelled by the Soviet Union could easily believe that it was a threat as well? And believe too, in the absolute necessity of America's guardianship and leadership of the world?

THE COLD WAR SYSTEM IN EUROPE

The logic of the Cold War involved the Soviet Union in other important respects in post-war Western stabilisation, most obviously, and possibly most significantly, in Europe. It remains true that by incorporating the whole of Eastern Europe and part of Germany, the USSR brought an equilibrium to Europe which had been absent since 1914, and which would have been impossible without the expansion of Soviet power after 1945. The subtraction of a part of the world system brought order to that area which remained within the world system. What became the Soviet bloc, although formally separate from the West, con-tributed to a new stability in the West. It required the partial extension of 'communism' therefore, to underpin security in Western Europe where the market system still prevailed. Further-more, what was then seen to exist under communism, as the alter-native to the West and capitalism, only reinforced the case for the market. Communism became a deterrent: its own worst enemy in the West. Socialism in one country – Russia – and its imposition in the mainly backward region of Eastern Europe, thus limited its further spread to the West. The historic alternative to capitalist democracy became, after World War II, the best argument for it. 'Actually existing socialism' developed into the ideological prop which sustained the West after the great traumas of the inter-war years; the warning which bourgeois society pointed at in the Cold War to deflect criticism and defeat history.

Ideologically and strategically the Cold War thus transformed unstable Europe into a stable entity, relatively untroubled by the internal and international struggles which had marked it from the late nineteenth century. Europe, the area of past class conflicts, within and between the bourgeois states, underwent a profound metamorphosis after World War II. Germany was divided[62] and its political and economic reach in Eastern Europe drastically reduced. West Germany was thereafter integrated into Western Europe and the Atlantic Alliance, a responsible and weakened force, rather than the rogue elephant of the world system. Internally it became a model of advanced capitalism, stabilised by its own division which cut off crucial sectors of the German working class in Saxony, Berlin and Thuringia. The thirteen million refugees from the East also made a crucial contri-bution to capitalism's stability and productivity in West Germany. Finally, in West Germany the disciplining impact of the Soviet threat was most effective and the fear of communism greatest. West Germany became the site where the Cold War was fought and won by the West. Who, after all, built the Berlin Wall? The case against socialism was clearly proved by the barbed-wire fence across Germany. A stable Germany, the result of Germany's bifurcation by the Cold War, also contributed to European stability as a whole. Germany could no longer threaten its neighbours. Its political quiescence and economic dynamism reinforced the accumulation process throughout Western Europe. Division in effect solved the German problem in Europe.[63]

The loss of Eastern Europe from the world system further reinforced the general equilibrium of Europe after 1947. This ironical result of the expansion of Soviet power occurred for several reasons. First, the problem of consolidating and stabilising Soviet rule there, throughout the post-war period, posed a major political headache for the USSR. In a peculiar way, therefore – although for different reasons than existed after 1919 – Eastern Europe helped discipline Russia. The new 'empire' was never stable, and undoubtedly expansion beyond it would have increased instability in the area. Eastern Europe effectively and efficiently tied down the USSR after the end of World War II. (It still does.) Furthermore, the removal of Eastern Europe from the international system reduced its traditionally destabilising impact upon Europe. Two world wars, it should be recalled, began in Eastern Europe. Historically, Eastern Europe had proved non-viable anyway; neither Britain nor America had ever regarded the area as essential[64] and its loss to 'communism' weakened Germany, not them. The sovietisation of Eastern Europe benefited West European capitalism in other ways as well. It made credible the claim that there was a 'threat' to the rest of Europe, which only increased and reinforced discipline and unity in Western Europe as a result. Furthermore, the creation of Soviet type systems in one part of Europe (not distant Asiatic Russia) made more actual and real the contrast between capitalism and communism. The result was extraordinarily important within the West. East Germany showed West Germany its future if it attempted to go beyond the market; Eastern Europe only proved why capitalism was necessary in Western Europe as a whole.

AMERICA AND THE COLD WAR IN EUROPE

American policy towards Europe and the Soviet bloc increasingly came to accept the new situation beyond the iron curtain as being stable, stabilising, and in American interest. American strategy throughout the Cold War therefore was essentially conservative. Of course at the rhetorical level US acquiescence in the Cold War system was denied. Formally America and Western Europe remained wedded to Soviet withdrawal from Europe, German reunification, and some alteration in the Soviet Union as well (note the goal of 'roll-back' in the fifties). However, this outward opposition to communism in Eastern Europe and the USSR, necessary for political reasons, was directly contradicted by the actual policies that America pursued; policies which firmly froze the situation and made all change in Europe and Russia impossible. America's real strategy was obscured for three fairly obvious reasons. First, because of domestic pressure which arose from the influential East European émigré population in the USA. Second, for fear that a total lack of commitment to the goals of European and German reunification by America would have loosened the Western Alliance and possibly even forced Europe and West Germany towards Russia in an attempt to resolve the Cold War, in spite of, and possibly even against, America. Third, because America's whole anti-communist and anti-Soviet rhetoric in the Cold War would have been undermined if America had openly accepted the new status quo in Europe and Russia. In short, politically the United States had to deny its strategic dependence upon the Cold War system in Europe.

At each and every point, America in the Cold War did nothing to change the new equilibrium: quite the opposite. Marshall Aid, it should be recalled, assumed, in fact was premised upon, Soviet and East European refusal.[65] The later Soviet offer on the reunification of Germany in 1952 was summarily dismissed by America (and Adenauer).[66] The disengagement proposal, the logic of which must have led to German reunification, was fiercely attacked by Acheson and Kissinger in 1958.[67] America obviously accepted the building of the Berlin wall with all its implications.[68] American policy towards Eastern Europe and the USSR after 1947 also reflected the same basically conservative character of American strategy during the Cold War. As several commentators pointed out at the time and later, US pressure upon the Soviet bloc from without only stifled change within. Dealing with Russia from an accepted position of strength, when this strength was mobilised directly against the system, could only reinforce Stalinism in Russia and Soviet control over Eastern Europe. Pressure created unity and cohesion beyond the iron curtain; it did not and could not encourage change. The net result of isolating the Soviet bloc, of waging economic and ideological warfare against it, and of America's massive military build-up after 1950, was to discourage any possible movement inside the Soviet bloc. The contradictions of the Stalinist systems remained, but could find no expression largely, if not only,

because of American policy. It is not surprising that the implications of Stalin's death in 1953, and Khrushchev's statements in
1956, were played down in the United States; neither provoked
any real policy change in Washington.[69]

There was a clear logic behind America's general strategy
towards Europe and Russia. By freezing the division of the first,
by exacerbating the difficulties of the second, and emphasising
the threat presented by Russia to Europe, America sought to
achieve the following ends. First, it clearly wished to perpetuate
the division and weakening of Germany and thus facilitate its
increased integration with the rest of Europe and dependence
upon America. Movement of any form would have upset all of
those aims. Second, America recognised that the division of
Europe as a whole was in itself a necessary price to pay for
European stability. A united Europe would have been more
unstable and powerful, and its western half less dependent upon
the United States. If, as one writer has argued, the United States
fears a more autonomous Europe seeking its own identity[70] (a
view accepted by the Director of the Office of Research for
Western Europe at the State Department as late as 1978),[71] it was
unlikely to have pursued policies in the Cold War which may have
fostered greater West European independence. In other words,
America's hegemony within Europe, and the new found unity of
the West, rested upon a divided, weakened, and therefore more
dependent Europe and Germany. The great success of America's
strategy was the degree to which it managed to reinforce this
double division, yet make it seem as if it were Russia alone who
was responsible for it. Equally effective too was American policy
towards the Soviet bloc which aimed to weaken but not
necessarily change the systems there. To some degree the strategy
was a dangerous one, for too much pressure might precipitate an
unwelcome explosion which America could then do little about.
Such was the case with Hungary.[72] Pressure had to be carefully
regulated therefore. Too little and it would have no impact. Too
much and there was the possibility of undesirable turmoil. The
break-up of the 'Soviet Empire', its roll-back, or liberation, was
not American policy.[73] It sought instead to increase Soviet bloc
problems in order to decrease its general attractiveness at home
and abroad. It was hoped that in the great competitive ideological struggle between the 'free world' and 'communism',
the horrors and inefficiencies of the latter would prevent what

Chomsky once referred to as 'contagion by copying'[74]. Each refugee, every escapee and émigré, even the maintenance of a powerful repressive apparatus in the USSR, all played a crucial part in rolling back socialism: in the West, not the East. By fighting the enemy 'over there', the result was to destroy it 'over here'. The strategy was a brilliant success. Brzezinski once observed, with a quite remarkable candour, that Stalin, 'by creating a particularly despotic model of communism...vitiated much of communism's appeal at a time when the susceptibility of the more advanced West – the area originally seen by Marx as ripest for historical transformation – might have made communism the truly dominant and vital force of our time'.[75] In the Cold War, American policy attempted to further decrease the appeal of communism in the world. Ironically, but inevitably, far from freeing the people in the Soviet bloc American actions in the Cold War only postponed their day of 'liberation'. They became sacrifices in many respects to the ultimately successful American quest for a new world after World War II that rested upon the maintenance of Soviet power, not its dissolution or destruction. To the populations of Eastern Europe and the Soviet Union – 'our secret allies' as Eugene Lyons had once defined them – America seemed to be holding out a hand and, it must be admitted, a hope as well. In reality, the offer of liberation was not only baseless, it made the political and economic conditions worse for the 'captive peoples' beyond the Iron Curtain, whose plight served only to warn those in the West what fate might await them too in any future communist society.[76]

American policy in the Cold War, Kennan once remarked, 'was seldom conducted for what appeared to be its ostensible ends'.[77] There can be little doubt about that. The United States contained a threat which did not exist; supported a European division it formally opposed; was repelled by a system which legitimised its own; talked of liberating the satellites, but assumed their existence in the new European equilibrium. Outwardly, a great conflict of two social systems and between two super powers was occurring. In reality the great contest was more apparent than real, conducted between forces of totally unequal economic and military capability. Real though the antagonism was in the broader historical sense, after 1947 the two poles within the world system effectively existed in an interdependent and functional relationship in which the mutual opposition between the two facilitated the stability and reproduction of both.

The American cat teased and played with the Soviet mouse for most of the Cold War. There was only one super power after 1947, not two. US rhetoric was invariably contradicted by its own intelligence. The great military threat was known to be weak; its 'satellites' an increasing burden; Soviet ability to project itself internationally always limited. Yet, once the 'threat' had become established at the centre of American foreign policy planning, it followed logically that America had to exaggerate, discover and rediscover it. As American strategy deliberately assumed the worse, it planned for the worse.[78] As American policy assumed Russia to be totalitarian, and therefore static, when change did begin to occur its significance had, by definition, to be denied. When all concrete analysis pointed to limited Soviet aims circumscribed by both the nature of the system and its very limited material basis, Cold War planners would then point to the system's ideology and its designs for a world state. The ideological approach to comprehending Soviet behaviour ('what they really believe and want') was the result, not the cause, of the Cold War. It was the inevitable outcome of Cold War thinking and the intellectual orthodoxy it created. It produced, as indeed was the intention, an absolute rigidity in US policy. Hence, when the Soviets started talking of peaceful coexistence, this was obviously a way of dividing the West; better to conquer it. When they looked for relaxation,[79] this was clearly a manoeuvre in the greater game of world domination. The simple fact is that throughout the Cold War the United States did not wish to relax the tension or the state of war which existed, for both were central to its broader strategy.

It is feasible that after Acheson (under Eisenhower), American policy makers even believed their own originally constructed view of the Soviet Union. In the atmosphere of America in the 1950s it would have been politically unwise not to have done so (at least in public). The device became the truth; a planning concept reality itself. Anything was feasible in America at the height of the Cold War. The point should not be pushed too far however. Even under Eisenhower (who was always a realist about the Soviet Union) there was a clear line of demarcation between rhetoric and real intelligence. Dulles talked of roll-back, but never practised it. They chastised Kennan in public for only wanting to contain Soviet power, but they often sought his advice in private.

There is little doubt of course that a large deal of the Cold War rhetoric was a function of domestic forces and electoral politics inside America. The Republicans used McCarthy to get back to power in 1952 (and disposed of him in 1954). Dulles (following Lubell's[80] analysis of American politics) used hard line anti-communism against Truman to detach key ethnic voting blocs from the Democrats. Kennedy utilised the missile gap to win in 1960. As Wolfe[81] and La Feber[82] have shown, there were powerful internal forces supporting the Soviet threat. For the FBI, the military, the Deep South, and all those states which were highly dependent upon military spending, there had to be a threat. Further, the ideological influence of ex-communists, the power of the East European émigrés of long standing and recent origin, the Jewish bloc, the trade unions as well, made any escape from the Cold War extraordinarily difficult. However, the Cold War was more than simply a by-product of American political economy. In historical terms it was no less than the vehicle through which the West as a whole was stabilised and disturbance purged from the central core areas of the world system. Unplanned at first, the Cold War's historic task was to create the conditions inside and between the advanced capitalist countries for class peace and international harmony. Conflict remained, but was increasingly peripheralised towards the Third World. The left did not disappear, but the pressure of Cold War propaganda (and rising living standards) either shifted it to the right, or led to its increasing marginalisation. By the late fifties, after a decade of conservative rule and anti-communist propaganda in Western Europe, many social democratic parties had already abandoned nationalisation; the communist movement had lost in influence and credibility. (Hungary and the Secret Speech in 1956 only deepened their problems and further ghettoisation.) The left did not become illegal in Europe or America, just irrelevant. Nor had the working class become 'embourgeoisified', simply confused and depoliticised. In 1945 the left seemed to be on the verge of a new era and the right totally discredited; a decade later the opposite was true. In this lay the real measure of the success of 'containment' and the Cold War system which administered to Marxism, under the guise of fighting the Soviet Union, a blow from which it has yet to recover.

BEYOND THE COLD WAR

It was perhaps symptomatic of the depth of the crisis of bourgeois society between 1917 and 1947 that throughout the Cold War the West had to seek security and comfort, indeed its very affirmation, not through a self-confident celebration of the market, but by a constant and repeated reference to the inefficiency and the terrors which the alternative might bring. That world capitalism after 1947 could only establish its legitimacy and stability by effectively resting upon the USSR was a mark of degeneracy, not confidence; weakness, not vitality. The staple diet of the Cold War in America in particular – fear, crisis, anxiety – was clear proof of a deep unease about its purpose. The fact that America, the most powerful nation in history, nevertheless required the perverted image of socialism to sustain it, was an index of insecurity. Equally, the inability of world capitalism to establish a new equilibrium after 1947 without the existence, and even extension of Soviet power into Europe, was illustrative of how potentially unstable and contradictory the post-war system was. The Cold War system could not last. Its origins and its nature presupposed a certain unique conjuncture in the world system. Change had undermined the nineteenth century equilibrium after 1914; it was bound to erode the Cold War system too. The Cold War system created a twin equilibrium: within the two 'camps' and in the world system as a whole. However, no equilibrium, however perfectly balanced it appears, is immune to the dynamic of change. Developments within the capitalist world and the Soviet bloc were, by the 1960s, conspiring to undermine the foundations of the house which America and Russia had built together. Change within the West, and in the East, gradually induced an alteration in the relationship between the two systems. Slowly but surely, the Cold War gradually began to crumble. The process of deconstruction began first in the two halves of Europe,[83] then in Russia itself as the costs of the Cold War and isolation became unbearable,[84] and finally within the United States itself. The movement towards something new was obviously uneven. The break with the Cold War was more problematic for America whose interests had been best protected by the system. However, once the process of change began, it was inevitable that the world would move beyond the Cold War. In the process it would expose many of the hidden problems and underlying tensions of a system which its critics had been aware of since 1947, and which were becoming uncontainable twenty years later. By the latter half of the 1960s the Cold War was in many respects regarded as being both unnecessary and impossible. As the Cold War broke down, American and European planners looked for a new framework upon which to construct a new equilibrium. This was bound to involve a new relationship with the communist world.[85] The Cold War was a contradictory system. There was something inherently unstable about a capitalist equilibrium being maintained by the existence of non-market societies in a large part of Europe. Ultimately there was an essential tension in America's strategy, for the West as a whole could never fully accept the loss of large areas of the globe. The relationship of interdependence could not escape this basic antagonism. The USSR and Eastern Europe were potentially huge markets and sources of raw materials. More generally, their reincorporation would clearly be regarded as a major political victory for the West. Therefore, dependent though Western capitalism was upon Stalinism, Eastern Europe and the USSR, when taken together, constituted an important overall loss to world capitalism which could never be completely acceptable to a market economic system which pre-supposed global dominance.[86]

By the sixties, pressure to seek the reincorporation of the Soviet bloc was strengthened by three post-war developments. First, by the fact that by the late fifties, the deterrent role of the Soviet Union had diminished in value: Stalinism had, by then, performed the historic task of undercutting socialism in the West. Second, by the process of industrialisation within the Soviet bloc which made the reintegration of these societies both more feasible and desirable.[87] Third, by deepening problems in the relations between the Soviet Union and Eastern Europe, and in the economies of the bloc as a whole. The 'crisis of communism', reflected in the growing nationalist fragmentation of the Stalinist monolith, the failure to raise the basic productivity of the economy, the hesitating but clear moves back to the market, and the evident shift away from economic autarchy, opened up major opportunities for the West which could not be ignored. As early as 1957 many Americans were arguing for a new strategy, termed 'peaceful engagement', the forerunner of détente. Change in the East therefore called for a change in America's strategy to exploit the contradictions of Stalinism.[88]

Freezing a large sector of the world system outside of the international division of labour was the major contradiction of the Cold War system. That the Cold War relationship gave Russia (or China) no reason for not directly or indirectly challenging Western interests where it was possible, was another. For a period this did not matter for a number of reasons. First, the opposition of the USSR and the communist movement was, as we have suggested, directly functional for the West anyway. Second, American power was so great after 1947 that it would 'contain' all the challenges thrown up by the Soviet Union on the basis of its own strength. Finally, it should not be forgotten that Soviet global reach was quite limited in the Cold War and constituted no major problem. However, by the later fifties the situation was changing, not because the communist movement had grown in influence (the opposite had occurred), but because of new developments within the Third World which challenged the stability of the international system, and which both China, and especially the USSR, attempted to exploit. Throughout the 1950s the United States did not confront a direct challenge in the Third World of any serious nature; nor was the USSR a serious economic, military or political force there. However, by the early 1960s nationalism, often but not always combined with a type of Third World socialism, was asserting itself globally. In the Middle-East, Latin America and South-East Asia, the USSR made a clear alliance with this anti-imperialist upsurge. In the cases of Cuba and Vietnam (in a halting, ambiguous, and self-interested way) the Soviet Union also gave vital economic and military support. Khrushchev thus made a clear orientation to the rising force of radical nationalism which in the 1960s proved relatively successful. Even though Soviet economic reach was highly limited (it did not have the resource base to supply aid or food in any serious quantity, and its goods and technology could not compete with the West), it could, and did, supply arms, some investment in large-scale projects, a market for some Third World raw materials, some aid, and, in a certain sense, a 'model' of development based on non-capitalist industrialisation. As a result the USSR was able to limit Western pressure upon some Third World countries. By linking itself with the colonial revolution, anti-zionism, and demands for development, the USSR extended its influence (unstable and shaky though it turned out to be). More important, it weakened – to some degree – direct Western control over events in the Third World. By the late 1960s America could no longer ignore the USSR (and China), who had acquired important points of external support and bargaining counters by allying themselves with nationalism in the Third World. The

United States, in short, had to find some means to reduce Soviet and Chinese support for change and disturbance in a world system which was becoming more unstable and less manageable on the basis of American power alone.[89]

The third problem of the Cold War system was that it rested upon an American nuclear monopoly which could not last. The logic of the arms race inevitably led the USSR to acquire some form of inter-continental nuclear capability by the late fifties. For the first time America, and not just Europe and the USSR, was vulnerable to attack. This did not produce an equivalent nuclear capability (it still has not), but by the 1960s, many years after Sputnik, some deliverable, probably very inaccurate and unreliable intercontinental missiles were in Soviet hands. The sense of panic which Soviet advances in nuclear weaponry produced was unfounded. However, the USA's new insecurity posed a number of problems which ultimately forced a change in the Cold War system. Most immediately, it created a clear division of interest within NATO, for America, as Kissinger admitted, was unlikely to 'commit suicide'[90] to defend Europe from the hypothetical Russian attack. A major question mark was thus placed under the value, and even the meaning, of the Atlantic relationship.[91] In turn this created demands within Europe for its own independent nuclear capability (which America opposed), and for negotiation with Russia for some regulation of the arms race. At the same time there emerged similar, albeit less urgent, demands for America to seek some regulation, if not elimination, of the arms race once it too became vulnerable. It was evident, however, that America never sought to stop the arms race. Moreover, it never effectively deviated from the goal of seeking to maintain some form of superiority over the USSR. Its clearly more advanced weapons technology;[92] the greater size of its economic base;[93] and the enormous burden the arms race placed upon the USSR,[94] precluded America from not constantly escalating the race. However, once Russia had weapons, and some delivery capability, the USA was pulled into negotiation. An uncontrolled and unregulated arms race was clearly unstable. By constantly pressuring the USSR from a position of strength a point could be reached which could trigger a confrontation. As events in Cuba demonstrated, under pressure the USSR might attempt to relieve the situation, not by a mass ICBM attack (Russia simply did not have the capability in

1962),[95] but by putting America under pressure in the one forward base position which directly threatened the USA. Kennedy's attempt to move America even further ahead of Russia after 1960 nearly ended in catastrophe. After Cuba demands grew for arms negotiation. In effect the fact that the USSR remained outside of the control of the USA raised a major problem in an age of nuclear weapons. Disciplining the USSR by an escalating arms race became more problematic once the American monopoly, if not its superiority, was undermined. American security demanded an alteration in the terms upon which the arms race should be based. However, given its superiority, America was bound to use any arms negotiation talks to exact political concessions from the USSR.[96]

Finally, it was clear that the Cold War system was premised on several assumptions which if changed could undermine America's post-war foreign policy strategy. By the mid sixties nearly every one of these had been brought into question. America's economic hegemony was increasingly being challenged by a more assertive Europe and Japan who were no longer willing to follow America on all questions, especially over the issue of trade with the communist countries.[97] Also, Europe, and West Germany in particular, were becoming increasingly dissatisfied with a system which effectively perpetuated their own division. By the mid sixties, as many influential figures realised, America would have to abandon the Cold War if it wished to maintain inter-capitalist unity.[98] Unless America was prepared to accompany the European rapprochement with the Soviet bloc, and Japan's desire for trade and accommodation with China,[99] the harmony which had been such an essential feature of post-war capitalist equilibrium would have been undermined. At home too, the domestic consensus which had supported the Cold War was rapidly disappearing through the 1960s, culminating in the great Vietnam crisis of 1968 and 1969. Vietnam marked a crucial watershed for America in two ways. Domestically it generated massive opposition and inflation and thus shattered the link which had traditionally existed between the people, their prosperity, and American imperialism abroad. Secondly, defeat in Vietnam meant that America's global policeman role was no longer possible. After Vietnam America could no longer underwrite stability in the world system by itself alone. Inevitably it was bound to look towards a new relationship with Russia and China to establish the conditions for peace in the world after the traumatic reverses America had clearly suffered in South-East Asia.

DÉTENTE AND THE COMMUNIST WORLD

The dangers of an uncontrolled arms race, the possibility of reintegrating the Soviet bloc, the logic of American decline,[100] the deepening crisis within the alliance system, and the internal and external ramifications of Vietnam, were the major reasons why the Cold War system was no longer sustainable for the USA. America could no longer control its allies, discipline the USSR and the Third World, or carry the political and economic costs of empire by the mid sixties. For nearly twenty-five years America had underwritten the world system on the basis of a stable America which no longer existed by 1968, through the projection of an economic and military power which in relative terms was no longer so great, and with the support of a Europe and Japan who were no longer willing to follow. 'The world of 1947 and 1948 had passed', observed Hoffman in 1968, 'and the vision with which we met its challenges and transformed it, is now inadequate'.[101] A new form of equilibrium, or concept of order[102] (to use Kissinger's term), had to be reconstructed in a rapidly changing and more unstable world. Crisis and the erosion of US hegemony created the need for rapprochement with the USSR and China – not choice.

American policy, as designed by Kissinger, sought to create a basis for world stability by incorporating rather than excluding the USSR and China. The aim was to exploit their various problems and needs – food, trade, arms limitation in the case of the USSR – in exchange for their support of the world status quo. There was something quite conscious about détente.[103] Kissinger was very specific about his objectives; indeed his plan rested upon an acute historical understanding of the problems and possibilities confronting the United States. The possibilities were, or seemed, as great as the problems. The divisions in the Alliance could be overcome; consensus could be reconstructed at home; and, new and potentially huge markets would open up in a period when the long boom was slowing down. Russia and China, it was hoped, would come to recognise the great advantages of co-operating with the West in the new world order rather than disturbing the international system's stability, or supporting those forces which did.[104] Finally, in the longer term, the new relationship would lay the basis (as Kissinger, Nixon, Pisar and Brzezinski were well aware) for exploiting the contradictions of the Soviet bloc in order to reintegrate it into the world system. The architects of détente were clear that the Soviet system had reached the end of an historical epoch which demanded a changed Western strategy to encourage tendencies which were already emerging. There was always therefore a deeper Western purpose behind détente. Kissinger and Nixon (and many of the advocates of détente) were unambiguously clear that they sought to change and reincorporate Eastern Europe and the USSR. In 1965 Brzezinski, for instance, had argued against European partition and hoped that through 'peaceful engagement' the iron curtain would come down, 'returning East Europe and Russia to the European civilization'.[105] In 1970 Samual Pisar believed that 'commerce and coexistence' would in the long term lead to a single world market.[106] Kissinger in his memoirs was also clear about the longer term ramifications of détente. 'Time was not necessarily on the Soviet side', he argued. 'The inherent stagnation of the Communist system (would) work its corrosion'. Détente was in reality the 'beginning of a process of transformation' that would permit 'a long period of peace' which 'would unleash more centrifugal tendencies in the totalitarian states than in the industrial democracies'. It would hold the West together while the USSR's 'increasingly intractable problems' would bring about profound change.[107] Kissinger, like Nixon, was looking for 'victory without war'[108] over a system whose deepening problems posed new chances for the West in the late sixties.

If the irreversible process of decline was producing pressure to change direction in the United States, the crisis of the Soviet system was bringing it to recognise that it could no longer continue in the old way. In a broad sense, the whole Stalinist industrialisation strategy, based on national self-sufficiency, had reached an impasse. Socialism in one country was no longer feasible. After World War II the USSR had certain options. Then, it could continue with its simple economic goal of building factories by brute methods of superexploitation of its working class and peasantry, for the system could still maintain a system of repression extensive enough to maintain its economic dynamism.

After 1948, for a period at least, it could also draw upon Eastern Europe to sustain its own industrialisation process. Equally, it still had a reliable communist support in Western Europe upon which it could depend. By the 1960s the Stalinist economic model was redundant, Eastern Europe was becoming an increasing economic burden, and the Communist movement of declining political value. By the late 1960s Russia's alternatives had narrowed down to one; a return to the world market, with the recognition, quite revolutionary in Soviet terms, of 'the practical value of the international division of labour'.[109] Fearing reform, it turned to the West in an attempt to solve its problems.

Several things had occurred between 1953 and 1968 to bring about the USSR's abandonment of autarchy: the success of world capitalism itself after 1948; growing technology lags with the West; an inability to transform or reform its own economy (because of the working class); the failure to dramatically improve agricultural production or expand the consumer goods sector; and finally, the double burden of its arms sector and Eastern Europe. Moving back to the West (for aid, not just barter trade), was an admission by the Soviet élite that the system had reached an historic impasse. In the short term, the USSR was seeking to solve its problems, not with dangerous reform, but through the import of technology, food and consumer goods, supported in turn by lessening the burden of Eastern Europe[110] and the arms race.[111] The long circuitous road away from the West had come to an end. In the immediate sense Russia looked for relief and aid. In the longer term the United States was bound to use Soviet weaknesses and problems (including the conflict with China) to serve a broader strategy.

Détente has caused as much confusion amongst writers as the Cold War itself. It was not an abandonment of world revolution by the USSR, that had occurred forty years previously. It was not a new form of 'appeasement' as its right wing critics argued. It did not entail, as most writers have assumed,[112] a recognition by West Germany and America of the status quo in Eastern Europe. Nor was it really very much to do with stopping the arms race. For the USSR, détente was a rather desperate attempt to overcome its very grave internal problems by looking to the West for support, in return for their recognition of the new world order Kissinger was trying to reconstruct after Vietnam. For America the aim was to establish a new equilibrium within the world system, not by

excluding the USSR, but by including it in it and, ov
breaking down the indispensable condition of its very existence
its closed character. By opening up the Soviet bloc, the advocates
of détente sought to gradually domesticate and integrate it. The
velvet glove of friendship only served to conceal the tight grip the
West aimed to apply to the Soviet system.

TOWARDS A NEW COLD WAR?

It has become normal to argue that détente has failed and that
there now exists a 'new cold war'.[113] To some extent this has
become the new accepted orthodoxy. Such a judgement obviously
reflects major critical problems in the process of détente. In the
USA these were evident from the beginning. Clearly there was
never a mass or stable social basis for détente. With the apparent
shift to the right in the 1970s it seemed to evaporate altogether.
The deepening world economic crisis and America's rapid decline
also affected détente. The crisis made America less, not more
sensitive to Europe and Japan; decline created an ideological shift
in the late seventies, accompanied by a reassertion of nationalism,
which fed a powerful demand to make America strong again.
This led, almost logically, to a reassertion of Cold War rhetoric.
The escalating anti-Soviet line was also a function of a mid
seventies struggle by a faction within the foreign policy élite who
saw in détente several dangers.[114] Whereas Kissinger saw détente
as a means of holding the alliance together, they regarded it as
leading to a breaking up of the West, and an undermining of the
discipline which the 'threat' and the Cold War had provided. If
Kissinger had envisaged détente as creating a new foreign policy
consensus in America after Vietnam, they argued that to
overcome the traumas of Vietnam only a clear anti-Soviet and
anti-Communist position could mobilise and reunite the United
States. The reemergence of the Soviet threat after the mid
seventies in America was therefore part of an attempt to establish
the lost legitimacy of American capitalism at home and abroad.
Opponents of détente also pointed to the fact that détente did not
prevent Soviet attempts to exploit the deepening world crisis of
the 1970s (Angola, S.E. Asia). Finally, it was evident that the
Soviet 'threat' was still a useful device. After the mid seventies it
was clearly being used to legitimise continued American support

for repression in the Third World and the new military expansion which had been planned throughout the 1970s. Dispensing with the Soviet threat proved extremely difficult for America given its proven historic value. Having defined itself around the threat, America discovered many problems in living without it.

There were other factors too which weakened the argument for détente in America. Economically, trade with the Soviet bloc remained less important for the USA than it was for Europe and West Germany. The economic case for détente was never as persuasive in the United States as in Western Europe.[115] There was also the entirely self-interested argument that slowing down détente would be a useful means (amongst others) to erode European and West German competitive strength; weakening détente would therefore strengthen the USA in relative economic terms (e.g. if the Europeans buy Soviet gas they may not buy US coal).[116] To some degree the general crisis of détente was also an index of the decline of traditional Eastern dominance in the determination of American foreign policy. For the Mid-West and Californian interests (areas heavily dependent on military contracts), the Kissinger sensitivity for Europe was less in evidence, an insensitivity which grew rapidly as the recession deepened and demands for protection grew. Finally, there was a certain ideological rationale in the new anti-Soviet line which clearly corresponded to the right's attack on traditional Keynesianism in the latter half of the seventies. The reassertion of the primacy of the market, of its self-evident and miraculous advantages for humanity, and of the dangers of creeping socialism (low productivity, too much welfare, high taxation) necessarily led them to point to the wonders of capitalism compared to the awfulness and inferiority of communism. At the ideological level at least, the crisis of late capitalism led to renewed emphasis on the 'threat' and the totalitarian character of the alternative.

The crisis of détente within the West has been mirrored, for different reasons, in the Soviet bloc. Détente created political problems for the USSR and confronted critical economic difficulties. At the political level détente undoubtedly loosened the Soviet bloc very considerably (as was planned by Bahr and Brandt, Kissinger and Nixon): the removal of the cohesive German threat made less legitimate Soviet control over Eastern Europe; capitalist encirclement was hardly a credible disciplining force in a period when trade and other East-West flows were growing. Détente aimed to break down isolation and was gradually achieving this, particularly in Eastern Europe, but to some degree in the USSR as well. Social control was bound to weaken in a post-Stalinist era of international rapprochement. The West also (through the Helsinki agreements) was deliberately using détente as a means of levering open the Soviet bloc with clear results, as Charter 77 and later Solidarity indicated. The Sonnenfeldt doctrine was working. Remove pressure, increase the Soviet sense of security, create links of interdependency, and evolution will occur within the Communist countries. 'Change through rapprochement' was taking place. Détente also raised critical problems for the USSR's 'revolutionary' credentials in the world. As the Soviet élite moved towards a dependency relationship with the Western bourgeoisie it inevitably confronted dilemmas in terms of its relations with the communist movement and Third World nationalist movements. The USSR could not have détente and at the same time obey the 'laws of the global class struggle'. In short, détente, if followed through fully, would compromise Russia's relationship with Eastern Europe, the communist movement and Third World nationalism; the Soviet élite was not prepared to abandon these for a dependency relationship with the West. The price of détente appeared too high, however essential it may have been.

In economic terms détente saw a massive expansion of trade with Western Europe, notably West Germany. Western technology solved certain bottle-necks, grain imports helped stabilise food supplies and consumer imports fed the Levi-Jean starved youth; but the strategy of 'modernisation' on the basis of importing foreign technology did not and could not work. Technology alone could not transform the labour process and raise productivity in any lasting way.[117] Soviet and East European goods still remained defective and non-competitive on the world market. Grain imports from the West staved off the food crisis and potential discontent, but it clearly did not solve the problems of agriculture.[118] The economic result of détente was debt,[119] made worse by imported inflation and Western recession, but certainly not caused by them. The only things which saved the USSR were gold, oil, and later, gas. Détente did not solve the underlying contradictions of the Soviet economy (which requires socialism which the élite oppose, or the market which the working class reject). After ten years of détente the Soviet bloc still cannot compete. Détente in many ways has only made the economic situation worse. Its most obvious political result has been the Polish crisis. Détente postponed reform, but over the longer term has not reduced the pressure for it. In many ways it has reinforced the case for change by showing there is no alternative to it.

It is evident that détente, in terms of what both the West and the Soviet élite hoped to achieve through it, is in crisis. It is also self-evident that many of the features of the Cold War system remain intact, including the arms race and the division of Europe. However, the conditions which made the Cold War feasible no longer pertain. The world has changed enormously. The Cold War was the product of a conjuncture which no longer exists. The American nuclear monopoly, its general control over Europe and Japan, and even the type of society America was in the Cold War; all these things have gone forever. It would be impossible to reconstruct Cold War America in anything like its original shape. Vietnam was not a problem: it marked the end of one epoch and the beginning of another. Clearly it would be extremely difficult to recreate the domestic consensus for direct US intervention in any part of the globe.[120] Furthermore, huge defence spending is by no means so easy, or unambiguously beneficial as it once seemed. Public spending, which remained extraordinarily low in the Cold War, cannot be cut back now so drastically in order to permit an easy expansion of the arms sector. Escalating arms spending upon the basis of what is now a low productivity and decreasingly competitive economy would increase inflation and further reduce the general viability and competitiveness of the productive sector of the US economy. Those fractions of capital not directly benefiting from arms spending would inevitably see it as a burden upon the rest of the economy.[121] Arms spending also does not produce high employment levels today in such an easy way, for the industry is highly capital intensive. Also, popular support for militarism is now less in America and opinion, twenty years behind Europe, will no longer easily acquiesce in an arms race that is now regarded as a direct danger and an economic burden.[122] This can only erode any possible consensus for a reconstructed Cold War in America. At the simple propaganda level too, selling the 'threat' is far more difficult in contemporary America. In 1947, and for a decade thereafter, communism seemed powerful and monolithic; today it is clearly recognised to be neither. Finally, a renewed Cold War in its original form would inevitably lead to a major conflict between Europe and America. Western Europe and West Germany in particular would oppose any American attempt to totally refreeze the division between the two camps. In the context of rising economic competition, both Europe and Japan would see American economic embargoes as simply a crude way of reducing their own economic potential and competitiveness. Far from creating unity amongst the advanced capitalist countries a 'new Cold War', fostered by the USA, would actually divide it even further. Far from establishing conditions for a new equilibrium it would undermine it. As the world recession grows and fractures within the West deepen, Western Europe in general, and West Germany especially, will resist all attempts by the USA to cut it off from useful markets and ready supplies of cheap energy. Equally, there will be total opposition to unilateral American efforts to deliberately maintain a frozen European status quo, regulated by constant reminders of the Soviet threat, whose only *raison d'être* seems to be to keep Europe dependent upon the United States.[123]

For the Soviet Union too there can be no return to the situation of the 1950s. Autarchy and isolation are no longer viable. Politically, it would be impossible to attempt to exploit Eastern Europe economically as it did before.[124] Also, the arms burden upon the Soviet system is now recognised to be critically high and this demands negotiation with the United States.[125] There is pressure for reform, possibly drastic, but not for a re-run of the Cold War. The system requires to maintain its links with the West and clearly could not afford to sever them. Importing technology and food cannot solve Soviet economic problems, but cutting them off could precipitate a crisis.[126] The simple scale of the Soviet bloc debt places pressure upon the USSR to keep open relations with the West (and vice versa). As its problems increase, which is recognised clearly in the West, the USSR will be forced to make some critical decisions. Under the threat of pressure by the United States to increase its arms burden, by the Western banks to repay Soviet bloc debts, and facing as it does enormous difficulties on all fronts, it has to negotiate with the West. The West is in crisis, it is more divided than ever, but in real terms it is still negotiating as before from positions of strength. The only question is what price will it ask and how much will the Soviet Union be prepared to pay politically?

Talk of a 'new Cold War' can be criticised therefore at several levels. The concept begs several questions and falsely identifies two different epochs. Often those who talk of a new Cold War falsely equate the Cold War system entirely with the arms race. To do so is historically misleading. The proposed massive American rearmament programme is not proof that the old system in its pure form can be recreated. In fact at the height of the Cold War in America, Eisenhower tried to cut arms spending and later attacked the military-industrial complex.[127] Kennedy, in some ways the apostle of détente, led an enormous arms build-up.[128] As a result of détente, nobody assumed there would be an end to the arms race, or less spent on arms.[129] Also, in the Cold War there was only one nuclear power which in some ways is why it was physically safer than the present. This was an indispensable feature of the Cold War system. Once that changed, there was no longer any possibility of returning to a Cold War system of simple US monopoly of nuclear weapons. Finally, it is not even clear that Reagan is aiming to achieve what the Cold War system achieved, that is to completely refreeze the USSR and Eastern Europe into place; although that may be the consequence of his policies. After 1948 it was assumed that little or nothing could be done to change the status quo beyond the iron curtain. There were, as we have argued, extremely good reasons for not doing so. Now the situation is very different, as Kissinger in 1969, and Reagan's advisers today, clearly understand. One of the reasons why American pressure is being remounted upon the USSR (similar in some but not every way to what occurred after 1948) is not to freeze it, but possibly to transform it.[130] Since 1975 the USA has become increasingly aware of how deep and wide Soviet problems are. The great 'threat' is more vulnerable now than it has ever been – as the CIA has admitted over the last seven years. It is far more amenable to pressure than it was in 1948 or the 1950s, when external hostility directly prevented change in Eastern Europe and the Soviet Union. Today, Russia's situation is truly critical, in many ways more so than in 1947 for then the system had more options and, in a special way, more choices. Then, no change was possible, or even desirable; today it is possible; many believe it is imminent. The Soviet Union and Eastern Europe can no longer continue in the same way indefinitely. In 1947 it seemed as if they were at the beginning of a new era, not, as it appears today, at the end of one.

There is in fact a real possibility that the Cold War system in

Europe as a whole could unwind, bringing change to Europe, Germany and the USSR. But does the United States desire it – that is the question? The one great outcome of the Cold War has never altered: the division of Europe with the Soviet Union behind its buffer zone. Now it might. American policy is effectively caught on the horns of a dilemma. If it seeks to change the Cold War system it hurts its own interests. If it does not, it may miss a great opportunity of pulling the Soviet bloc back into the world market. The conflict between its dependency upon Stalinism and European-German division, and the pressures and historic possibilities to reconstitute and reconstruct a world system of capitalism, is at the root of the manifest incoherence in its 'Russian policy'. However, both America and Russia are caught in an unresolvable dilemma. Neither power can any longer continue with the Cold War system, yet to abandon it would bring about far-reaching change. For the USSR and for the USA moving beyond the Cold War has proved a necessity, but for the moment at least it is extremely problematic as well. Irreversible changes in the world no longer make the Cold War feasible, but both the USA and the USSR have been moulded by the Cold War relationship: to alter that fundamentally means altering themselves and the world system which they shaped after 1947.

TOWARDS A SOCIALIST ALTERNATIVE

The post-war crisis produced specific responses by America and the USSR which led to strategies seen as essential for their own reproduction. In effect, America expanded while the Soviet Union retreated behind a number of defensive shields. The Cold War legitimised the former and rationalised the latter. The Cold War was not caused by America or Russia alone. It was a process of interaction created by two systems as they re-established control at home and equilibrium within their own spheres of influence. Détente was only an index that American power had reached a limit and that Soviet separation from the world system was no longer possible. In fact, although it was not fully appreciated at the time, détente was a rather desperate attempt by a declining American super power to forestall further decline, and by the Soviet élite to avoid reform by 'solving' their own internal problems by looking to the West. In some ways it was only a different form of the dependency relationship which had existed throughout the Cold War. The strategy could not work. America's decline continued and the Soviet bloc's internal problems deepened. It is this which has led to the crisis of détente.

However, to assert that détente could not stop American decline, or raise Soviet and East European labour productivity, is not the same as assuming the world will once again return to the Cold War. This, as we have suggested, is impossible. Further crisis within capitalism and the Soviet system, something which is now universally expected throughout the 1980s, will make the possibility of a return to the old system even more remote. Soviet problems in the bloc, both in political and economic terms, will almost certainly increase. As the costs of holding on to Eastern Europe grow the Soviet élite may try to seek disengagement. In the West the identity of Europe with America can only be reduced further as competition between them grows and their policies and aims diverge even more. Pressure will grow in Western Europe to move even further away from America, especially as America takes measures increasingly at variance with the interests of Western Europe, and West Germany in particular. This unwinding of the Cold War system could have massive ramifications in Europe as a whole, especially in Germany where the loosening of both blocs will raise the German question anew.

If the Cold War was a means of disciplining Europe, nowhere was that more acutely felt than in West Germany. If détente was a sign of American decline, for West Germany it was an index of assertion. More than that, it was viewed as the beginning of a long process by which Germany could be reunited. As Birnbaum has put it, 'Deutschland politik became the heart of Bonn's Ostpolitik'.[131] The SPD mayor of West Berlin made it clear in 1969 when he argued that 'the subject matter of Ostpolitik is Germany itself'.[132] Kissinger was well aware of this, but realised that if America did not accompany the process of bridge-building to the East, Western Europe and West Germany might well go it alone.[133] This is why Ostpolitik was a problem for America: it threatened to unlock a European and German division which benefited the United States. More obviously, it made West Germany more assertive and independent. Furthermore, as the crisis within the Soviet bloc unfolds (and Poland is only the tip of that iceberg); as the burden rate of holding Eastern Europe for the USSR grows (now calculated at $20 billion);[134] and as demands for the market reform[135] become more audible once again in the Soviet bloc, it is West Germany which is better placed to gain than the United States. This presents the United States with a major dilemma which it will find difficult to resolve. If it attempts to freeze the process of evolution within Europe as a whole it can only do so by coming into greater conflict with Europe. However, if it accedes to change, Germany could clearly move beyond American control and re-emerge as the great threat to US interests in the world. The Soviet élite, when faced with its own crisis in Eastern Europe, may well offer West Germany (as it did in 1952), the lure of reunification in return for neutrality. As one aspect of the Soviet crisis is the escalating costs it is confronting as a result of over-extension on a world scale, costly forms of external support (including Eastern Europe), could easily be seen as increasingly dispensable in the 1980s. The process of 'Finlandisation' in Eastern Europe is clearly an option for the USSR if some form of rapprochement with West Germany takes place. Possibly the main question confronting the United States in the 1980s will be how to come to terms with change in Europe and Germany's role within it. Whichever strategy it chooses, and in the end it will almost certainly veer between the policy of preventing and accepting change, it is bound to lead to a further weakening of its hegemony over Europe.

There is little doubt therefore that changes in East and West will move the world system beyond the Cold War. However, the international system which follows may be less stable; possibly more dangerous. As Hackett has observed, 'a world in which there are two superpower blocs in abrasive but more or less stable equilibrium is likely to be a safer world than if one of them collapses'.[136] Both blocs are in transition. The stable equilibrium which was the Cold War system is finished. Yet the outcome may not be the rosy one sought by those who believe that by moving 'beyond the Cold War' we will solve the main questions of our time. It will only pose them in a different way. Overcoming the division of Europe will not of itself lead to the end of the arms race. It could even increase the proliferation of nuclear weapons. Also, it will deepen instability in general throughout the continent. A new Europe need not be more pacific, indeed as Hackett suggests it could be more susceptible to war. A 'new Russia' may become competitive and expansionary, unlike the present regime.[137] Eastern Europe could once again become a major area of instability. A reunited Germany could assert its hegemony in Europe as a whole, with all the implications of that. In short, getting the Russians and the Americans 'out of Europe' will solve little in itself. Ending the Cold War division of the continent, without specifying for what end, could lead to even greater danger than that which already exists. For those who are opposed to the Cold War it is essential to state more than simply than they are against it. Those who favour 'peace' might oppose the arms race, but may have to accept the Cold War division of Europe which has at least brought an equilibrium to the continent which never existed before. Those, however, who do advocate 'one Europe' will have to spell out clearly what its implications may be and, more obviously, what sort of structures they believe will be necessary in a new united Europe to guarantee that it will not be the battleground for the sort of international conflicts which existed during the great inter-war crisis.[138] In short the struggle to overcome the division of Europe must be linked to fundamental change within Europe as well as the Soviet Union.

For socialists in particular the Cold War division of Europe raises major problems and questions. Socialists have to confront the simple fact that their weakness and decline in the post-war period – in both camps – is largely a function of the Cold War. To overcome the Cold War is thus a precondition for socialist renewal on both sides of the divide. It will of course mean that those socialists in particular who have held on to cherished illusions about the workers' states and their progressive historical character will have to abandon such positions. The 'socialist' camp is part of the problem and must be seen as such. Without Stalinism, capitalism could not have been so massively successful as it was in the post-war period; its continuation, even in a modified form, still makes the future look hopeless for those struggling in the West. Major change beyond the 'iron curtain' is therefore crucial if there is to be a chance of change in the West. But in turn, change in the West is essential if there is to be genuine renewal in the East. There is little doubt that the arrival of the oft-heralded crisis of European capitalism has done much already to undermine popular East European and Soviet illusions in the Western market system. The resulting and almost inevitable escalation of international and internal class conflicts in the West will further that process. It is almost certain that these developments will feed into the systems of Eastern Europe and the Soviet Union, systems it should be recalled that are also entering into a new critical phase, with social structures now dominated for the first time by an hereditary working class which is alienated from its own system, but not attracted towards the market either. Those who believe that we have now entered into a new Cold War not only mis-understand the complexities of the modern epoch, they also forget that renewed working class struggles in both parts of Europe, however unconnected and inchoate, will also erode the Cold War division further by making actual and obvious the similarity of workers' respective positions in the two types of society. This deep geological shift will only make the vast chasm which has hitherto separated East from West appear less vital and important; indeed, as a result of these joint struggles, something new may emerge. That long lost and discarded *mot d'ordre*, 'workers of the world unite', may seem utopian to many after decades of defeat. In fact it is, and remains, the only real solution to Europe's division and Russia's tragedy.

NOTES

1. James Burnham, *The Managerial Revolution* (Harmondsworth: Penguin, 1962) p. 43.
2. Many leading State Department experts argued strongly that Stalin opposed foreign CP's taking power for fear this would increase their independence from Moscow – which later happened with Tito and Mao. See C. Bohlen, *The Transformation Of American Foreign Policy* (New York: W. W. Norton, 1969) pp. 104–106; G. F. Kennan, *The Realities Of American Foreign Policy* (Oxford University Press, 1954) pp. 74–75; G. F. Kennan, *Soviet Foreign Policy* (New York: Anvil, 1960) p. 54.
3. 'These soldiers coming home are simply not going to understand our boasting about our capitalist economy if it can't deliver the goods in terms of the opportunity for work': R. E. Sherwood (ed.), *Roosevelt and Hopkins* (New York: Grosset and Dunlap, 1950) p. 926. The words were Hopkins'.
4. America, according to the US ambassador in Finland, 'intended to fore-stall the revolutionary disintegration of Europe upon conclusion of war by preparations now being made to meet urgent supply needs of European populations at that time': US Department of State, *Foreign Relations Of The United States 1941* (Washington, 1958) p. 59.
5. H. S. Truman, *Year of Decisions 1945* (Sevenoaks: Hodder and Stoughton, 1955) pp. 398–415. As one writer has argued, 'The First World War ended suddenly...and caught statesman...unprepared with plans either for relief or reconstruction...During the Second World War, government

officials in London and Washington were anxious to prevent a repetition of this error': E. F. Penrose, *Economic Planning for the Peace* (Princeton University Press, 1953) p. 11.

6. '...The economic potential of the United States of America has enormously increased during the war, while that of many other important industrial centres has considerably diminished': *United Nations Economic Report. Salient Features of The World Economic Situation 1945–1947* (New York: United Nations 1948) p. 3. In 1945 America controlled 50% of global GNP and most of its aid resources; the economy had doubled in size between 1941 and 1945.

7. Contrary to what is normally accepted among historians of the Second World War, America did an enormous amount of planning for the post-war world. Not all those plans were fulfilled, but the underlying goal of creating an open world economy remained constant throughout. This goal was not the invention of later revisionist historians, but of the US State Department and its economic advisers in the thirties and forties. For a short critical examination of planning for 'peace' see L. Shoup and W. Mintner, *Imperial Brain Trust* (New York: Monthly Review Press, 1977) pp. 117–187. A longer more orthodox account can be found in R. N. Gardner, *Sterling – Dollar Diplomacy* (New York: McGraw-Hill, 1969).

8. On US military superiority in 1945, see B. Brodie, 'The Atom Bomb as Policy Maker', *Foreign Affairs* (Oct. 1948) pp. 28–29; E. Teller, 'Alternatives for Security', *Foreign Affairs* (Jan. 1958) p. 201; J. Deane, *The Strange Alliance* (London: John Murray, 1947) pp. 122, 126; Clark Clifford, 'American Relations with the Soviet Union', in A. Crock, *Memoirs* (New York: Funk and Wagnalls, 1968) pp. 477–8. The US Navy and Air Force discounted Soviet military capability: see V. Davis, *Postwar Defence Policy and the U. S. Navy 1943–1946* (University of North Carolina Press, 1966) and P. McCoy Smith, *Air Force Plans for the Peace* (Baltimore: Johns Hopkins Press, 1970).

9. J.F. Dulles admitted in January 1947 that war 'is one thing which the Soviet leadership does not want and would not consciously risk. Economically the nation is still weak in consequence of war devastation. Also, for the time being, the Soviet military establishment is completely outmatched by the mechanized weapons – particularly the atomic weapons – available to the United States'. Cited in G. Kolko, *The Limits of Power* (New York: Harper & Row, 1972) p. 33. Arnold Toynbee, a central figure in the British foreign policy establishment, noted in October of the same year: 'The United States at any rate, with her overwhelming superiority in industrial potential and her monopoly of the "Know-how" of the atom bomb, is at present impregnable against military attack by the Soviet Union. For Moscow it would be sheer suicide to make the attempt and there is no evidence that the Kremlin has any intention of committing such a folly'. 'The Present Point in History', *Foreign Affairs*, 24 (1947) p. 191.

10. Several official reports made it clear that Russia was not a major military menace. See G. Kolko, *The Limits Of Power* (New York: Harper & Row, 1972) pp. 33, 480–481, 499; D. Yergin, *Shattered Peace* (Harmondsworth: Penguin, 1980) p. 467 fn. 20, 23; L. Freedman, *U.S. Intelligence And The Soviet Strategic Threat* (London: Macmillan, 1974) pp. 63–64. John

Deane, former head of the American military mission in Moscow, argued that Russia had neither the intention nor the capability to launch a military offensive; Deane, op. cit., pp. 122, 126, 325–329. *The Forrestal Diaries; The Inner History Of The Cold War*, W. Millis (ed.), (London: Cassell, 1952) show conclusively that American policy makers did not expect Russia to expand after WWII, pp. 174, 184, 196, 211, 260, 336, 374–375, 387, 434, 440–441, 444, 475, 478, 505. In 1947 the CIA discounted any chance of Soviet aggression, L. Farago, *War Of Wits. The Anatomy Of Espionage and Intelligence* (New York: Funk and Wagnalls, 1954) p. 81. In 1948 and 1949 the CIA denied there was any grand Russian 'masterplan for global domination'; see T. Barnes, 'The Secret Cold War: The C.I.A. and American Foreign Policy in Europe 1946–1956', II, *The Historical Journal*, 25, 3 (1982) pp. 650–651. In 1951 Truman confided to Arthur Crock that the USSR did not have the economic capacity to launch an offensive and faced too much 'trouble with the satellites and also at home' to initiate war. A. Crock, *Memoirs* (New York: Funk and Wagnalls, 1968) p. 261. Soviet economic potential was known to be very weak compared to America and West Europe; see the accounts in *The American Economic Review*, 37 (1947) pp. 611–623, and later in Vol. 41, May 1951) pp. 475–494. *The Annals of the American Academy of Political and Social Science* (May 1949) carried important material on Soviet economic weakness, pp. 52–84.

11. In 1945 a US loan of $10 billion to Russia was being discussed by Harriman and Morgenthau. *F.R.U.S. The Conference of Malta and Yalta* (Washington, 1955) pp. 309–324. Harriman noted 'that our co-operation will depend upon their behaviour in international matters' (ibid., p. 313). 'Co-operation would necessitate [their] abandonment of interference in the internal affairs of other nations' argued Cordell Hull, *Memoirs*, vol. 2 (Sevenoaks: Hodder & Stoughton, 1948) p. 1468.

12. Roosevelt told worried US Senators, 'The Russians had the power in Eastern Europe. The only practicable course was to use what influence we had to ameliorate the situation'. Yergin, op. cit., p. 58. He confessed to Berle that Eastern Europe was already in the Soviet sphere of control: R. Dallek, *Roosevelt and American Foreign Policy 1932–1945* (Oxford University Press, 1979) pp. 521, 524.

13. Cited in G. Kolko, *The Politics of War* (London: Weidenfeld & Nicolson, 1969) p. 334.

14. Later Cold War charges that Roosevelt was simply naive or worse, 'sold out the West', totally miss the point of Roosevelt's longer term co-operative strategy. For brief but clear presentations of his attempt to open up and change Soviet society see the recollections of some of his closest advisers: Sumner Welles, *Where Are We Heading?* (London: Hamish Hamilton, 1947) pp. 87, 317–321; E. Stettinius, *Roosevelt and The Russians* (New York: Doubleday, 1949) pp. 323–324; W. A. Harriman and E. Abel, *Special Envoy To Churchill and Stalin 1941–1946* (New York: Random House, 1975). The similarities between Roosevelt's approach and that advocated later by the supporters of détente and Ostpolitik is striking.

15. 'The Soviet regime and the lives of its rulers might be imperilled by allowing free, easy and friendly intermingling with the outer world. An

endless series of quarrels, a vehement and violent antagonism, the consciousness of an outside enemy in the minds of the masses, may be regarded by the Soviets as a necessary precautionary element in maintaining the existence of communist power'. *House of Commons Debate*, vol. 473, 28 March 1950, col. 199. Churchill was only repeating the Kennan thesis which the American had advanced earlier in his famous 'x' article of July 1947 in *Foreign Affairs*.

16. Soviet society presupposed isolation and separation from the more advanced West. This was, as Deutscher, amongst others, has pointed out, 'the indispensable condition for its very existence': *Stalin* (Harmondsworth: Penguin, 1966) p. 544. The war had led to a breach in the closed character of the USSR which required resealing after WWII. On the impact of, and reaction to, the breaking down of the iron curtain after 1941 see F. C. Barghoorn, *The Soviet Image of the United States* (New York: Harcourt Brace & Co., 1950); J. Fischer, *The Scared Men in The Kremlin* (London: Hamish Hamilton, 1947) and W. B. Smith, *Moscow Mission 1946–1949* (London: Heinemann, 1950) pp. 279–292. More recently, N. Tolstoy, *Stalin's Secret War* (London: Heinemann, 1981) has drawn our attention to the fact that Stalin's 'European conquests aroused as many fears as they allayed', p. 272. The dilemma of expansion outside of the Soviet Union has also been discussed by V. Mastny in his 'Spheres of Influence and Soviet War Aims', in S. Sinanian *et al* (eds), *Eastern Europe In The 1970's* (New York: Praeger, 1974) pp. 87–107. Mastny notes that from 'Stalin's point of view, the path of military conquest entailed the incalculable risk of exposing his troops to the allurement of different ways of life, from which he had tried so hard to shelter all his subjects', p. 88. Is it feasible therefore that Stalin would have envisaged expansion into *advanced* Western Europe, after WWII?

17. The House Committee on Un-American Activities was revived in 1946 following the victories gained by the Republicans for the 80th Congress. It was controlled by the GOP and Southern Democrats and its main political function was 'to badger the State Department and attack the New Deal': R. Carr, *The House Committee on Un-American Activities 1945–1950* (New York: Cornell, 1952) p. 42.

18. In his attempt to provide a neat conceptual framework upon which to hang his impressive empiricism, Yergin, in *Shattered Peace*, manages to make Kennan the author of the Cold War, a believer in what Yergin terms the 'Riga Axioms'. According to Yergin, Kennan was the 'chief ideologue' (p. 27) of this school which argued that 'doctrine and ideology and a spirit of innate aggressiveness shaped Soviet policy' (p. 35) making the USSR 'a world revolutionary state' (p. 38). In fact Kennan argued no such thing. The main Kennan 'thesis' was that the nature of the Soviet system made Roosevelt's co-operative strategy impossible. To make Kennan the father of the Cold War cannot explain why he became a major critic of the Truman Doctrine, had, by the early 1950s, been marginalised from the State Department, and was to be one of the earliest advocates of détente. See his *Memoirs 1925–1950* (London: Hutchinson, 1968), *Memoirs 1950–1963* (London: Hutchinson, 1973).

19. Macmillan provided an excellent summary of the realist interpretation of

Soviet behaviour when in a Commons debate on foreign affairs in 1946 he asked: 'May it not be that the apparent chauvinism of Soviet policy is a form of insurance, not expansion, that security not imperialism is their instinctive goal?' He continued: 'It may well be, therefore, that the ultimate cause of these recent manifestations of Soviet policy are, at bottom isolationist and not expansionist, and that their purpose is not to dominate the world either as Russian imperialists, or as militant international communists, but to secure the soil of Holy Russia'. *House of Commons Debates*, vol. 419, 20 Feb. 1946, cols. 1167–1168. A glance through Hansard before 1947 shows that this was the generally accepted view by both parties.

20. See Kennan's discussion of the Soviet Union's major problems in 'Russia – Seven Years Later' (September 1944); 'Russia's International Position at the Close of the War with Germany' (May 1945); 'Telegraphic Message from Moscow of February 22, 1946'; 'The United States and Russia' (Winter 1946): all cited in *Memoirs* (1968) pp. 503–563; 'The Sources of Soviet Conduct', in *Foreign Affairs* (July 1947) esp. pp. 577–578; 'The Soviet Union and The Atlantic Pact' (September 1952) in *Memoirs* (1973) pp. 327–351.

21. Hugh de Santis, *Diplomacy Of Silence* (University of Chicago Press, 1980) shows that Kennan denied Russia was guided by ideology or belief in world revolution, and assumed some form of co-existence or realistic cooperation was feasible. These were hardly the premises of the Cold War.

22. Kennan himself believed that his advice was rejected because it became increasingly unacceptable domestically. Thereafter a 'domestically inspired foreign policy' prevailed: *Memoirs* (1972) p. 320. Kennan was particularly vehement against the influence of the East European ethnics upon US policy towards the Soviet bloc, ibid., pp. 97–102.

23. 'Only slowly did it dawn upon us that the whole world structure and order we had inherited from the 19th century was gone and that the struggle to replace it would be directed from two bitterly opposed and ideologically irreconcilable power centers': Dean Acheson, *Present At The Creation* (New York: W. W. Norton, 1969) p. 726.

24. P. A. Moseley, 'Kremlin's Foreign Policy', in *Foreign Affairs* (Oct. 1953) pp. 4–5. Moseley distinguished between two Western schools of thought in relation to the Soviet Union. One, which seeks to discipline the system from without and the other, which has attempted to pull the USSR into a close relationship with the West. Moseley, it goes without saying, was a member of the first.

25. In fact the 'threat' was first used to ensure the passage through Congress of the British Loan of 1946. As Gardner has shown there was much conservative opposition to the $3.75 billion loan. The Soviet menace became, a year before the Truman Doctrine, the 'new factor in American policy': Gardner, op. cit., pp. 248–254. The best study on the relationship between domestic resistance to foreign aid and the Russian 'factor' remains Richard M. Freeland, *The Truman Doctrine and the Origins of McCarthyism* (New York: Knopf, 1972).

26. 'There are many indications that Stalin fully appreciated the disastrous consequences of an overt move against Western Europe; [also he] was not

prepared to encourage the French and Italian Communist parties to seize power': Marshall Shulman, *Beyond The Cold War* (Yale University Press, 1966) pp. 9–10. (Shulman was special Soviet adviser to Carter after 1978)

27. 'Historicus', 'Stalin On Revolution', in *Foreign Affairs*, 27,2 (Jan. 1949) pp. 198–199. Before 1947 'ideology' was hardly considered relevant to understanding the Soviet Union; after the Truman Doctrine nothing else seemed to matter. An official American statement on the world revolutionary role of the USSR can be found in *The Strategy and Tactics of World Revolution. Committee on Foreign Affairs*, May 1947 (Washington, 1948). A 'classic' statement of the Cold War view that world domination remained the ultimate Soviet goal can be found in Elliot R. Goodman *The Soviet Design For A World State* (Columbia University Press, 1957). In the sixties the picture was rather complicated by the outwardly more militant policies of China; however the official line remained clear. Russia was still the 'greatest menace'. See 'The Reality of The Russian Threat' (interview with William Griffith) in *The Reader's Digest*, Feb 1967. The CIA, according to two former employees, backed the publication of Walt Rostow's *The Dynamics of Soviet Society* in 1953 because it 'promoted the thesis that the Soviet Union is an imperialistic power bent on world conquest': V. Marchetti and J. D. Marks, *The C.I.A. and the Cult of Intelligence* (London: Coronet, 1976) p. 203. One of the most influential books written on communism, by R. F. Carew-Hunt, a career officer in the Foreign Office and intelligence, argued that expansion was a substitute for revolution: 'The promotion of revolution by increasing the power of Russia is the inevitable result of failure of the communist parties to bring it about for themselves': *The Theory And Practice of Communism* (1950, Harmondsworth: Penguin, 1968) p. 243. For Stalin, according to Robert Tucker, 'the international communist revolution would grow by accretion from the centre', *Slavic Review* (Dec. 1977) p. 571.

28. The 'early' Kissinger argued that it was 'futile to seek to deal with a revolutionary power by ordinary diplomatic methods', *Nuclear Weapons And Foreign Policy* (New York: Oxford University Press, 1957) p. 337; a view he repeated in *The Necessity For Choice* (New York: Harper, 1960) 'Barring the evolution of the Soviet system negotiations were futile', p. 191

29. In 1956 the young Brzezinski was predicting 'no fundamental mellowing of the Soviet system: Z. Brzezinski, *The Permanent Purge in Soviet Politics* (Harvard University Press, 1956) p. 173. In a co-authored study published in the same year he thought 'there might conceivably be internal transformation' (p. 302), but it was more likely for the Soviet system 'to become more total' (p. 306), in C. J. Friedrich and Z. Brzezinski, *Totalitarian Dictatorship and Autocracy* (Harvard University Press, 1956).

30. 'What we must do is to create situations of strength; we must build strength and if we create that strength then I think the whole situation in the world begins to change . . . I should hope there would be a willingness on the part of the Kremlin to recognize the facts': *U.S. Congress, Senate Committee On Armed Services And Committee On Foreign Relations* 82nd Congress, 1st sess. 1951, p. 2083.

31. 'I pleaded with people to recognize . . . that the Russians . . . were weaker than we supposed; that they had many internal problems of their own; that they had no "grand design" . . . ': G. F. Kennan, *Memoirs* (1973) p. 92.

32. 'The task of a public officer seeking to explain and gain support for a major policy is not that of the writer of a doctoral thesis. Qualification must give way to simplicity of statement, nicety and nuance to bluntness, almost brutality in carrying home a point...If we made our points clearer than the truth, we did not differ from most other educators...' Acheson, *Present At The Creation*, op. cit., p. 375.

33. *Pravda*, 1 Feb. 1948. A. Bergson, 'Russian Defence Expenditures', *Foreign Affairs* (Jan. 1948) believed that 'urgent reconstruction tasks' made any Soviet action very unlikely. 'Perhaps', he argued, 'the Russians have not yet finished demobilizing [and that] further cuts in defence outlays still may be in prospect' (p. 375).

34. H. Schwartz, *Russia's Postwar Economy* (Syracuse University Press, 1947) estimated that ten million veterans had returned to the civilian labour force between 1945 and 1947, pp. 69–70. R. Garthoff has calculated a reduction in the Soviet army from 11 to 3 million between 1945 and 1948: *Soviet Military Policy* (London: Faber, 1966) p. 23.

35. See the series in the *Economist*, 15 March 1947; 22 March 1947; 29 March 1947. As the first of these argued, 'There can be no doubt that the Soviet Union is in the throes of an economic crisis [related to] a crisis in the morale of the working population, a crisis due to disastrous housing conditions, to shortages of food and consumer goods, and also to general postwar frustration' (p. 380).

36. W. B. Smith, *Moscow Mission 1946–1949*, op. cit., pp. 126–127. Smith succeeded Harriman as ambassador to Moscow and in 1950 became head of the CIA. He was much admired by Philby! See *My Silent War* (London: Panther, 1976) p. 163.

37. Farago, *War of Wits*, op. cit., p. 81.

38. *F.R.U.S., 1945*, op. cit., p. 322.

39. M. L. Tamarchenko, *Sovetskie finansy v period Velikoi Otechestvennoi voiny* (Moscow) p. 135. Kennan, in *Memoirs* (1973) p. 327. According to N. A. Voznesensky, total losses of all sorts amounted to about two-thirds of the total wealth existing before the war in the territories subject to occupation. *The Economy of the U.S.S.R. during World War II* (Washington, 1948) p. 87. War death estimates range between 20 million, in A. Nove, *An Economic History of the U.S.S.R.* (Harmondsworth: Penguin, 1975) p. 285, and 22–27 million, J. A. Newth, *Soviet Studies*, XV, 3 (January 1964) p. 347. The total deficit of population made up of deaths, as well as those not born, or who died prematurely because of wartime conditions has been calculated at 45 million: W. Eason, 'The Soviet Population Today', *Foreign Affairs*, 37 (July 1959) pp. 598–606. The OSS study was carried out by A. Bergson and W. Leontieff, see *Soviet Economy In a New Perspective* (Washington: USGPO, 1976) p. 251.

40. The threat was constructed, but succeeded to the degree that the Soviet system could be portrayed as alien to all that was human and progressive. Thus the threat was 'associated with the prospect of an imminent general breakdown of civilization and the obliteration of all that made life worth living, or even possible, under the Muscovite tyranny that was spreading from the East': L. J. Halle, *The Cold War As History* (New York: Harper & Row, 1967) p. 138, fn 3.

41. Every empire in history has attempted to validate itself by an appeal to a

higher mission while at the same time obscuring the nature and extent of its own expansion. 'It is precisely in this falsification of the real import of motives that the gravest vice and the most signal peril of imperialism reside': J. Hobson, *Imperialism* (1902, London: George Allen & Unwin 1968) p. 198.

42. In 1945 and 1946, however, there was distinct tolerance towards the USSR and the American CP, a tolerance that was undermined by the Truman Doctrine and Loyalty Programmes in the following years. The change did not 'happen', it was created by government policy and the virulent opposition campaign conducted by the GOP. A. Theoharis, *Seeds of Repression* (Chicago: Quadrangle, 1971) pp. 3–12, 194–206.

43. The defeat of Wallace in 1948 (facilitated by intimidation, harassment police hostility, and his association with the CPUSA), marked the death of the New Deal and its associated liberal foreign policy in America. K. M. Schmidt, *Quixotic Crusade 1948* (Syracuse University Press, 1960). R. J. Walton, *Henry Wallace, Harry Truman and The Cold War* (New York: Viking, 1976).

44. Theoharis, op. cit.; Freeland, op. cit., p. 369; Gardner, op, cit. pp. 192–194, 236–239. In his study of Marshall Aid, Jones stresses that the great problem in late 1946 and early 1947 was 'American attitudes' which 'lagged far behind reality...weighing down policy decision and action'. WWII had changed the world, 'but there had been no genuine national conversion to the attitudes and policies and specific requirements...of world leadership': J. M. Jones, *The Fifteen Weeks* (New York: Harbinger, 1955) pp. 9–10.

45. Block characterises the victory of internationalism over isolationism as defeat for the fiscal conservatives (who opposed aid and the costs of empire) and national capitalist interests who were against free trade. Victory was achieved, he reminds us, by 'the intensification of the Cold War', without which 'it would have been impossible even to contemplate sending such a massive aid programme to Congress': F. Block, *The Origins Of The International Economic Disorders* (University of California Press, 1977) pp. 9–10, 70–92.

46. H. D. Lasswell, 'The Garrison State', *The American Journal of Sociology*, XLVI (1941) pp. 455–468.

47. After 1950 military spending accounted (on average) for 10% of USGNP. Between 1946 and 1970 approximately 70% of federal expenditure went into national security. In 1965 defence-related work accounted for 10% of total direct employment. J. L. Clayton (ed.), *The Economic Impact of The Cold War* (New York: Brace & World, 1970). Military Keynesianism thus underwrote economic growth after 1950 and acted as a central disciplining agency in American society.

48. The Cold War produced, in the words of one writer, 'a stamp of passive conformity for a whole age': C. Solberg, *Riding High In The Cold War*, (New York: Mason & Lipscomb, 1973) pp. 56–64.

49. The specific strength of 'Americanism' was the historical consequence of the immigrant character of a society where each new wave had to *prove* and demonstrate its loyalty to the state.

50. T. J. Lowi, *The Politics of Disorder* (New York, 1971) esp. pp. 102–119.

51. Acheson, op. cit., pp. 347–348. Acheson approvingly quoted Oliver Wendell Holmes who had noted (in another context) that there are times when 'we need education in the obvious more than investigation of the obscure', pp. 374–375. See Acheson's revealing remarks on NSC-68 and his discussion of the nature and role of the Soviet threat, pp. 373–381.

52. J. Sanders, 'Shaping The Cold War Consensus: The Soviet Threat, Interelite Conflict and Mass Politics in the Korean War Era', in *Berkeley Journal of Sociology*, XXV (1980) pp. 67–136.

53. Leahy noted in his diary in February 1947, 'The consensus of opinion of members of Congress was that such action [aid to Greece and Turkey] could obtain the support of the American people only by a frank, open, public announcement that the action was taken for the purpose of preventing the overthrow of subject governments by the Communists'; quoted in H. Feis, *From Trust To Terror* (London: Blond, 1970). See Feis' valuable discussion of the background to Truman's speech, pp. 189–200. Marshall, in fact, believed that Truman had overstated the 'case a bit' but was informed by Truman that a bold presentation of the problems in global terms 'was the only way' in which aid to Greece and Turkey would be passed. See C. Bohlen, *The Transformation of American Foreign Policy* (New York: W. W. Norton, 1969) p. 87. Gimbel in his study of Marshall Aid shows how the State Department used the Soviet 'card' to ensure Congressional support for Europe: J. Gimbel, *The Origins Of The Marshall Plan* (Stanford University Press, 1976) pp. 4, 279. See also Freeland, op. cit., 'March 1947 had its origins in American politics rather than the developments in Greece' (p. 93); and Gardner, op. cit., 'American acceptance of the loan had been secured out of concern with the Soviet factor' (p. 254).

54. Freeland, ibid., 'The war scare of 1948 terminated the problem of achieving House authorization . . . for the European Recovery Programme', p. 275.

55. H. S. Truman, op. cit., pp. 127–139.

56. Acheson, op. cit., pp. 403–477. See the essay by W. La Feber in L. H. Miller and R. W. Pruessen (eds), *Reflections On The Cold War* (Temple University Press, 1974) which shows how Korea strengthened America's position in Europe and temporarily helped to modify Franco-German conflict.

57. D. Healey, 'Cominform and World Communism', in *International Affairs*, 24 (July 1948) pp. 339–349; H. Butler, 'A New World Takes Shape', in *Foreign Affairs* (July 1948) pp. 604–612, noted that Russia's verbal bellicosity and its policies in Eastern Europe created 'the political and psychological conditions without which there could be no prospect of pulling the West together', p. 612.

58. The head of the CIA had pointed out to Truman in October 1947 that the identity of the CP's with the USSR 'was more a help than hindrance because [they] would appear puppets of the Kremlin', in T. Barnes, op. cit., II, p. 407. By December 1947 the CIA felt the communist danger had passed in France and Italy: *Forrestal Diaries*, op. cit., p. 334.

59. See Acheson's rather disparaging remarks about Kennan in *Present At The Creation*, op. cit., esp. pp. 151, 202–3, 367, 445–6.

60. The crucial study of the NSC-68 discussions is Paul Y. Hammond, 'NSC-68 Prologue To Rearmament', pp. 265–378 in W. R. Schilling, P. Y. Hammond, G. Snyder, *Strategy, Politics and Defence Budgets* (Columbia University Press, 1962). All quotes in the preceding paragraph are taken from Hammond's summary of NSC-68.

61. *Forrestal Diaries*, op. cit., pp. 412–418; S. P. Huntington, *The Common Defence* (Columbia University Press, 1961) connects 'Soviet Power' with the creation of 'stability' in US military planning, pp. 29–32.

62. R. Steel, *The End Of The Alliance* (London: André Deutsch, 1964) pp. 103–124, contains an excellent discussion on the 'Two Germanies'. Halle concludes that 'privately it was widely recognized that most of the principal political and economic interests in West Germany would view reunification with alarm': Halle, op. cit., pp. 393–394.

63. Adenauer, whatever his outward rhetoric, was not primarily interested in German reunification. His main goal was domestic stability, European integration and the American connection: W. A. Paterson, *The S.P.D. and European Integration* (Lexington: Saxon House, 1974); R. Morgan, *The United States and West Germany 1945–1973* (Oxford University Press, 1974); J. L. Richardson, *Germany And The Atlantic Alliance* (Harvard University Press, 1966).

64. On Britain's indifference to Eastern Europe in the 1930s see M. Gilbert and R. Gott, *The Appeasers* (London: Weidenfeld & Nicolson, 1963) pp. 49, 55; H. Seton-Watson, *Eastern Europe Between The Wars 1918–1941* (Cambridge University Press, 1945) pp. 382–384. On America's lack of interests in the area, L. E. Davies, *The Cold War Begins* (Princeton University Press, 1974) and more recently G. Lundestad, *The American Non-Policy Towards Eastern Europe 1943–1947* (Oslo: Forlaget, 1978). It is true that the economic loss of the region was seen as problematic in the context of European recovery as a whole, but it had the advantage, for America at least, of reinforcing West European dependence upon the USA.

65. H. Feis, op. cit., pp. 227–247; T. G. Paterson, *Soviet-American Confrontation* (Baltimore: Johns Hopkins Press, 1973) pp. 211–220; J. Jones, op. cit., 'If the Russians came in, the whole project would probably be unworkable because the amount of money involved in restoring both Eastern and Western Europe would be so colossal it could never be got from Congress...', p. 253.

66. C. Bell, *Negotiation From Strength* (New York: Knopf, 1963) pp. 105, 124; Helmut Schmidt, *Verteidigung oder Vergeltung?* (Stuttgart: Seewald Verlag, 1961) p. 101; Richardson, op. cit., pp. 25–30. Anthony Eden admitted that West German integration with Europe was the main priority, not reunification. See his comments in *Full Circle* (London: Cassell, 1960) and Acheson's in *Present At The Creation*, op. cit.

67. D. Acheson, 'The Illusion of Disengagement', in *Foreign Affairs* (April 1958) pp. 371–382; H. A. Kissinger, 'Missiles And The Western Alliance', ibid., pp. 383–400.

68. Greville Wynne argues that Western intelligence was aware that the wall was going up some time before it was constructed. *Man From Odessa* (London: Robert Hale, 1980) pp. 208–209.

69. R. Divine, *Eisenhower and the Cold War* (Oxford University Press, 1981) p. 107.

70. A. Stent, *From Embargo to Ostpolitik* (Cambridge University Press, 1981) p. 251.

71. A. W. Deporte, *Europe Between The Super Powers* (Yale University Press, 1978).

72. V. Marchetti and J. Marks argue that after Hungary the German radios (Radios Free Europe and Liberation) were ordered to drop the 'liberation' rhetoric and emphasise 'liberalization within the communist systems through peaceful change', op. cit., pp. 195–199. See the discussion on the role of US Cold War rhetoric in the Hungarian events in D. Wise and T. B. Ross, *The Invisible Government* (New York: Vintage, 1974) pp. 324–329; and D. Irving, *Uprising* (London: Hodder & Stoughton, 1981) pp. 155–159, pp. 560–561 fn. 11.

73. Kennan, *Memoirs 1950–1963*, pp. 181–182; Halle, op. cit., pp. 267–272, 307–330. It is interesting that the classic documents advocating liberation of the captive peoples of Eastern Europe nowhere suggest how this might be achieved. E. Lyons, *Our Secret Allies* (London: Arco Publications, 1954); James Burnham, *Containment or Liberation* (New York: Viking, 1953).

74. *New York Review of Books*, 15 June 1972, pp. 23–31. The essence of the Cold War, as defined by both sides, was a competition which existed at every level, from development to sport, culture to space exploration. A central feature of US strategy involved forms of 'squeeze play' against the Soviet bloc to reduce its competitive political and economic attraction for its own people, as well as for those living in the West.

75. Z. Brzezinski, *Between Two Ages* (Harmondsworth: Penguin, 1977) p. 138.

76. The twofold and somewhat contradictory message presented to the West was that the USSR was both 'a menace', yet at the same time 'inferior'. Around the struggle against 'communism', the West 'organised itself and won stability'. For individuals in the West the result was reflected in apathy and acceptance of the status quo, 'not because they approve, but because they have no alternative': R. Aronson, 'Socialism: The Sustaining Menace', in K. Fann and D. Hodges (eds), *Readings in U.S. Imperialism* (Boston: Peter Sargent, 1971) pp. 327–343.

77. *Memoirs 1950–1963*, p. 320.

78. Worse case military planning ('inflate the enemy and minimize one's own capability') was built into the Cold War, for it guaranteed the military superiority which was essential to American Cold War strategy. 'Gaps' which did not exist were an inevitable consequence. As McNamara has recently admitted. 'We overstate the Soviets force and we understate ours, and we therefore greatly overstate the imbalance. This is not something that is new; it has been going on for years': 'The Declining Strength of the Soviets' in the *Guardian* (summer 1982).

79. Shulman has shown that even before Stalin's death the USSR was looking for a relaxation of tension, a policy clearly pursued after 1953 with little success. M. D. Shulman, *Stalin's Foreign Policy Reappraised* (Harvard University Press, 1963).

80. S. Lubell, *The Future of American Politics* (London: Hamish Hamilton 1952) argued that if Republicans did not wish to remain permanently out of power, the immigrant (mainly Catholic) base of the New Deal had to be eroded.

81. Alan Wolfe, *The Rise and Fall of the 'Soviet Threat'* (Washington Institute for Policy Studies, 1979).

82. W. La Feber, *America, Russia and The Cold War 1945–1980* (Cornel University Press, 1980). The conclusion arrived at by Divine in his two volume study was that during elections the parties 'exploit foreign policy issues to gain maximum political advantage' but 'once elected, they turn diplomatic issues back to the small cadre of experts who repair the damage and strive to preserve their domain from the ravage of political discussion for another four years'. R. Divine, *Foreign Policy and United States Presidential Elections*, Vol. I (New York: Franklin Watts, 1974) p. xv.

83. Gaullism and the reassertion of nationalism within Eastern Europe were related signs that the hegemony of both America and Russia was under challenge.

84. 'Khrushchevism' was a halting recognition that Stalinism in its classic form had reached a limit internally and externally.

85. 'Beyond the Cold War' analysis is to be found in T. Paterson (ed.), *Cold War Critics* (Chicago: Quadrangle, 1979); W. Lippmann, *The Cold War* (1947, New York: Harper & Row, 1972); R. Steel, *The End of Alliance* (London: André Deutsch, 1964); R. Steel, *Walter Lippmann and The American Century* (London: Bodley Head, 1981); L. J. Halle, *The Cold War As History* (New York: Harper & Row, 1967); G. F. Kennan, *The Realities of American Foreign Policy* (Oxford University Press, 1954); *Russia, The Atom and The West* (Oxford University Press, 1958); *On Dealing With The Communist World* (New York: Harper & Row, 1964); Marshall D. Shulman, *Beyond The Cold War* (Yale University Press, 1966); Z. Brzezinski, *Alternative To Partition* (New York: McGraw-Hill, 1965); H. A. Kissinger, *The Troubled Partnership* (New York: McGraw-Hill, 1965); S. Hoffman, *Gulliver's Troubles: The Setting of American Foreign Policy* (New York: McGraw-Hill, 1968); Hans J. Morgenthau, *A New Foreign Policy for the United States* (London: Pallmall, 1969); E. J. Hughes, *America The Vincible* (Harmondsworth: Penguin, 1960); Leo Perla, *Can We End The Cold War?* (New York: Macmillan, 1960); J. William Fulbright, *The Arrogance of Power* (1966 Harmondsworth: Penguin, 1967). This list only refers to American critiques of different aspects of the Cold War system written from within the framework of establishment thinking. Long before Kissinger it was evident that the Cold War was no longer intellectually credible or defensible.

86. The West never accepted the basic legitimacy of 'communist' systems. It fought to prevent their emergence, and did as much as possible to hinder their development and stabilisation. Significantly, Bohlen referred to the USSR as 'this unnatural organization of human society [in which] sooner or later there is bound to be change': op. cit., p. 121. Kennedy spoke in 1957 of 'slowly [undercutting] the foundations of the Soviet order' in 'A Democrat Looks at Foreign Policy', *Foreign Affairs* (Oct. 1957) p. 48.

Acheson's famous statement that the aim of American policy was 'to maintain as spacious an environment as possible in which free states might exist and flourish' (op. cit., p. 727) certainly indicates that the West's longer term goal remained global monopoly. As Barghoorn has argued, 'we cannot merely dam the surging tide of totalitarianism but eventually must roll it back. For in the long run a dynamic democracy is both a more revolutionary and a more satisfactory philosophy than communism': op. cit., pp. 284–5.

87. Industrialisation also transformed the social structure of the Soviet bloc, creating, as a result, a mass intelligentsia who came to dominate the economy, party and state. Their emergence solved a fundamental problem, namely, to which group could the West orient and successfully appeal? Not surprisingly the intelligentsia became the most favoured Soviet bloc group in the West. On the special place allotted to the intelligentsia see F. Barghoorn, ibid., p. 290, and his later *Detente and the Democratic Movement in the U.S.S.R.* (New York: The Free Press, Macmillan, 1976). Pisar argued that: 'The single most important action for human rights activists [would be] to encourage the Soviet Union's integration into the world market': S. Pisar, *Of Blood and Hope* (London: Cassell, 1980) p. 270. The human rights dimension of the Helsinki agreements only formalised the intelligentsia's role in the West's integrationist strategy, a role which Brzezinski had advocated in 1963 when he argued that through peaceful engagement 'Eastern Europe should act as a transmission belt [for the West] reaching ever wider circles of Soviet society, especially the intelligentsia': 'Threat and Opportunity in the Communist Schism', *Foreign Affairs* (April 1963) p. 522.

88. On the developing strategy of bridge building and engagement see J. F. Kennedy, ibid., pp. 44–59; Adlai Stevenson, 'Putting Things First', *Foreign Affairs* (Jan. 1960) pp. 191–208; Z. Brzezinski, 'The Challenge Of Change In The Soviet Bloc', *Foreign Affairs* (April 1961) pp. 430–443; with W. E. Griffith, 'Peaceful Engagement In Eastern Europe', *Foreign Affairs* (July 1961) pp. 642–654.

89. It was not Soviet economic competition in the Third World which could have worried the West in the Cold War or indeed since. In spite of Khrushchev's bravado the actual degree of serious Soviet economic extension into the Third World was extremely small. His 'vision' as one writer has put it, 'exceeded the Soviet Union's power to fulfil it': F. Ermath, 'The Soviet Union in the Third World: Purpose in Search of Power', in *Annals of the American Academy of Political and Social Sciences*, November 1969, p. 31. In spite of a concerted economic and political drive towards the Third World since 1954, the USSR has lost many of its former political allies and clearly has not substituted itself economically for the West. On Soviet failure in the Third World see the recent review by W. I. Zartman, 'The U.S.S.R. in The Third World', in *Problems of Communism* (Sept.-Oct. 1982) pp. 76–80; Y. Roi (ed.), *The Limits To Power: Soviet Policy In The Middle East* (London: Croom Helm, 1979); R. H. Donaldson, *The Soviet Union In The Third World, Success and Failure* (London: Croom Helm, 1981). One recent US report has argued that the USSR was most likely to retreat from the pretensions of

globalism in the 1980s: *The Soviet Union and The Third World: A Watershed In Great Power Policy?* (U.S. House of Reps., 8 May 1977). In 1980 the Soviet bloc accounted for only 1/15th of LDC trade and contributed only 0.05% of its GNP in aid, the bulk of which went to Cuba, N. Korea, Vietnam, Afghanistan, Kampuchea and Laos, *O.E.C.D. Review* (1981). What concerned Kissinger and his successors therefore was not Soviet economic penetration, nor the fact that it created instability, but its political and military support to anti-Western forces in unstable situations. For Kissinger the problem areas were the Middle-East and South-East Asia to which he not unnaturally devotes an enormous amount of space in his memoirs, *The White House Years* (London: Weidenfeld & Nicolson, 1979); *Years of Upheaval* (London: Weidenfeld & Nicolson, 1982).

90. 'The Search for Stability', *Foreign Affairs* (July 1959) p. 518. Kissinger in earlier writings had openly admitted that Soviet acquisition of intercontinental capability meant that America would be very 'reluctant to invoke its own destruction for the defense of Europe': 'Nuclear Testing and The Problem of Peace, *Foreign Affairs* (Oct. 1958) p. 12. He assumed that 'as the United States grows more vulnerable fewer and fewer objectives will seem worth all-out war.... even Europe may not appear important enough': 'Missiles and The Western Alliance', *Foreign Affairs* (April 1958) p. 389.

91. 'Thus the development of weapons technology seemed to work to the disadvantage of the free world' argued Pierre Gallois, for Americans 'were forced to realize that henceforth it could commit itself to the defense of other nations only at considerable risk. And America's allies, aware of the dangers she must be willing to accept on their behalf, began to question the worth of that guarantee': 'New Teeth For N.A.T.O.', *Foreign Affairs*, (1960) pp. 68–69. See also Pierre Gallois' classic argument for independent nuclear deterrents in *Stratégie de L'Âge Nucléaire* (Paris 1960).

92. For a recent evaluation of American technological superiority in conventional and nuclear weaponry see the evidence presented by American intelligence and others to the Joint Economic Committee in 1977 and 1978: *Allocation of Resources In The Soviet Union and China – 1977. Pts 1, 2, 3.* (Washington: USGPO, 1977); *Allocation Of Resources In The Soviet Union and China – 1978* (Washington: USGPO, 1978).

93. In 1955, the USSR's GNP was 40% of American GNP; by the late 70s it stood between 50–60% of American GNP. Soviet per capita consumption was 29% of the US level in 1955 and 36% in 1977. The economic weight of the West as a whole compared to the Soviet bloc is of course much greater. Total GNP of the 'big 4' in W. Europe & Japan is $1818 billion. The total GNP of the five largest East European countries in the Warsaw Pact was $234 billion in the same year. Figures from *Soviet Economy In A New Perspective* (Washington: USGPO, 1976) pp. 243–300; *Soviet Economy In A Time Of Change* 2 vols. (Washington: USGPO, 1979) pp. 369–401; *The Military Balance 1978–1979* (International Institute for Strategic Studies, 1978).

94. Until the mid 70s the 'burden-rate' of the military sector on the Soviet economy was calculated at between 6–8%. In 1975 the CIA revised the figure up to 13–15%. This did not reflect a doubling of Soviet capability

but a belated recognition of the degree of inefficiency in the Soviet defence sector. 'There is then some evidence that past official analyses have over-estimated the relative efficiency of Soviet military production and thereby systematically underestimated the ruble value of the resources devoted to Soviet defense activity': *Allocation of Resources In The Soviet Union and China – 1975* (Washington: Joint Economic Committee, 1975) p. 63. In 1977 the CIA was arguing that 'as the economy slows . . . ways to reduce the growth of defense expenditures could become increasingly pressing for some elements of the Soviet leaderships': *Soviet Economic Problems and Prospects* (Washington: Joint Economic Committee, 1977) p. X.

95. In 1962 the official figures put Soviet ICBM numbers at 50–75 and America's at between 200–250. America also possessed 144 missiles in Polaris submarines, and 600 or more intercontinental bombers (the Soviets only about 200); in R. F. Weigley, *The American Way Of War* (New York: Macmillan, 1973) pp. 452–3. Daniel Ellsberg argues that American superiority was even greater than the offical figures show. See his intro-duction to the US edition of *Protest and Survive* (New York Monthly Review, 1982). Certainly after the Kennedy build-up, by the mid 60s, the United States had something close to a first-strike capability: D. Ball, *Politics and Force Levels: The Strategic Missile Program of The Kennedy Administration* (California University Press, 1981).

96. Détente still presupposed both a real American advantage militarily, as well as a threat to increase that advantage, for without these 'bargaining counters' the Soviet Union would not make concessions in other fields. SALT aimed, as Kissinger admitted, to 'create the conditions for [Soviet] political constraint' internationally. This was the essence of his concept of 'linkage': *White House Years*, p. 550. Aspaturian has put the point very well arguing that 'Washington perceived the S.A.L.T. I agreements as instruments designed to domesticate and contain Soviet power, not unleash it. Of this fact, Moscow is exceedingly conscious': V. Aspaturian, 'Soviet Global Power and The Correlation of Forces', *Problems of Communism* (May-June 1980) p. 4.

97. Europe had always resented trade embargoes, but its economic and political dependence upon America meant that only when this was reduced could it ignore American controls over East-West trade; which it did increasingly through the late 1950s and early 1960s. On trade embargoes and their (disputed) effectiveness see J. Wilczynski, *The Economics and Politics of East-West Trade* (London: Macmillan, 1969) pp. 236–252, 271–293; G. Adler-Karlsson, *Western Economic Warfare 1947–1967* (Stockholm: Almquist & Wiksell, 1968); M. Goldman, *Detente and Dollars* (New York: Basic Books, 1975).

98. 'If however, the United States fails to lead the West in building bridges to the East, then Western Europe will almost certainly continue to build bridges of its own, drawing away from the United States in the process': J. W. Fulbright, op. cit., pp. 204–205.

99. See E. O. Reischauer, *Beyond Vietnam. The United States and Asia* (New York: Vintage, 1967) and E. H. Burnell (ed.), *Asia Dilemma: United States, Japan and China* (California University Press, 1969) plead for a new US foreign policy in Asia and towards China.

100. Kissinger returns to the problems of American decline in nearly all his writings of the 1970s. In his memoirs he argued, 'The deepest cause of our national unease was the realization – as yet dimly perceived [in 1969] – that we were becoming like other nations...our power, while vast, had limits': *White House Years*, p. 57. He noted in a lecture given in 1977, 'Our foreign policy difficulties are often described as the legacy of Vietnam. But the Vietnam ordeal was not a cause but a symptom. The late 1960's, coinciding with Vietnam, marked the end of the period when America was overwhelmingly more powerful than any other nation. Vietnam was a catharsis. It taught us that our power while great is finite': *For The Record* (London: Weidenfeld & Nicolson; Michael Joseph, 1981) p. 73. Kissinger was, in essence, a theorist of American decline.

101. In *Gulliver's Travels*, op. cit., p. 343.

102. Writing in 1968 Kissinger argued, 'The greatest need of the contemporary international system is an agreed concept of order [made more difficult by the late 1960's because] the age of superpowers is now drawing to an end'. 'Central Issues In American Foreign Policy' in H. A. Kissinger (ed)., *American Foreign Policy* (New York: W. W. Norton, 1977) pp. 56–7.

103. 'The most sensitive thinkers of the West have recognized that excessive empiricism may lead to stagnation' ... 'we will never be able to contribute to building a stable and creative world order unless we first form some conception of it': ibid, pp. 50, 97.

104. 'We were quite deliberately creating a network of interdependencies that would give us more leverage in future crises. We wanted the Soviets to think twice about the potential economic costs of provoking us by troublemaking adventurism': R. Nixon, *The Real War* (London: Sidgwick & Jackson, 1980) p. 207–8. Nixon saw the need 'to link progress in such areas of Soviet concern as strategic arms limitation and increased trade with progress in areas that were important to us – Vietnam, Mid-East, Berlin...': *The Memoirs of Richard Nixon* (London: Arrow, 1978) p. 346. The aim of détente as defined by Sonnenfeldt (Kissinger's adviser on Soviet affairs) was to 'draw the Soviet Union into the constraints and disciplines, but also the advantages of the international system': 'Russia, America and Detente', *Foreign Affairs* (Jan. 1978) p. 291.

105. *Alternative To Partition For A Broader Conception Of America's Role In Europe* (New York: McGraw-Hill, 1965) p. ix. Brzezinski also called for a new Marshall Plan to create 'all-European economic cooperation' which would 'bind us all together' in 'a future cooperative community', pp. 172, 174, 175. A year earlier Brzezinski had advised America to join with Western Europe 'to reunite Europe and reintegrate Russia into the Western civilizations'. This was the logical outcome of his ideas on peaceful engagement. See his 'Russia and Europe', *Foreign Affairs*, 3 (April 1964) pp. 428–444.

106. *Coexistence and Commerce Guidelines for Transactions between East and West* (London: Allen Lane, 1970). Also see his earlier attempt to persuade the Kennedy administration to use trade as part of America's strategy towards the Soviet bloc. *A New Look at Trade Policy Toward the Communist Bloc* (Washington: Joint Economic Committee, 1961). As he makes it abundantly clear in his autobiography, *Of Blood and Hope*, op.

cit., the aim was to use the attractive power of the world market to undercut the closed character of the Soviet Union and Eastern Europe. Interestingly he congratulated Nixon on reviving his strategy: ibid., pp. 184, 193.

107. See the comments by Kissinger in *White House Years*, pp. 800–801; *Years Of Upheaval*, pp. 235–245; 983. In September 1974 before the Senate Foreign Relations Committee he argued 'that economic boycott would not transform the Soviet system', and pointed out that 'over time, trade and investment may lessen the autarchic tendencies of the Soviet system, and invite gradual association of the Soviet economy with the world economy': *American Foreign Policy*, pp. 156, 158. In an interview with James Reston he believed 'that transformation of the communist societies [was] inevitable': *New York Times*, 13 Oct. 1974, p. 35. On Kissinger's assessment of the Soviet future, which in his view was bleak and bound to lead to change, see *For The Record*, pp. 28, 43, 44, 76, 146, 147, 248, 263, 264–265, 273, 295–296.

108. See Nixon's revealing comments on détente in *The Real War*. Nixon was pleading for renewed détente after Afghanistan, for a 'successful detente can help make victory for the West possible without war': p. 281. John Hardt (senior specialist in the US Congress Research Service) urged the West to break down the USSR's attachment to autarchy. The result would mean that 'Stalin's world of two markets becomes one market and the spirit of the Helsinki Final Act is carried forward', making the new Russia both economically competitive and materially powerful for the first time: G. Kirk and N. H. Wessell (eds), *The Soviet Threat, Myths and Realities* (New York: Praeger, 1978) pp. 122, 134.

109. Pisar, *Commerce and Coexistence*, p. 3. See his excellent discussion of the reasons why the Soviet Union was forced to turn to the West, pp. 1–57. The Soviet grain crisis of 1963 and the purchase of 12 million tons of foreign grain, the building of the Fiat carplant in Togliatigrad in 1965, the retreat from economic reform between 1968 and 1970, and, finally the Czech and Polish crises of 1968 and 1970 were some of the key events along the road to détente. By 1974 the 'two world' theory had finally been replaced by the concept of a 'single world economy'. See E. Valkenier, 'The U.S.S.R., the Third World, and the Global Economy', *Problems of Communism* (July-August 1979) pp. 19–20.

110. The escalating costs of subsidising, controlling, and trading solely with Eastern Europe are discussed by G. Wynn, 'Trade and Politics', *Survey* (Oct.-Dec. 1958) pp. 40–45; V. Winston, 'The Soviet Satellites. Economic Liability', *Problems of Communism* (1958) pp. 14–20; P. Marer in C. Gati (ed.), *The International Politics Of Eastern Europe* (New York: Praeger, 1976) pp. 59–81; M. Lavigne, '*Stratégies des pays socialistes dans l'échange international*' (Paris, 1979). See also *East European Economies Post-Helsinki* (Washington: USGPO, 1977) and *East European Economic Assessment. Pts 1 and 2* (Washington: USGPO, 1981).

111. *Economic Performance and The Military Burden in the Soviet Union* (Washington: USGPO, 1970).

112. The (widespread) belief that détente and the Helsinki agreements marked Western acceptance of the Cold War division of Europe, and, as some

writers have argued, of West Germany's renunciation of the goal of national unity, stands history on its head. *The Times* at least got it right. 'The Final [Helsinki] Act was a very considerable diplomatic victory for the West. It did not give the Russians the confirmation of the status quo which they sought. Instead it provided a charter for more than relations between east and west Europe... It embodies and legitimizes aspirations for a freer Europe': 'Keeping Alive The Helsinki Process', 9 Feb 1982. A representative of the German embassy in Washington stated in one discussion, 'The division of the German nation can be surmounted only when the division of Europe is successfully surmounted [and] we have [not] renounced reunification' in S. Sinanian *et al*, op. cit., pp. 235–236. See the arguments by Willy Brandt for German unity through rapprochement: *A Peace Policy for Europe* (New York: Rinehart & Winston, 1969).

113. The 'new Cold War' thesis has been advanced in one form or another by Noam Chomsky, Jonathan Steele, John Gittings, *Superpowers In Collision. The New Cold War* (Harmondsworth: Penguin, 1982); Fred Halliday, *The Making Of The Second Cold War* (London: Verso, 1983); E. P. Thompson *et al*, *Exterminism and Cold War* (London: New Left Books/Verso, 1982); W. La Feber, *America, Russia and The Cold War* (New York: John Wiley & Sons, 1980 ed.) pp. 279–305; J. Cox, 'Goodbye to Detente' in *Marxism Today* (September 1980) pp. 5–11. The new cold war argument has also been used to legitimise the peace movement, and has been generally accepted on the left. See Dan Smith and Ron Smith, 'The New Cold War' in *Capital and Class*, 12 (Winter 1980–81) pp. 37–42.

114. The 'Committee on the Present Danger' was formed in 1976 including most of the so-called 'Team B' analysts who had been warning of the Soviet military build-up since the early 1970s. On the intellectual struggle to upset détente see the *Defending America* collection published by the Institute for Contemporary Studies California 1977 with contributions by Nitze, Conquest, Luttwak, Rostow, Schapiro and James Schlesinger *et al*.

115. There is a more obvious complementarity between Western Europe and the Soviet bloc economically. Also America in general is far less dependent upon trade with the world economy than Western Europe. The failure by the Soviet Union to achieve Most Favoured Nation status and access to US Government credit put a ceiling on US-Soviet trade in 1974.

116. In the 1950s and 1960s Western Europe and Japan had often complained against the USA, arguing that trade embargoes against the Soviet bloc only helped to limit their competitiveness. S. Sternheimer, *East-West Technology Transfer: Japan and the Communist Bloc* (Washington: Sage, 1980); A.S. Yergin, *East-West Technology Transfer: European Perspectives* (Washington: Sage, 1980).

117. P. Hanson, 'International Technology Transfer from the West to the U.S.S.R.; in *Soviet Economy In A New Perspective*, op. cit., pp. 786–812; and with M. R. Hill, 'Soviet Assimilation of Western Technology', in *Soviet Economy In a Time of Change: II*, op. cit., pp. 582–604, examines many of the indigestion problems of Western technology transfers into Soviet-type economies.

118. Witness the several failed harvests in and after 1972. On the cause of the agricultural crisis see G. A. E. Smith, 'The Industrial Problems of Soviet Agriculture' in *Critique*, no. 14 (1982).

119. The estimated Soviet bloc debt (made by Wharton Econometric Forecasting Associates) – excluding Yugoslavia – was $69.5 billion for 1980;
forecast to rise to $123–140 bn in 1985. See 'Poland: how the Western
banks played into Soviet hands', *The Times* 14 Jan. 1982.
120. Note American difficulties in Angola, Iran and Central America.
121. The classic arguments against the burden of arms spending upon the
American economy were first advanced by Seymour Melman in *Our
Depleted Society* (New York: Holt, 1965) and *Pentagon Capitalism* (New
York: McGraw-Hill, 1970) and have been recently revived by Mary
Kaldor, *The Baroque Arsenal* (London: André Deutsch, 1982), as well as
Lester Thurrow, Galbraith and Emma Rothschild in America, Dan and
Ron Smith in Britain. American business is today clearly opposing massive
arms expenditure. See R. Halloran, 'Reagan Facing Growing Resistance
From Public and Congress to Military Spending', *International Herald
Tribune*, 6 Nov. 1982.
122. Congressional hesitation over the MX-missile and the growing weight of
the nuclear freeze movement in America are clear indications that Cold
War militarism is not being reconstructed with any great success in the
United States.
123. All recent American efforts to either limit Western technology transfers or
prevent the gas pipeline deal have been defeated, with the United States
retreating before a fairly united West European opposition. For a general
discussion of the issues see S. Woolcock, *Western Policies on East-West
Trade* (London: Chatham House, 1982) and T. Gustafson, *Selling The
Russians The Rope* (New York: RAND, 1981).
124. Renewed attempts at 'integration' within Comecon have met with failure
as well. See J. M. van Brabant, *Socialist Economic Integration* (Cambridge
University Press, 1980). Soviet and East European demand for Western
technology, and the very autarchic nature of the several 'socialisms' in one
country, preclude integration as any solution to Soviet bloc problems. See
L. Collit, 'Shift to Comecon looks short-lived', *Financial Times*, 6 Sept.
1982.
125. Although the CIA does not predict 'reduced growth on defense
spending...at least through 1985', it suggests 'that Moscow is becoming
more anxious about the near term decisions that it might feel compelled to
make in order to counter U.S. programs'. Any additional investments
'could impinge on the Soviet civilian economy...the pressures indeed will
be there...to reduce rather than to expand. They face really quite a
dilemma...the Soviet economy is in real trouble and its problems are
becoming progressively more severe'. Cited in *Allocation of Resources In
The Soviet Union And China – 1981* (Washington Joint Economic
Committee, 1981) pp. 257, 259, 267.
126. See especially K. E. Wädekin, 'Soviet Agriculture's Dependence On The
West', *Foreign Affairs* (Spring 1982) pp. 882–903. M. I. Goldman,
'Autarchy or Integration – The U.S.S.R. and The World Economy' in
Soviet Economy In a New Perspective, op. cit., pp. 81–96. However if the
USSR and Eastern Europe wishes to take full advantage of the technology
transfers it must, as liberal pro-market economists have pointed out, go
over to the market. See H. Hunter, 'Soviet Economic Problems and Alternative Policy Responses' in *Soviet Economy In A Time Of Change, I*, op.

cit., 1979, pp. 23–37.

127. See the essay by G. Snyder, 'The "New Look" of 1953' in W. Schilling; P. Hammond, G. Snyder, op. cit., pp. 380–524.

128. D. Ball, *Politics and Force Levels*, op. cit.

129. See Paul Warnke's comments in *Allocation of Resources In The Soviet Union and China – 1977.* 'Saving money is not the primary objective of arms control [which] is the security of the United States', p. 119.

130. See the assessments made of Reagan's 'pressure' strategy by N. Ashford, 'U.S. tightens noose around Russia', *The Times*, 1 July 1982 and H. Brandon in the *The Sunday Times*, 8 August 1982. Ashford argues that senior advisers believe that the growing Soviet crisis presents an 'opportunity...to force the Soviet Union to implement radical political and economic reform'. See also Richard Owen, 'Could Reagan really rattle the Kremlin?' *The Times*, 26 April 1982 who argues that Reagan's advisers believe a 'window of opportunity' now exists 'to precipitate a crisis of the Soviet system'. In an interview Haig argued that 'the Soviet Union presents clear signs of being in historical decline'. *Paris Match* 5 June 1981. Such an assessment could not have been made and believed in 1947.

131. Birnbaum, *East and West Germany: A Modus Vivendi* (Saxon House, 1978) p. 30.

132. Ibid, p. 30.

133. Henry Kissinger, *White House Years* (New York: Little) pp. 400–410.

134. *Allocation of Resources In The Soviet Union and China – 1981* (Washington: USGPO, 1981) p. 250.

135. See S. Bialer's assessment of the future in, 'The Politics of Stringency in the U.S.S.R.' in *Problems of Communism* (May-June 1980): 'Yet something will have to give [and] speaking with Soviet economists and political scientists, one is struck by the extent to which the need for major reform is recognized and the introduction of one is expected', pp. 24, 30.

136. Sir John Hackett expressed this position very well in a recent interview. 'But we have to make do with [the Soviet] regime, barbarian, brutal and based on butchery as it is, because a world in which there are two superpower blocs in abrasive but more or less stable equilibrium is likely to be a safer world than if one of them collapses'. 'The Soldier's Cautionary Tale', *Observer*, 4 July 1982.

137. A problem recognised by Brzezinski in *Between Two Ages*, op. cit. See his comments on Stalinism as a 'blessing in disguise' for the West. 'The historical function of Stalinist communism may have been to restrain and redefine a phase in which the Russian people went through an intense nationalist, even imperialist awakening', p. 137.

138. Interestingly Lord Carver, a critic of the arms race, supports the division of Europe in the name of peace and stability. 'The most likely cause of war in Europe would be the instability created by any attempt to juggle the kaleidoscope through changing the rigid pattern of frontiers established at the end of the Second World War': *A Policy For Peace* (London: Faber, 1982). Being a military man it is certain that he regards Soviet power in Europe as less problematic than a revived Germany.

7 The Political Economy of British Defence Policy

DAN SMITH

Despite the fact that the word 'crisis' is much over-used, it seems fair to say that in the early 1980s British defence policy is in a state of crisis. This essay will attempt to explain the nature of that crisis in terms of the long-run patterns of policy and the pressures and tensions on it and within it. A crisis is, at least potentially, a turning-point, a moment of change, whether for good or ill. The ability of the British State to manage crises by suppressing them, and to resolve crises by muddling through, should never be underestimated, least of all in the field of defence policy. Yet it seems that the combination of problems within defence policy coming to a head, together with a profound international economic and political crisis and a large and determined disarmament movement, could provide an unprecedented, and possibly unrepeatable, moment of change. At present, in defence policy, almost all the questions are unanswered and an extraordinarily wide range of options is open.

This is more than a little ironic, since the Conservative Government elected in 1979 entered office with a set of very definite answers to the problems of defence which, one would have expected, should have closed the subject off, setting defence policy on a clear and stable course. In broad terms, the Conservatives identified the problem of defence as not spending or buying enough; the solution was clear – spend more, buy more. That this simple solution has turned out to be no solution is due to a number of factors, not least to the fact that it rested on a profound misperception of the constraints on British defence policy.

The elements of the crisis of defence policy can be swiftly summarised. First, the broader, international crisis, which can be understood as the crisis of the US-led post-1945 world order of capitalism, is naturally felt in relations within NATO, in tensions between Western Europe and the USA as well as within Western Europe. The setting of British defence policy, the Atlantic Alliance and the Western European Atlanticist consensus, is itself facing a potentially decisive moment of change. Second, long-run economic decline, combined with long-run cost increases in military technology, have caught Conservative defence policy between the scissor-blades. Increasing military expenditure by politically feasible degrees through the 1980s will not prevent a diminution of deployed armed forces, and will nonetheless deepen Britain's economic malaise. Third, change in British defence policy over the past three decades has largely been accomplished by withdrawal from military Empire and a corresponding shift of resources into the NATO commitment. But virtually no further room for manoeuvre can be found in this way, since the withdrawal process has gone so far, and Conservative ideology in any case seeks a relative reversal of the process. Finally, the resurgence of CND since early 1980 has imposed unexpectedly powerful pressure on crucial aspects of the defence programme and is, of course, but one part of a gathering pressure throughout Western Europe.

For one group of people, the claim that British defence policy is in crisis will seem especially inappropriate. I am referring to senior serving officers and defence civil servants, who have more than three decades behind them of dealing with apparent crises in defence policy, through a series of defence reviews (Korean War, 1957, 1964, 1966, 1974 and 1981) and a seemingly unending process of chopping and changing, adjusting policy, shifting and stretching resources, withdrawing forces and cancelling weapons projects, at the same time as British forces have been almost constantly in combat in one part of the world or another. For this group, things which outside commentators call 'crises' may seem to be their daily routine. Through all these fluctuations, however, there have been persistent themes which denote areas of relative stability in policy – and all of these themes are now themselves in question.

THEMES IN BRITISH DEFENCE POLICY

Four constant themes in policy can be identified. First, there has been the withdrawal from military Empire. Most of the armed forces' involvement in combat has been related to this withdrawal, often as a holding action, while political arrangements for an 'acceptable' post-colonial state could be completed. The withdrawal of most forces from 'East of Suez' in the 1960s, and the withdrawal from the Malta base and large Mediterranean deployments in the 1970s have taken this process almost to the point of completion. British forces have remained in Hong Kong and Brunei, the Indian Ocean, the Caribbean, Cyprus, Gibraltar and the South Atlantic. But these holdovers from the former global role are fairly small and account for a very small proportion of expenditure: British forces in the Falkland Isles amounted to 78 men in April 1982 when Argentina invaded.

The concomitant of this has been the increasing relative importance of the NATO commitment, now absorbing about ninety per cent of annual military spending. The third theme is the determination, maintained under successive administrations since 1945, to have a major nuclear force. Embodied first in the 'V-bombers' (Valiants, Victors and Vulcans) and then, after a couple of technological hiccups (Blue Streak and the American Skybolt), in the four Polaris missile-firing submarines since the late 1960s, this theme is planned to continue with the purchase of Trident missiles from the USA. Britain also has a large tactical nuclear arsenal which includes artillery, short-range missiles, bombs and depth-bombs.

Finally, there is the allocation of economic resources to the military.[1] Military expenditure itself shows a number of fluctuations in medium-term trends. In the early 1950s, the Korean War boom hiked up military spending by 53 per cent in real terms in two years. There followed a period of reduced budgets under Conservative Governments until the late 1950s when spending was again increased. The Labour Government elected in 1964 first stabilised and then reduced spending, so that in 1970 it was at just about the same real level as it has been at in 1960. At the start of the 1970s, the Conservatives again increased spending, and Labour, entering office in 1974, again stabilised it, but this time followed this up with new increases in its final defence budget, with the current government's own increases following that. Military spending in 1979 was some seventy per cent higher than in 1950 (before the Korean War boom), but only sixteen per cent higher than in 1955, though twenty three per cent higher than in 1970. These fluctuations are smoothed out, however, if one looks at the proportion of Gross Domestic Product allocated to the military. In 1950 it was about ten per cent; in the mid-1950s, over seven per cent; by the early 1960s, rather over six per cent; and by the mid-1970s it was around five per cent. This relatively steady decline was first slowed by the slow-down in the economy and by the higher plateau of military spending in the 1970s compared to the previous decade. Under the Conservatives, the decline in the military share of GDP is being reversed, as it would have been had the Labour Government been re-elected in 1979.

NEW DEPARTURES AND HALF-FORGOTTEN ECHOES

The issue of defence has been extremely important in the construction of Thatcherism as a political force. Indeed, in 1975 about the only policy on which the Conservatives were united was the need to increase military spending to respond to what was so strenuously proclaimed to be an increasing Soviet threat. A series of strident speeches on this issue by Mrs Thatcher not only set out the policy and ideology of defence, but also served as a rallying cry for party unity. While occasionally replaced in the centre-stage of Thatcherism by other themes, strong defence remains a cardinal tenet. The effects of Conservative defence policy are thus the more deliciously ironic.

The commitment to NATO has, of course, been maintained and, in terms of expenditure, increased. The target for real increases in military spending of three per cent per year is, however, only what was bequeathed to the Conservatives by their Labour predecessors, and in the current recession they are finding it hard to meet. Moreover, the centrality of the commitment to NATO is effectively challenged by Conservative policy on two other fronts.

While a definite effort to return to military Empire seems neither intended nor likely, except with 'Fortress Falklands', the Conservative Government finds itself trapped by the current Western ideology of the Soviet threat. For this threat is seen to be global, requiring a global response. In its first White Paper on defence, the Government set out its views about Britain's 'Wider Defence Interests'.[2] Near the end of 1980, a naval patrol was despatched to watch over the Iran-Iraq war. In early 1981, Mrs

Thatcher embraced the notion of NATO participation in a Rapid Deployment Force to rush to trouble-spots around the world and 'sort them out'. In April 1982, the Government found itself sending out a strong naval force to the Falkland Isles, though not to fight the Soviets.

Despite the Government's own talk of supporting an allied RDF, it has recognised that

Resource constraints and our primary commitment to NATO rule out any idea of creating a substantial standing 'intervention' force.[3]

However, as the fleet which went to the Falkland Isles shows, Britain remains surprisingly well-equipped for naval deployments abroad, and the Navy has never fully restructured itself out of the imperial image. The case of the Invincible-class of anti-submarine warfare (ASW) cruisers is important here. In the late 1960s, in the light of withdrawal from 'East of Suez', the decision was taken to do without aircraft carriers. But the Navy successfully fought for a new class of ship – then called Through Deck Cruisers – which looked extraordinarily like small aircraft carriers. The cruisers were approved under a Conservative Government and then, when Labour returned to office in 1974, swiftly and tactfully renamed ASW cruisers. The Navy then won another battle; to equip these cruisers not only with ASW helicopters but also with modified Harrier aircraft, supposedly to provide air cover for ASW task forces despite the Harrier's low claims to any role as an air-to-air combat fighter. By 1981, it was known that these Sea Harriers would be equipped with nuclear weapons and it was clear that their most rational use would not be against other aircraft, but against surface ships or targets on the land. Around the ASW cruisers, the Navy has also retained the full supporting cast of ocean-going destroyers and frigates and support vessels.

I doubt that this force structure results from subtle covert planning by the Navy, calculating well in advance that it might support a global anti-Soviet force or have to take on Argentina. Rather, the ASW cruisers reflect the difficulty the Navy has had in revising its self-image. Tradition runs deep in armed services and is an important force in their self-perception and identification. The Navy has never forgotten it was once the supreme instrument and symbol of a supreme world power; it has never attuned to the setting of the imperial sun. The consequence of this is that a government which wants to behave as if that sun never did set has some capability to do so. But if it does behave in that way, in the South Atlantic or anywhere else, one of the issues which is raised is that when the Navy sails away, it does indeed sail away, absenting itself from the Eastern Atlantic, the Channel and North Sea areas of its main deployment, weakening the British commitment to NATO.

Similar themes arise when one looks at the purchase of Trident. The arguments for and against the purchase of Trident have received a considerable airing. Few enthusiastic supporters of it can be found outside the Ministry of Defence (and not a lot inside it). Even supporters of nuclear weapons and, among them, even those who support a semi-independent, semi-strategic, semi-British, nuclear force have expressed their doubts. As an independent weapon of last resort, Trident's deterrent function must be impaired by the presence in Britain of US nuclear bases (but remove those bases and Trident could not be purchased). As a contribution to NATO, it is a peripheral addition to existing 'overkill' capabilities. And the argument that it is both an independent weapon of last resort and a contribution to NATO is untenable: what if NATO requires the use of Trident before the British Government thinks it has reached the last resort? Despite the confused and contradictory arguments in favour of Trident, it appears the Government still wants to spend in the region of ten to twelve billion pounds on it.

This sum of money will, of course, be spent over a period of perhaps fifteen years, not all at once, and the Government has made much play of the argument that even in the peak years the project will consume only around three per cent of the annual military budget and ten per cent of the military equipment budget; true, but misleading. Military budgeting in any year or period of years is constrained by previously made commitments and investments. Budgetary room for manoeuvre is inherently limited. It is difficult and highly disruptive to shift resources at short notice from one budgetary category to another. The category into which Trident expenditure will fall is a sub-section of the equipment budget devoted to new production: even if the total military budget rises in real terms by three per cent annually throughout the 1980s (and that is more ambitious than current plans), peak years of Trident expenditure could see it consuming forty per cent of expenditure on all new production.[4] In 1981, a defence review reduced the Navy's surface fleet: this was the first minor nibble of Trident into the defence budget. By the late 1980s, if the project survives, it will not be nibbling at other armed forces, but taking huge bites out of them. And that will unavoidably reduce the ability of the government of the time to meet its NATO commitments.

To explain such a phenomenon, one must seek a very powerful driving force with massive influence in the British State. The identifiable political advantages of having possessed Polaris are, to put it mildly, elusive. It has not arrested political decline; it has been of no help in any important political or economic conflicts or negotiations; it has fooled nobody into believing Britain is still a great power. Identifiable economic and institutional interests in procurement of Trident are also hard to come by. The missiles will be made in the USA. All the British contractors and sub-contractors for the submarines would be contractors for con-ventionally-armed nuclear submarines if Trident were cancelled. To be sure, the Navy would lose its strategic nuclear role, but it is having to pay a high price to keep it. And Aldermaston could go out of business, but it is hard to believe that it, even combined with part of the Navy, could swing the project through against determined resistance.

Accordingly, I have concluded that explaining Trident in terms of political, economic or institutional interests is fruitless. It is necessary to turn to an ideological explanation, seeing it as the reflection of post-imperial inertia, a desire to turn backwards rather than forwards, to see Britain as a great power with the right to appropriate appurtenances of power, an entirely inter-nalised image of power and status, a deep refusal to come to terms with the realities of the late twentieth century. As awesomely destructive as Trident will be, there is nonetheless something deeply ludicrous about Britain's purchase of it: it represents the most archaic tendencies within the British State, and we should have no doubt that these retain a powerful ideo-logical pull.

The decision to purchase Trident will thus affect the central commitment to NATO not only by reducing Britain's input of conventional forces – at sea and on the central front in Europe – but also at a more diffuse level of strategy and ideology. Trident embodies the perception of British specialness, a state which is a cut above the run-of-the-mill NATO member. This is explicitly reflected in some advocacies of Trident which see it as creating a 'nuclear sanctuary' of Britain: while Europe burns, we shall be safe. Needless to say, this is a highly unrealistic strategic assumption, but it is a powerful one. As an independent weapon of last resort, Trident, like Polaris, represents a break in the NATO chain, a fracture in the concept of collective defence.

What complicates this picture, and makes these post-imperial pretensions particularly shallow, is that Britain can only have this magnificent symbol of independence courtesy of the USA. A factor which will complicate and possibly sink the Trident procurement is that Britain will have to take the more sophisticated and physically larger Trident II missiles from the USA, and in order to build the boats to carry them will very likely have to adapt its submarine-building yards. Britain has to take Trident II because that is what is on offer from the USA, however unnecessary and unsuitable it is to Britain's own stated strategic requirements. If Trident is a symbol of an illusory power and independence, that illusion is most graphically revealed in the way in which it is tied to American technology. In other words, the archaism of the British State provides only the illusion of independence, not the actuality.

Similarly, while the Navy's difficulty in adapting to the post-imperial era provides the capability for some limited return to global deployment, this is only possible and only makes any kind of sense within the globalistic concept of the Soviet threat held by both the Thatcher and Reagan Governments. Throughout the 1970s the USA was trailing a coat in front of its NATO allies, seeking Western European participation in world-wide military deployment. This was the effect of the post-Vietnam political constraints on use of US armed force abroad and of the economic burden of continuing solo international police action. If the Thatcher Government wishes to pick that coat up, it will affect the commitment to NATO in and around Europe in terms both of resources and strategic priorities. But while the motivation for that may come in part from harking back to former glories, it will also tie Britain more tightly in to the USA and its strategic perceptions and priorities. Paradoxically then, Trident and military action outside the NATO area restrict the NATO commitment but deepen the ties of the Atlantic Alliance.

Naturally enough, the Government has not faced up to this set of problems. Ignoring the costs to the NATO commitment of other aspects of its military programmes is accomplished in two ways. At the level of strategy and ideology, it is accomplished by a version of the 'seamless web' theory of international communism and Western interests: the world is seen in starkly bi-polar terms; 'our' interests are global; the threat to them is global and unified; the response to the threats must be global and unified. Thus, since NATO is directed at resisting the threatening Soviet giant, it is perfectly consistent to resist the giant elsewhere around the world, and anything which resists the giant is compatible with the commitment to NATO and is part of the same continuum. At the level of available resources to support military policy, ignoring the costs is accomplished by believing the entire bill can be paid.

In 1980, the Ministry of Defence's expenditure plans for the 1980s assumed real military expenditure would increase by three per cent each year to 1986 and one per cent annually thereafter.[5] On the optimistic assumption that the British economy grew by one per cent annually through the 1980s, the result would be increasing the military share of GDP to about six per cent by 1985 and nearly seven per cent by 1990, thus decisively reversing the pattern of declining shares of GDP since the Korean War boom. This shift of resources into military expenditure will have to be accomplished at the cost of civil industrial investment, public expenditure or private consumption – or a combination of all three. Given the cogent evidence that high military expenditure (high as a proportion of GDP) is associated over the long-run with lower rates of investment, productivity growth and economic growth, current plans for the military budget appear to be a good way of ensuring the economy fails to recover from recession.[6]

Moreover, the government of the day does not have a free hand in setting military spending levels, either to increase or reduce them. Social and economic constraints on allocative priorities are established over time; are expressed both politically and bureaucratically; and create real limits on any government's room for manoeuvre. It is possible to have some idea of the effects of these constraints in the 1980s by considering patterns of expenditure in the past. An economic model which fits military spending by Britain from 1951–75 explains it in terms of the relationship between real national income, US and perceived Soviet military spending and the relative price effect (the difference between the price of military goods and services and civil goods and services). Applying this model to the 1980s, assuming one per cent annual economic growth, indicates that if those earlier socio-economic patterns held the outcome would be a reduction in military spending over the decade by an average of 1.5 per cent annually, with the military share of GDP dropping by a couple of decimal points.[7]

Accordingly, we can conclude that current expenditure plans would be economically punitive and that their full implementation must be in doubt; to achieve them, a major political onslaught would be required to gain acceptance. However, it must be added that, in any case, they would not be enough.

This conclusion is unavoidable if attention is paid to two factors. First, the real costs of major items of military equipment have risen and are continuing to rise exponentially. Second, within constrained budgets, one effect of this has been to squeeze other elements of the budget, leading to a crescendo of complaints in the late 1970s about service pay, conditions and morale, and about the availability of spares and support equipment. By and large, the 1974–9 Labour Government managed to maintain expenditure on the major weapon projects, but in doing so it allowed expenditure on other less visible aspects of military preparations to lag. It is no surprise that this created a profound crisis of morale within the armed forces. The Government was in danger of creating a generation of service people who saw the civilian government as their main enemy. Naturally enough, the Conservatives committed themselves to avoiding a repeat. But to avoid a repeat, it is necessary to shift resources within the budget back towards salaries, conditions and support functions, which is only possible if the equipment budget is squeezed. Yet the pressure of rising equipment costs, moving much faster than three per cent a year, demands more resources in that part of the overall budget. Add into this picture the proportion of the new production budget which Trident will consume in the late 1980s and it should be starkly clear that current expenditure plans are not adequate to support all commitments, now including Fortress Falklands. Sooner or later, something will have to give, and the sharper the constraints upon the overall budget, the sooner that day will come.

Suppose for a moment that the Conservatives remain in office throughout the 1980s. Suppose that they successfully mount a political campaign which gains consent to shifting resources into military preparations to sustain an increase in spending of three per cent annually. The picture which emerges is of a wrecked economy, a widespread war psychology, possibly coercive measures against dissenters and/or censorship, movement towards a new major nuclear force, geographically wider military deployments, and a crumbling defence effort despite it all.

RESOURCES, CAPABILITIES AND INDUSTRY

British defence policy has thus arrived at a particularly unstable situation. However, around the areas of relative stability within policy, there has for thirty years been a series of chops and changes – as one commentator has put it, referring to Conservative policy in the early 1960s, 'a succession of tacks and jibes and course corrections, some of them very coarse corrections'.[8] This process, and the particularly parlous present position, has been dictated by a long-run inability to reconcile two major contradictions.

On the one hand, the economic resources which have been made available for military preparations have consistently been inadequate to provide the military capabilities desired by the forces, the defence bureaucracy and successive governments. Through the 1950s, 1960s and 1970s forces and commitments have been successively trimmed. Hitherto, this has taken the form of the withdrawal of forces from far-flung global deployments. Even major defence reviews, initiated specifically to survey the whole range of commitments, have not been followed by greater smoothness in policy: the 1964 Labour defence review was no sooner completed than it was followed by another; the 1974 defence review (also Labour) was followed by a series of minor adjustments to budgets, squeezes on spending, penny-pinching on spares and so on. British governments have constantly been unable to provide the economic resources necessary to sustain the forces they have said they wanted, but unable to set force levels which would be consistently sustainable given the level of resources available.

On the other hand, economic resources have also been inadequate to the task of providing a market for the products of military industry. Once a broad military industrial capability is seen as an essential element of strategy and policy, the state is committed to sustaining that capability. To do this it must provide a market for it. But to provide a market it must also support the process of marginal improvement from one weapon system to its successor, which means supporting an increasingly costly process since improvement tends to take the form of increasingly sophisticated variations on a theme, requiring more development capacity and producing ever more expensive equipment. Within constrained budgets, this process cannot be allowed to go unchecked. Attempts to check the expansion of capacity and manage the problems of sustaining it have included major industrial reorganisation, a series of cancellations of major projects, promoting international (especially European) collaborative projects, and promoting arms exports. Even so, the demands of industrial capacity place tremendous pressure on the budget. While collaborative projects share the costs of maintaining development capacity, they still require a major investment and, since they are harder to cancel, a major outlay on procurement. The British-German-Italian Tornado aircraft will cost in total about the same as the procurement of Trident. Similarly, arms exports may be a way of exporting some of the costs of maintaining the arms industry, but the international arms market is highly competitive and an exporting government normally needs to procure equipment itself before export orders can be gained. It was the pressure of industrial capacity on military budgets in the 1970s which led to the squeeze on non-procurement items of expenditure, which in turn led to the crisis of morale in the armed forces at the end of that decade.

These two contradictions – available resources versus desired capabilities, and available resources versus excess industrial capacity – exacerbate each other. The military, the civil servants and government ministers have tended to be as wedded to the philosophy of continual technological sophistication as the industry is. Expensive procurement projects not only put pressure on the overall budget but tend, as most starkly in the case of Trident, to squeeze expenditure for the normal operations of the armed forces. Recognition of this problem is evident within the British Ministry of Defence, which has itself published figures showing real cost increases from one weapon system to its successor of up to 300 per cent;[9] it is also evident in the US Department of Defense, with increasingly loud dissident voices pointing out how the more costly and sophisticated systems are less reliable, harder to operate and maintain, and over-demanding of overall budgetary resources.[10] Resolution of the problem, however, requires more than simply recognising it. Indeed, it requires a wholesale and revolutionising reform of the standard operating procedures and underlying technological philosophies of the military and military industrial establishments.

TENDENCIES AND TENSIONS

Across three decades, British defence policy has succeeded in managing these two basic contradictions, but not in resolving them. The equilibrium arrived at in policy at any moment is inherently unstable and transient, despite the persistence of the basic themes. This is partly due to the power of the different elements in these contradictions: it has neither been possible to revitalise the British domestic economy nor to gain consent for a much greater allocation of resources to the military; industry has been reorganised, and internationalised, but not revolutionised; forces have been trimmed, and have adapted to absorb new technologies and new sophistications, but they have not been fundamentally re-shaped. Possibly the one change in British armed forces of the kind of significance which would be required to resolve these economic, industrial and institutional contra-dictions was the abandonment of conscription at the end of the 1950s. Yet this can be seen as ending a practice which is atypical of British military history, marking a return to the professional forces which Britain has had for by far the greater part of its modern history. Otherwise, reshaping defence policy has proved difficult and slow at best, has often been overturned when attempted (as in the cases of the decisions to do without manned bombers in the 1950s and without aircraft carriers in the 1960s) and has often been impossible.

Resolution of these problems is made the harder by the tension within the British State and political leaderships between three conflicting political tendencies. This conflict has similarly been managed rather than resolved. The tendencies can be summarised as post-imperialism, Atlanticism and Europeanism.

The first derives from the historic role, and therefore the

shape, of British armed forces. The second stems from the basic shape of the international order since 1945, with the advanced capitalist states grouped under American leadership, providing for many years a relatively stable international economic environment, eliminating the possibility of repeating European conflicts which produced two global wars in the first half of this century, and confronting the USSR and its developing political and strategic bloc of states. The third tendency reflects the basic economic and political trajectory of Western European states, diminishing American economic dominance and political leadership.

Each tendency is reflected in current developments in policy. Post-imperialism provides some of the driving force for the ASW cruisers and most of the motivation for procuring Trident. Atlanticism continues to provide the basic underpinning for British strategy – reliance on US nuclear strategy and capabilities, trans-Atlantic unity as the precondition for Western European security. British basing for cruise missiles, American nuclear bombers and missile-firing submarines all follow from these basic assumptions. Europeanism is fed both by the increasing concentration of British forces onto their deployments in and around Europe, and by the development of Western European collaborative projects such as Tornado (with Italy and West Germany), Jaguar aircraft and three types of helicopter (with France), armoured vehicles (with Belgium), artillery (with West Germany and Italy). In fact, British military industry is probably agnostic as between these three tendencies; what matters to it is the provision of a market. It will sell to the USA and participate in essentially American weapons development as happily as it will sell to and collaborate with the Western Europeans, as happily as it will produce purely British equipment for the national government and later export. But the logic of collaboration as a way of managing the costs of industrial capacity leads to greater emphasis on collaboration with Western European states and companies rather than to being swamped in the much larger US military market and business.

These tendencies do not conflict in the sense that it is impossible for them to co-exist. We have seen how ASW cruisers, a renewed world military role and procurement of Trident can fit post-imperial echoes with new Atlanticist departures. A Europeanist orientation in weapons procurement can be squared with commitment to an over-arching Atlantic unity in which the USA welcomes a militarily strong Western Europe as long as it remains under US leadership expressed in the strategic nuclear 'umbrella'. But these tendencies do reflect different fundamental assumptions about Britain and its world role, and in a sense could be said to represent different periods of Britain's modern history. At root, post-imperialism represents a turning back to the attitudes of a great power, away from either subordination to the USA or absorption within Western Europe. Atlanticism stresses the paramountcy of the alliance with the USA (in the post-imperialist variation on Atlanticism, this took the form of nostalgia for the 'special relationship'). It is incompatible with the Europeanist identification of the Western European link as the paramount one, as the necessary guiding theme of British international policy to the extent that, if it comes to it, perceived Western European interests must have pride of place over US interests in British policy. It is in this sense that the three tendencies conflict, providing further dimensions to be held in balance in defence policy alongside the tensions between the level of available resources, the military capabilities which are desired and the pressure of industrial capacity. And while these tendencies can co-exist, the different priorities they place on deployment of forces and on procurement are becoming increasingly difficult to contain as the economy stagnates and weapon costs rise. Their continued co-existence provides no clear route out of the crunch towards which they are pushing defence policy.

THE NUCLEAR DIMENSION

The political or bureaucratic managers of defence policy might be forgiven for thinking they have enough on their plate with these various contradictions and conflicting tendencies, without having to bother about CND as well. Unfortunately for their peace of mind, they do have to bother about CND. And what is most bothersome is that what have hitherto been relatively uncontentious aspects of defence policy have now become highly controversial. The search for and maintenance of a major British nuclear force has been one of the enduring themes of British defence policy; reliance on US nuclear capability as the strategic underpinning of policy has provided the context for British defence planning. Inclusion beneath the USA's nuclear 'umbrella' and the operation of various delivery systems which would use US nuclear munitions have been the binding constituents cementing British policy into the Atlanticist framework. Britain's own nuclear capabilities have nourished the post-imperial self-image. There have been debates and controversies within the state over some of the details of these positions, but the basic principles have not, with the exception of the 'first wave' of CND from 1958 to 1963, been severely challenged either within the state or without.

CND's resurgence since early 1980 has been based on a mixture of fears about current strategy and policy and the directions they are taking us, together with a vision of the necessity and potential to do something about it, sustained by a series of mainly moral and strategic arguments. It would be superfluous to rehearse those arguments here. What is important at this point is to understand CND as a force disruptive to British defence policy, not at the level where the main economic and industrial issues have to be confronted, but beyond that in the fundamental assumptions of policy.

This disruption is not limited to a disagreement about strategy, the ins and outs of nuclear deterrence, limited nuclear war, nuclear first-use, the meaning of different items of hardware, and so on. Certainly, the disruption is real at those levels. The current Government has been pushed further than any predecessor to justify its strategic perspectives, to debate them publicly. What is most important about CND in political terms is that its success would mean an upheaval in the political economy of British defence policy. In the present crisis of policy, the basic impetus of the state must be to re-establish some form of equilibrium between the different terms of the crisis; the basic impetus of CND must be to discard those terms.

This challenge is the most direct and has the greatest leverage in its confrontation with Atlanticism. US nuclear weapons remain potent symbols and instruments of US power and influence in Europe, sustaining the USA's strategic hegemony in NATO despite its long-run relative economic decline and the weakening of its political leadership in the 1970s. Atlanticism is in a profound crisis in which nuclear weapons have changed from being a unifying force in the alliance to being the most divisive issue at present.[11] It is more than a little amusing to witness the frustration and shifts in established American opinion in the face of this crisis, and especially to watch the blame being put on the different styles of successive presidents: when Carter was in office he was criticised for vacillation and not providing a strong lead; now Reagan is in office he is criticised for striking out on his own too much and not consulting properly with the European allies. The fact is that the crisis of Atlanticism derives not from problems of diplomacy but from the underlying economic and political trajectory of Western Europe away from its former dependence on the USA. Yet Western European defence policies remain predicated on US nuclear capabilities and strategy. Thus, political movements focusing on nuclear disarmament get straight to the political heart of the matter: their success, even partial successes, will transform the relationship between the USA and Western Europe, and thus also shift the terms in which it is possible to think the political possibilities in Western Europe and Europe as a whole.

It is, however, the political cogency of the Western European disarmament movements which determines the ultimate bedrock of resistance to them. We see this already: the deployment of cruise and Pershing II missiles is now advocated not for any very precise military or strategic reasons, but in order to sustain the unity of NATO – a political advocacy, which is only strategic in a secondary and derivative sense and has no need of an operational military argument. Within the British Ministry of Defence, military establishments and political leaderships (outside the current Government) there is a growing resistance to Trident. There is also an awareness of the military and strategic dangers of short-range or battlefield nuclear weapons, and of NATO's reliance on a strategy which places the option of first use of nuclear weapons in the foreground. For different reasons, in other words, there is actually quite an amount of common ground between CND's opposition to nuclear weapons and specific objections in some official circles to particular nuclear weapons. But these tactical and strategic doubters are unreliable allies of CND, even in the short-term, because of the political challenge to Atlanticism, to continued American strategic hegemony, which is the unavoidable concomitant of basic change in NATO's nuclear strategy.

It would be short-sighted and self-defeating of the disarmament movements in Western Europe to attempt to disguise this political challenge. It is not mounted because of particular ways of arguing for nuclear disarmament; it is mounted as a direct consequence of arguing for nuclear disarmament at all. In Western Europe, nuclear disarmament cannot be an apolitical question. Instead of ducking this, we have to argue that, since nuclear weapons, the nuclear confrontation with the USSR and the threats they pose to our survival are integral to the Western European political order, we can only improve our chances of avoiding nuclear war if basic political changes are carried through.

At the same time, it can be argued that, because of this political effect, the Western European disarmament movements sit in the mainstream of Western European political development. The defence policies which bring dependence on the USA are in a definite sense out of 'sync' with the overall economic and political trajectory away from dependence. The disarmament campaigns are politically consistent with that overall trajectory where the defence policies are not.

These considerations both indicate why it may be possible to cohere the necessary social and political majority for nuclear disarmament, and reveal the importance of sustained disarmament movements. For, in seeking a way to turn, Atlanticism may reorient more strongly towards Europeanism, while retaining the nuclear component of the ideology. Few conceivable outcomes of the present crisis are worse than the prospect of a new nuclear-armed military bloc of the current European members of NATO. The vision of Europe which is promoted by the disarmament movements must close the door to the possibility of a nuclear-armed 'third force' in international politics.

OUTCOMES

The current Conservative Government's defence policy cannot be successful. That is, planned expenditure is inadequate to sustain planned forces and deployments, and expenditure plans are almost certainly over-ambitious. To be successful in a more limited sense; that is, to be able to spend the money it wants to spend (assuming it stays in office), the British people will have to accept even more drastic attacks on living standards, health facilities, educational standards, welfare, public transport and all amenities. It does not seem likely that this consent will be gained without a major propaganda war and an expansion of the security state. Even under these grim circumstances, the question about defence policy is not whether it will change, but when and how. In all probability, the moment for change will be when a new government is elected, even if it is a coalition government, even if the coalition includes the Conservatives.

The resulting change in policy will have to establish a new, though certainly transient and unstable, equilibrium between the competing tendencies of post-imperialism, Atlanticism and Europeanism. The first of these seems the most vulnerable, and if it is attacked in favour of a new and more 'modern' balance between Atlanticism and Europeanism, the brunt will probably fall on the Navy, both its general purpose forces and Trident.

Such a change, however, would neither defuse the disarmament movement, although it would concede some ground to it, nor would it establish a lasting resolution of the contradictions between available economic resources, military industrial capacity and desired military capabilities. Some breathing space would be gained by naval reductions but the underlying problems would certainly reappear unless the British economy were to enter a sustained period of major growth. Yet, one condition for this is probably a demilitarisation of the British economy on a scale greater than is implied by merely cutting the Navy's long-range capabilities. More ground could be conceded to the disarmament movement by a major effort to shift NATO strategy away from its current nuclear emphasis. To do this properly, however, would require a major restructuring of land and air forces and, of course, it could not be done unilaterally by Britain. Should such a strategic shift and restructuring of forces be undertaken, the orthodox wisdom argues that more military expenditure would be required because nuclear weapons in Europe are seen as a cheap way of compensating for inferiority to the Warsaw Pact in non-nuclear forces. Though powerful, the orthodox wisdom is wrong: non-nuclear inferiority has been widely and hugely exaggerated, largely by concentrating on numerical comparisions of tanks and ignoring NATO's strengths, the weaknesses of the Soviet army and the unreliability of the USSR's Warsaw Pact allies; even if this inferiority did exist, it is now well known that use of nuclear weapons on the battlefield cannot compensate for it. Moreover, the outcome of this orthodox wisdom would be to throw British defence policy straight back into the contradiction between available resources and desired capabilities with which it has been plagued for thirty years. Yet this shift in strategy would be possible, if land and air forces were restructured away from being organised around high technology, and highly expensive, major weapon systems. This itself would only be possible on the basis of a fundamental restructuring of military industry. It is doubtful that such major departures from current practices could be effected on the basis of seeking only shifts and modifications within the terms of the political economy of British defence policy. But in the absence of these major changes, policy will only stave off crisis and pile up more problems for later solution.

Finally, therefore, one must seek the possibility of changes which reject the basic terms of current policy. The disarmament movements provide the social and political force for such change, though it is political parties which will have to define the new policy. The appropriate answer to the question, 'What do you think about defence?' is the same as Ghandi's when he was asked what he thought of Western civilisation and replied, 'I think it would be a good idea'. What is required is a policy which makes sense out of the word 'defence', which does not rely on threatening to blow up the world, which is as obviously non-threatening to other states as is possible, and which does not require a war psychology for public legitimation. Such a policy would have to grapple with the three basic problems of current policy: it would need to be based on a level of resources which can be assumed to be available over the long-run on the basis of unambitious assumptions both about the state of the economy and the proportion of resources which can be allocated to the military; it would have to seek a way out of the process of replacing existing equipment by ever more sophisticated, expensive, complex and unreliable systems; it would have to include a political strategy for reducing NATO's reliance on nuclear weapons and eventually eliminating them from Europe. Addressing these basic problems will involve and necessitate a resolution of the basic contradictions of British defence policy hitherto and the development of new political stances towards the USA, the rest of Western Europe, the Eastern European states and the USSR. It will probably also involve its own form of unstable equilibrium and balancing of competing political tendencies.

This alternative policy need not be tied to a precipitate withdrawal from NATO. As much as possible, the development of a sane defence policy in Britain should partner similar developments elsewhere in Western Europe: the more states which together opt for sanity, the better. In several Western European countries, the prospects and the forces for this kind of change exist and the movement in Britain is neither more nor less powerful. Change in NATO, not change in one country alone, is the key to avoiding nuclear war in Europe. Should European NATO states reduce their reliance on nuclear weapons at all levels, and thus emerge in a guise which is genuinely less threatening to the USSR, it is then (and, probably, only then) that the possibility of Soviet reciprocation would exist which could make the USSR less threatening to us.

One thing is clear after all this. If the disarmament movements continue to grow, if they can be sustained over the long haul, it will be impossible for the problems of defence policy to be resolved within the state as they always have been. Should the movements weaken, should they be relegated or relegate themselves to the political periphery, the driving force for far-reaching change will be utterly lost. In that dismal case, the political economy of British defence policy would be no different fundamentally, though it would certainly have changed in detail, ten years hence. Since the forces which shape current policy are pushing it and the rest of us towards deepening economic ruin, political repression and nuclear war, there could hardly be a stronger case for the imperative of sustaining the disarmament movements.

NOTES

1. Figures in this paragraph are taken from, '*World Armaments & Disarmament*', *SIPRI Yearbook* (London: Taylor & Francis, 1981).
2. *Defence in the 1980s: Statement on the Defence Estimates 1980*, Cmnd 7826-I (London: HMSO, 1980) ch. 4.
3. *Statement on the Defence Estimates 1981*, Cmnd 8212-I (London: HMSO, 1981) para. 415.
4. See D. Smith and R. Smith, 'Polaris Replacement and the Defence Budget in the 1980s', in Appendices to the Minutes of Evidence, *Strategic Nuclear Weapons Policy, Fourth Report from the Defence Committee, Session 1980–81*, 674 (London: HMSO, 1981).

5. Evidence of M. E. Quinlan to the House of Commons Defence Committee, 4 November 1980, Minutes of Evidence, *Strategic Nuclear Weapons Policy*, p. 113.

6. R. Smith, 'Military Expenditure and Capitalism', *Cambridge Journal of Economics*, 1, 1 (March 1977).

7. See D. Smith and R. Smith, 'Polaris Replacement and the Defence Budget in the 1980s'; the same calculations are reported in idem, 'British Military Expenditure in the 1980s', in E. P. Thompson and D. Smith (eds), *Protest and Survive* (Harmondsworth: Penguin, 1980).

8. D. Greenwood, 'Defence and National Priorities Since 1945', in J. Baylis (ed.), *British Defence Policy in a Changing World* (London: Croom Helm, 1977) pp. 195-6.

9. Cmnd 8212-I, p. 45.

10. See especially, F. C. Spinney, *Defense Facts of Life* (US Department of Defense Staff Paper, mimeo, December 1980); also J. Fallows, *National Defense* (New York: Random House, 1981).

11. See M. Kaldor, 'The Role of Nuclear Weapons in Western Relations', in M. Kaldor and D. Smith (eds), *Disarming Europe* (London: Merlin, 1982).

8 Defence Budgeting and Accountability in Britain and America: Executive Innovation and Legislative Response in the 1970s

STEPHEN KIRBY AND ANDREW COX

The accountability of the defence establishment in advanced industrial societies has always been a problem for legislatures and individuals concerned to discover the rationale of defence spending. This of course has grown as a problem with the advent of the Cold War and the use of nuclear technology. These twin developments have led the armed services and their respective bureaucratic agencies to become excessively concerned with security and the minimisation of public access to defence decision-making. Something of this fear was expressed by President Eisenhower in his final address when he spoke of the growth of a 'military-industrial complex', which was able to subvert the democratic process. This was at the end of the 1950s, but the perception that defence policy-making and expenditure decisions are not effectively controlled by the representatives of the people has been a continuing theme since that time. The distortion of the truth in the USA during the Vietnam War merely served to reinforce this fear. More recently, the ability of the defence establishment in Britain to present mis-information as truth to Parliament during the Falklands War, indicates that this problem is not confined to the USA.

The possibility that the defence establishment can dupe legislatures raises a series of questions which this paper attempts to

address. Do the political heads of the defence establishment fully
control defence decision-making and the allocation of resources
among the services? Do the services dominate the allocation of
budgetary resources for the defence establishment? How effective
have recent attempts at legislative reform been in making defence
decision-making more accountable to democratic scrutiny and
control? Does the provision of more information actually assist or
hinder effective scrutiny of defence? Does the development of
output budgeting systems in the defence area serve to provide
more or less opportunity for legislatures to check and control
defence spending? In particular, this paper will attempt to assess
the impact of innovations in defence budgeting in an era when
legislatures in Britain and the USA were gradually coming to
realise their own inability to control, or even to stay fully
informed of, new developments in the armed services.

The Department of Defence (DoD) and the Ministry of Defence
(MOD) have been in the forefront of attempts in America and
Britain to devise management structures and budgetary techniques that make central departments more efficient and, it has
been argued, more accountable. The MOD introduced a form of
output budgeting in 1952, and under McNamara a full-blown
Planning, Programming and Budgeting System (PPBS) was
introduced into the DoD in 1961. The experiment was regarded
as so successful by President Johnson that in 1967 the system was
extended to all other federal departments. The defence departments in Britain and America have also experimented with sub-
optimising techniques such as systems-analysis and cost-benefit
analysis, and with various forms of accounting and auditing procedures. These management and budgeting methods have
undergone continuous reform and refinement as problems have
been encountered and as revelations, like the excessive profits
earned on government defence contracts by Ferranti in 1964 and
Bristol Siddley in 1965, and the spectacular cost over-runs on
defence contracts throughout the 1960s in America, produced
political demands for change. Indeed, the operating problems of
PPBS were so great that the experiment has been terminated in
the 'domestic' departments of the American administration, and
the technique has not spread widely in British departments.
However, the DoD has retained the system, and also attempted to
build in zero-base budgeting (ZBB) methods from 1977. The
MOD has also retained output budgeting as part of its methods,

although it operates a more traditional input budget process in parallel with it.

Output budgeting is claimed to offer advantages in formulating departmental policy and budgets, and in making departmental management more efficient.[1] One of its major virtues is that it requires political heads of departments to spell out goals or objectives and to devise programmes to achieve them, and this should allow them to relate ends to means in a comprehensive way, and also to consider the budget as a whole as programmes compete for funds. Since programmes are related to objectives, which tend to cut across the structure of departmental organisations, the budget can be formulated only by the political head and senior executives. As Wildavsky says of the American system, 'Program budgeting contains an extreme centralising bias',[2] and of Britain, David Howell commented that 'one undisputed advantage (of PPBS) is that it provides more information and control at the top and therefore less opportunity for the growth of publically unauthorised or non-accountable bureaucratic activity'.[3] Centralisation, it seems, allows political heads and senior executives to formulate, and if necessary re-order priorities within the budget, and also to ensure that accountable programmes are established. Another virtue is that with such methods the policy implications of budgeting are emphasised, and this allows alternative programmes to be compared and selected in terms of their effectiveness in, and cost of, achieving objectives. Comparison, it is claimed, promotes better and more 'rational' policy-making.

These techniques should allow budgets to be formulated and priorities re-ordered centrally, and should ensure that the most effective programmes and policies are adopted. Furthermore, output budgeting requires a clear definition of programmes and a clear assignment of programme responsibilities to civil service and military managers, and allows the real programme costs to be calculated, and also allows departmental heads to assess how successfully responsibilities are being discharged. This provides an extra-departmental benefit since it enables legislatures to exercise programme accountability in respect of defence. David Howell considering the British system in the early 1970s addressed the American system as well when he wrote:

...by forcing the executive to spell out its objectives and

apportion them, (it) gives Parliament a better chance to know
what programmes are being undertaken, what their cost is and
who is in charge of them, and thus to work positively for the
improvement of executive government as well as to exert more
systematic control on behalf of the public and the tax-payer.[4]

Paradoxically, new management techniques like PPBS were
viewed with some scepticism by legislators, for they created
programme management units in departments that were semi-
autonomous and one step removed from the minister, and therefore one further step removed from the legislature. Sophisticated
management and budgeting methods were also too complex for
legislators, especially British legislators with very small staff and
research facilities, to master or often to comprehend. This
problem was hinted at in the Fulton Report when it presented its
proposals for departmental organisations and management on
the basis of accountable units:

> These proposals entail clear delegation of responsibility and
> corresponding authority. In devising a new pattern for a more
> purposive association with government departments, Parlia-
> ment and its committees will need to give full weight to these
> changes.[5]

In the United States, successive reports recognised the need for
reform in Congress if it was to come to terms with the federal
spending departments and their management and budgeting
methods.[6]

A major part of this response in Britain was the creation in the
1970/71 session of the Select Committee on Expenditure (SCOE),
one sub-committee of which was concerned with defence and external affairs (DEASC). The sub-committee was able to study any
defence estimates and relevant public expenditure papers. It
could also discuss the policy behind expenditures and call
ministers and civil servants to give evidence. All this was specifically intended to improve Parliament's ability to scrutinise the
MOD effectively and, some reformers hoped, to consider the
priority attached to defence in the context of other public
spending programmes; it was not, however, intended to give
Parliament any defence policy-making powers. In the United
States, Congress was already able to influence the formulation of

defence policy and could rework the annual defence budget, but the Budget and Impoundment Control Act of 1974 introduced a new congressional budget cycle, created Budget Committees in the House and Senate and established the Congressional Budget Office (CBO), all of which were intended to regain control of congressional budgeting which had become excessively fragmented, unco-ordinated and unbalanced. The Act aimed to relate expenditures to resources, but above all '... to establish national budget priorities'. Of particular concern to Congress in the 1970s was the desire to be able to establish a priority for defence as against welfare spending.

This article will examine the development of defence budgeting in America and Britain in the 1970s and assess the extent to which defence budgets were formulated and priorities reordered centrally, and the extent to which policies were selected more effectively than before. It will also examine the extent to which these same developments provided Congress and Parliament with new opportunities to exercise more effective scrutiny and control of defence, and how well such opportunities were exploited.

INNOVATIONS IN DEFENCE BUDGETING IN BRITAIN AND AMERICA

1. The American system

Decisions about the allocation of resources among the various public spending programmes, and decisions about the allocation of resources within each programme have been shared in America since 1921 by the executive and the legislature. Within the executive, decisions about the defence budget involve the Department of Defense, the Office of Management and Budget (OMB), and the President and his staff, especially the National Security Council (NSC) and the Council of Economic Advisors (CEA). Within Congress, the defence budget is handled by the House and Senate Armed Services Committees (HASC and SASC), the defence sub-committees of the House and Senate Appropriations Committees (HAC and SAC) and, since 1974, by the newly created Budget Committees in the House and Senate (HBC and SBC). These committees may draw upon the resources and support of the Congressional Budget Office (CBO), the General

Accounting Office (GAO), the Congressional Research Service (CRS), the Office of Technology Assessment (OTA), as well as their own considerable staffs. The Executive Budget, submitted in January each year, expresses priorities for national spending as well as detailed budgets for each government agency, including defence, but Congress is able to alter the President's spending priorities and to rework substantially agency budgets. In practice, the congressional budget that emerges in October has frequently resembled that of the President, but Congress' potential to make changes clearly exists.

The DoD budget cycle has been based on PPBS since 1961, but has been modified to some extent by each Secretary of Defense.[7] The last major revision of the 1970s was carried out by Harold Brown in September 1977, and contained the following stages:

PLANNING STAGE:
November
The Joint Chiefs of Staff (JCS) prepare and submit to the Secretary of Defense (SecDef) the *Joint Strategic Planning Document* (JSPD) which makes a comprehensive appraisal of the military threat to US interest and commitments throughout the world, and sets out military objectives and a strategy to protect them. It also contains recommendations on force levels and an assessment of their adequacy to carry out military strategy. The feature of this stage is that the JSPD represents the JCS's fiscally *un*constrained advice to the SecDef on military threats and objectives, however it is carried out with full knowledge of the existing Five Year Defense Plan (FYDP) which itself reflects the fiscal constraints of past years. The JSPD constitutes the advice and recommendations of the JCS to the SecDef to assist and guide him in drawing up the *Consolidated Guidance* (CG) which is the major planning document of the DoD.

December to January
The Office of Secretary of Defense (OSD) drafts the CG which contains defence policy and strategic guidance, but at this stage it does not provide fiscal guidance. The CG is sent to the Service Departments and to the JCS for review and comment. (After Brown had drawn up his first CG, relatively few modifications were made to it in successive planning cycles.)

March

The SecDef holds a single meeting with the JCS and the Service heads in early March (in the preparation of Brown's first CG, separate meetings were held for the JCS and the Service heads) to discuss any disagreements about policy or military objectives. A summary of the CG is also sent to the White House for review by the President and the National Security Council. The President, with the advice of the OMB, the Secretary of the Treasury, and the CEA conducts the 'Spring Review' to set the broad outlines of fiscal policy. The OMB estimates the likely spending of the 13 largest domestic agencies and takes advice from the SecDef and uses past experience of defence spending levels to calculate a total for defence. At this stage the OMB does not review the merits of programmes, but sets aggregate totals which it hopes will withstand the vicissitudes of the 10 months before the budget is submitted to Congress, and will provide agencies with acceptable budget totals which the domestic economy can support. In late March, when the differences with the Services have been reconciled and the President's views taken into account, the final version of the CG is issued and fiscal guidance is added. It is significant that domestic departments are issued with appropriation and expenditure targets by the OMB, but Defense receives fiscal guidance which, although intended to 'stick', is guidance and not an unbreachable ceiling. This culminates the planning stage, and the CG provides definitive guidance on policy, planning and programme issues, and also sets fiscal constraints for the development of Service programmes in each of the next five years.

PROGRAMMING STAGE:

This stage is intended to translate the approved concepts and objectives set out in the CG into time-phased requirements of men, moneys and material, and it proceeds by approving decisions that 'cost out' force objectives for financial and manpower resources five years into the future, and also displays forces for an additional three years so that the impact of current decisions can be seen on the future defence posture.

March to May

The JCS submit a *Joint Forces Memorandum* (JFM) which is a

fiscally constrained examination of the ten programme categories into which the defence budget is divided. It assesses what forces can be provided within the guidelines of the CG, and the risks associated with deploying forces at those levels for each of the ten programmes. It is at this stage that the JCS make a strong case for additional defence funds. (During the programme phase of the Fiscal Year 1981 budget, the SecDef decided that the CG should not be substantially revised, and no formal provision was made in the PPBS schedule for the submission of the JFM after definitive fiscal guidance was issued.[8] This gave rise to fears that the JCS was being downgraded in the preparation of defence budget.[9])

May
Each military department and defence agency prepares and submits to the SecDef a *Program Objective Memorandum* (POM). They are based on the strategic concepts and guidance contained in the CG, and express total programme requirements for the next five years. If such requirements affect the FYDP base, the POM must also provide a rationale for the change. POMs also identify major issues in programming that must be resolved in the current round of submissions, and include requests for forces and support resources with rationals for the levels and balance of forces requested.

May to June
The JCS submit the *Joint Program Assessment Memorandum* (JPAM) which provides a risk assessment based upon all the POM force requests, and also assesses the balance of forces and the overall force and support levels requested in the POMs against their ability to execute the approval national military strategy. The JCS may again recommend improvements in overall defence capacity at this stage. (This stage was also formally deleted from the Fiscal Year 1981 PPBS schedule.)

The OSD drafts *Issue Papers* which analyse the POMs in relation to the CG, the balance between force structures, modernisation and readiness, and efficiency trade-offs. The Issue Papers identify problems in the POMs that will require SecDef resolution, and also list alternative solutions to problems identified in the POMs in terms of the cost and capacity to implement DoD missions. Issue Papers are developed in conjunction with the Service departments and also take account of the JCS view of the risks involved in the POM requests. The Issue Papers are also reviewed by the NSC and the OMB. From April 1979, NSC and OMB personnel along with the SecDef sitting in his capacity as the chairman of the Committee of the JCS make up the Defense Resources Board and this body now reviews Issue Papers. This allows the OMB to exert some influence on programme issues before final decisions have been taken.

July to August
SecDef revises Issue Papers in consultation with OSD staff, and on the basis of these and the JCS risk assessment, the Secretary issues draft *Program Decision Memorandum* (PDM) which are sent to the Services and the defence agencies for review and comment. In early August the OSD prepares the *Reclama* book which is used to record Service appeals against the draft PDMs. The Service heads are also able to meet individually with the SecDef to resolve disagreements about their programmes. At the end of August, final and, if necessary, revised PDMs are issued and sent to the Services to guide the drawing up of Service budget estimates.

THE BUDGET STAGE:
15 September
Using the programme levels established in the POM/PDM process, the Services and defence agencies submit detailed budget estimates for the budget years of their programmes. Budget estimates are based upon the approved programmes and upon economic assumptions about pay and pricing policies which are contained in the PDM or in specific budget guidance issued by the SecDef.

October to December
These estimates are reviewed jointly (Fall Review) by the OSD and the OMB to ensure that requests are correctly priced, that production targets are realistic, and that estimates square with the Secretary's readiness objectives. As estimates are approved, they are listed by the SecDef in Budget Decision Documents and include the current year, the budget year, the authorisation year (budget year + 1) and an estimate of the

resource impact on the succeeding programme years. (This was to meet President Carter's decision of 1978 to implement multi-year planning estimates.)

The reclama process continues through the budget review and the JCS and Service heads may meet the SecDef to appeal against any decision and to resolve other outstanding issues.

December

The SecDef presents his budget to the President for review within the context of the overall federal budget, and any changes are incorporated into the DoD submission. At this point the OMB is obliged to make its 'hard choices' on defence and is constantly lobbied whilst it is doing so. The OMB/DoD trade-off responds to changes in dcmestic spending and the performance of the economy, which allows marginal, and usually upward, revisions of defence spending to be made almost to the eve of presenting the Executive's budget to Congress. After this the budget documents are finalised. The Defence Controller and the Service Controllers then translate the programme budget requests, expressed in the DoD's ten programme budget categories, into the six appropriation accounts and thousands of 'line items' that are handled by Congress. This apparently 'technical' function is very important since the translation is not easy, and also offers the opportunity to make costing decisions that can and do have programme effects. The FYDP is updated to reflect the President's budget and this becomes the new base for the ensuing PPBS cycle.

It is also worth noting that in 1977 President Carter instructed each federal agency to introduce zero-based budgeting (ZBB) to help eliminate waste and unnecessary programmes from budgets by reviewing and justifying each agency programme and budget from 'zero dollar' upwards. The attempt to incorporate ZBB into the DoD was a long and costly one, with two budgets being prepared in 1977. However, the end result was that only a few of the ZBB techniques and concepts were grafted onto the PPB system, and then only in terms of budgeting at the margin. By 1978 the OSD had established three budget levels, a minimum level, ten per cent below the current year budget in real terms, at which the department could only just operate without overwhelming dislocation, a base budget level which would allow current services to continue at their present level by taking into account inflation and other cost increases, and an enhanced budget, ten per cent above the current year budget in real terms, which would represent a significant real increase in resources for defence. Within this range only, the DoD produced ZBB 'decision packages' for each programme, which were then ranked in order of priority. This allows the DoD to increase or decrease defence spending within this range and still retain a balance between its programmes and protect its priorities. (The first Reagan defence budget seems to have exceeded even the DoD's enhanced budget level and helps explain the rather frantic search for programmes on which to spend the embarrassment of riches that DoD received in the summer of 1981, and the ensuing decisions to refit and re-engine several World War II battleships.) Below the minimum level, which represents the greater part of the defence budget, programmes are considered to be both essential and cost-effective.

This outline of the DoD's PPB system suggests that the department is concerned, in the main, with output budgeting, and several studies describe the planning phase as not fiscally constrained, and show that the JCS are able to make an objective assessment of military threats, needs and missions.[10] However, this is misleading and overlooks the fact that budget cycles overlap and that budgeting is a continuous and political process. The central document in the DoD process is in fact the FYDP which identifies defence missions in terms of major force programmes which are further broken down into programme element codes. It also provides a bridge from strategic planning to defence budgeting and gives the Secretary of Defense a coherent guide to the relationship between the military strategy and resources, and between resources and costs. The FYDP is revised at the end of each PPBS cycle and becomes the base for the next round of budgeting. In the planning phase the JCS are obliged to operate from the FYDP base which enshrines recent fiscal guidance and budget decisions. They are also obliged to exercise 'fiscal responsibility' when estimating the attainability of planning force levels in the JSPD.[11] Over and above this the Consolidated Guidance, the final version of which contains fiscal limits, stands until revised or modified by the Secretary of Defense, and even though the planning stage precedes the formal announcement of any year's *specific* fiscal guidance, the CG remains a powerful benchmark in JCS thinking and DoD planning. Under Brown the final revision or confirmation of the CG came earlier in the PPBs cycle in successive years, and thereby allowed presidential fiscal consideration to be expessed at a very early stage in the planning process. All this suggests that the budget phase is in effect the beginning of the cycle, and that it informs the ensuing stages of planning and programming; indeed this is a view supported by a recent Director of Program and Financial Control in the DoD.[12] In addition, the restriction of ZBB methods to the upper margin of the defence budget means that the base is continually approved, and this ensures the continuation of the operational plan that it represents. The acceptance of the base budget necessarily forecloses many planning options.

The importance of the FYDP base and the definition of a base budget level in the ZBB process, reveal that DoD budgeting is essentially input-based and incremental. In the executive's 'Spring Review', the defence total is established by political negotiations with the Secretary of Defense and a review of past defence spending levels. These factors are measured against the demands of other agencies and against the economy's ability to provide resources. Similar calculations are made when reallocating resources among agencies during the 'Fall Review' in December; a clearer case of budgeting incrementally and by input is difficult to find. If further confirmation were needed, it is provided in full by the DoD's preference for converting the product of its internal programme budgeting into the appropriating accounts and line items, requesting men, moneys and material, that are dealt with by Congress. This is partly to provide Congress with a budget that it can recognise and deal with, but also because DoD recognises that incrementalism, or making adjustments to a base that is 'given', is the most successful way to protect or increase the defence budget. The DoD's annual demand for more is not diluted by a justification of what it already has.

The PPB system was also introduced by McNamara to reassert civilian control over the service departments and the military, and to exert central control over the budget process and policy formulation. Clearly, under the McNamara regime this was achieved and his relationship with the JCS and service heads became so bad that all four members of the JCS were sacked or resigned within a year of his arrival. Melvin Laird attempted to restore a good deal of service and military autonomy over pro- gramme and budget decisions by introducing 'participatory management' which invited JCS and service contributions to the formulation of planning documents, and gave them great weight. Laird also gave the service heads almost complete autonomy in programming within fiscal limits set by him at the end of the planning stage. Brown ended the 'participatory management' experiment and his revisions of 1977 were intended to allow pre- sidential preferences to enter the DoD budget system at an early stage. They were also intended to produce a tighter and more centralised management of the budget. There were fears that at Carter's direction, Brown was bringing back McNamara style budget 'whiz kids' and that the President and Secretary of Defense were 'muzzling' the military. Brown was aware however that Congress would not accept the undermining of JCS and service influence, and conceded that he would not inhibit their initiatives and innovations.[13]

Fears that the military were being 'muzzled' proved groundless and overlooked the fact the services play an important part in the planning stage by drawing up the JSPD, even though it is done with fiscal limits in mind. There is no doubt, however, that when political circumstances are favourable for the expansion or redirection of the defence role, as with the election of Ronald Reagan in November 1980, that the JSPD and JCS statements to Congress are important devices for pointing the Secretary of Defense in the direction that the JCS would like to go. By their own admission, the JCS testimony on SALT in the summer of 1979, and their posture statement of 1980, only weeks after Afghanistan, were critical in redefining the executive's defence policies.[14] The speed of that policy re-orientation belies any claim that alternatives were exhaustively or comprehensively examined and compared.

The services also play a vital role in programming by producing the POMs and by contributing to the drafting of Issue Papers. The service-generated POMs are the core of the programming phase and, although they are based upon the strategic con- cepts and guidance contained in the CG, are flexible enough to accommodate frequent and substantial changes in programming requirements; changes that reflect the interaction of OSD, service and congressional interests rather than a 'rational' comparison of alternative ways of achieving mission goals. Within a period of less than five years it was programmed that the USAF was to contribute to the Strategic Offensive Mission with a new manned bomber under Ford, without one under Carter, and with the possibility of two under Reagan. Programmes seem to respond to political circumstances rather than to analysis or comparison.

The reclama system provides the services with access to the Secretary of Defense, to the OMB and to the President to reverse programme and budget decisions that go against them. These opportunities for service lobbying exist within the executive budget cycle, and the strength of that lobby is demonstrated by the fact that the OMB refuses to take any 'hard' decisions during the 'Spring Review' for fear that they will be inundated by service pressure.[15] The OMB exercises its influence during the November/December budget phase when such decisions become unavoidable. Even when the executive budget is complete, the services still have ample opportunity to fight their 'lost' causes in Congress and during Carter's presidency were very successful in restoring programmes deleted in the programming and budgeting phases.[16]

The PPB system is a lengthy process, taking some fifteen months to complete and with congressional action, the budget cycle occupies nearly two years. In this space of time many political and economic circumstances develop that alter the planning assumptions upon which programme and budget decisions are supposed to rest. For example, the 1974 mid-term elections brought to Congress many new members pledged to restrain defence expenditure, but within a year Cambodia and South Vietnam had fallen, and the United States was embarrassed by the Mayaguz affair, and the public and congressional mood began to change; so much so that by 1976 President Ford found it politic not to refer to détente and he directed that the Fiscal Year 1977 defence budget be increased dramatically to appease rising congressional demands and to underwrite a hawkish campaign designed to win over that element of the Republican Party that favoured the hard-line defence policies of Ronald Reagan. Carter, too, found that the public and congressional ground swell for a strong defence was irresistible despite his election pledge to cut defence spending by five per cent each year. In May 1977 he accepted a NATO obligation to increase defence spending by three per cent in real terms per annum, and was asking for a 7.9 per cent real increase by 1979. At the same time, the momentum for a balanced budget required him to increase defence spending at the expense of social welfare programmes. Such politically induced presidential decisions divorce budgeting from planning and programming, and have long-term effects on the FYDP base. In recent years such pressure and presidential responses to it have enabled the services to acquire resources that will affect the defence posture for many years to come, and in ways that did not appear in the FYDP or policy documents.

Congressional budget action itself has other effects upon the initial PPBS process of the DoD in that changes in the budget requests made by Congress require an extensive re-programming exercise by the services, including transfer of funds from one account to another. Inflation accounting also has effects upon the process after January when the executive budget is submitted to Congress and as inflation estimates vary so the services are able to adjust their budget requests to meet changing circumstances in the most favourable way. Indeed the problem of inflation has become so severe that the Fiscal Year 1981 Consolidated Guidance did not contain definitive fiscal guidance to give the services and the OSD some flexibility to respond to rapidly changing circumstances. For similar reasons the 'Current services' budget which used to be submitted to Congress in November to inform it of the cost of continuing agency services at current levels, is now submitted with the President's budget in January because inflation in the November to January period made the presidential request appear greater than it was in real terms. If political and economic realities and service preferences serve to obscure a truly 'rational' or 'managed' approach to defence budgeting in the USA then similar problems have been experienced in Britain in recent years.

2. The British system

Both the inter-governmental allocation of resources amongst alternative commitments, as well as the intra-departmental allocation of defence resources amongst the services and Procurement Executive in Britain are centralised. Parliament's role in defence budgeting is, and has always been, limited to the scrutiny of defence estimates and legitimation of defence policies through the approval of estimates and the passing of the annual Appro-priation Act.[17] In very general terms we can argue that primary responsibility for inter-governmental allocations (guns versus butter) rests with the Cabinet, assisted by the Treasury with its control over the Public Expenditure Survey Committee. The latter institution – PESC – entails a five year 'rolling' pro-gramme/review of the public expenditure consequences of existing policy commitments, against the best estimate/forecast of the future trends in the economy.[18] From this basis of future forecasting it is possible – in theory, anyway – for the government to assess where its policies will lead and whether or not there is scope for additional expenditure in new or existing areas, or whether existing policies will have to be cut as a result of poor economic performances.

Feeding into this system are, of course, the intra-departmental allocation decisions which for defence, are the responsibility of the Secretary of State and the senior civil servants and servicemen in the Ministry of Defence and Procurement Executive.[19] The process of allocating within defence is normally enshrined within the civil service and Procurement Executive generation of 'bids' for new expenditure programmes – known as ten year long-term costings (LTCs), which are then set against the Treasury's best estimate of the likely defence allocation by the Central Staffs (civilian) within the MOD. If the allocation arrived at is regarded as insufficient the individual services then have scope to press their case for more within the Chiefs of Staff Committee (Defence Staff) and with the Secretary of State – who can ultimately take any such requests to Cabinet for preferential treatment if he thinks he can make a justifiable case. Parliament's role in this process is 'post hoc', in the sense that it simply assesses the rectitude in 'value for money' terms of decisions already arrived at, without the ability to change any item within the government's defence budget: it is a scrutiny and informational role.

The way in which inter-governmental and intra-departmental allocations come together has been summarised in some detail by Richard Burt and David Greenwood,[20] and a short summary of their accounts will be presented here before a number of additional points are raised which these two authorities have perhaps ignored and which are important in fully appreciating the limited role and information accorded to the legislature in Britain.

While it is difficult to pinpoint any one date to be the starting point for defence budgeting, due to the sequential parallel and continuous nature of the process – which is always approximately sixteen months in advance of the existing financial year – Burt has taken the beginning of the PESC cycle as a convenient starting place. While it can be argued that this is not correct, for the moment this starting point will serve to illustrate British defence budgeting:

December
The Treasury sends its PESC instructions and forecasts to the MOD to guide the MOD's budget request for the next but one April (sixteen months on) as it is already preparing the final estimates for Parliamentary approval for the coming year.

January
MOD Central Staff (Programme and Budget Division) gives Service Departments and Procurement Executive tentative ceilings to guide them in their preparation of ten year LTCs. Since Service and Procurement Executive LTCs (bids) will always be above the tentative ceiling for defence spending from the Treasury this begins the process of intra-departmental allocation conflicts, as each Service fights to include its bids in the defence ceiling.

February – March
Tentative LTC bids are sent to the Treasury for its consideration by MOD (Programmes and Budget) staff, who also ask Services to make cuts in their own bids and to defend only those which they wish to retain as first priority. For information purposes the MOD (P & B) staff prepare an output budget in 12 functional headings (missions) with 550 Element Costings. This is the output (PPB system) budgeting process in Britain, but it tends to follow rather than lead or influence the input budgeting of the LTCs; it is therefore for informational and presentational purposes to guide difficult decisions over 'marginal' bids later in the process.

April – May
MOD (P & B) discuss alternative spending ceilings and bid allocations with Service Departments, Treasury, FCO and Pro-

curement Executive. Internally, the centralised Operational Requirements and Defence Equipment Committees as well as the Chiefs of Staff discuss the various alternatives available. The Chiefs of Staff prepare their own report on the implications of alternative spending allocations. This is the crunch point for intra-departmental allocation battles because the end result is the final MOD bid to be sent to the PESC in the Treasury.

June

PESC bids are sent to the Treasury by each department, normally most spending departments are including additional bids above the tentative ceilings given to them in January/February and it is at this level that the inter-governmental battle (guns versus butter) commences as the Permanent Secretaries fight over which departments will obtain, either the marginal increases in expenditure which are available, or the minimum cuts given the need to reduce expenditure. Clearly, the success of the MOD's Permanent Secretary in winning this inter-governmental battle will have implications for intra-departmental bids above the initial tentative ceilings.

July – September

PESC Report is sent to Cabinet and the summer is spent in Ministers re-thrashing out the decisions and compromises reached by their officials. This means, of course, that Cabinet becomes the final court of appeal for departments either to try to win battles they have lost earlier in the process or to introduce new arguments to overturn or modify earlier decisions. Clearly, the necessity for departments to have a Minister who is able to defend his department and stand up to the Treasury is crucial because the Cabinet can overturn decisions arrived at in the PESC Report, if it so wishes. Clearly, however, while Cabinet is the court of final appeal, the scope for Cabinet innovation is limited by the incremental nature of the process: the Cabinet is not discussing fundamental policy changes normally, but who gets the marginal increase in funds available.[21] The battle is not over particular spending programmes but marginal adjustments to aggregate spending levels. The MOD will use any argument available to it – the

Soviet menace, the NATO commitment, favourable Parliamentary Reports, etc. – at this stage to defend its position and attempt to increase its allocation. The inter-governmental budgetary allocation ends with the publication of the Public Expenditure White Paper, which is presented on a five year forward basis for expenditure.

October
The Cabinet decisions are then transmitted back to departments. The General Finance Division (GF), in MOD, then begins the process of preparing the estimates, which are input-based for presentation to Parliament to appropriation approval and scrutiny. The estimates are generally regarded as presentational and after October it is generally held that there is little scope for either inter-governmental or intra-departmental adjustments of defence expenditure. While it is the case that there is no scope for such alterations by appeals to Parliament there is scope for some modification as will be seen later when discussions are carried out on the problems of defence management in the context of inflation and cash limits.

November – December
MOD (GF) sends the draft estimates to the Treasury and the final estimates are prepared in conjunction with the Annual Defence White Paper, which draws heavily on the functional/output budget format generated for presentational purposes by MOD (P & B) in the previous March. The Central Staff are by now involved in the next financial year's bid preparation for PESC.

January – April
Estimates and White Paper presented to Parliament for debate and approval through the annual Appropriation Act.

Post-Hoc Review
The Estimates Committee (1912–1970) normally scrutinised the annual Estimates to assess 'value for money' of expenditure and since 1966 the Public Accounts Committee in conjunction with the Controller and Auditor-General's Department has audited the accounts of the departments to check

whether the money voted for particular functions has in fact been spent on those functions.

While this is a useful summary of the process for defence budgeting in Britain, as outlined by recent analysts, there are a number of points which have perhaps been under-played or ignored and which ought to be included for a full account. Firstly, it has been argued by Greenwood that there are two budgeting processes taking place in the MOD along parallel lines – input budgeting (LTCs) and output budgeting (Element Costings on a mission basis).[22] But, as we have seen the output budget process comes *after* arguments over LTCs (bids) by the services and Central Staff (P & B). Thus the output budgeting system in the MOD is for information and presentational purposes; it does not guide decision-making or operate in parallel, but as an aid to an input-biased budget system which has always been in operation. This does not mean of course that Greenwood is wrong to argue that there is far more use made of cost-benefit analysis through the Defence Operations Analysis Establishment at West Byfleet, nor that the new Operational Requirements and Defence Equipment Committees or the moves to centralisation after 1963 and the creation of the Procurement Executive in 1970 are examples of a move to more rational/functional decision-making. Rather we wish to argue that this takes place at a level which precludes the generation of a truly 'planned' approach to Britain's fundamental policy commitments for defence. This is simply another way of saying that Greenwood does not emphasise enough the fact that this output budgeting is at a sub-optimal level in the MOD. A fact illustrated by a recent central co-ordinator of defence allocation decisions in the MOD, John Bourn, who has argued:[23]

> . . . these systems (output budgeting) have not in themselves been successful in either central or local government in the United Kingdom or elsewhere. We may have looked for too much. We may have made the mistake of believing that to institute new procedures would itself solve our problems. We have had to learn again that technique is no substitute for analysis, debate and dialogue.

Such an admission indicates quite clearly that, whatever form of budgeting is taking place in Britain, it is far removed from the theories of PPB systems outlined in the 1950s and 1960s.

This conclusion is apposite because it leads us back to a consideration of a second tendency in recent analyses of defence organisation and budgeting: the tendency to overstate the degree of centralisation and therefore over-estimate the diminution of the role of the separate services (Army, Navy and RAF) in budgeting. This error is most glaringly made by Howard and Burt in their otherwise excellent accounts, but it is not made by Greenwood, who rightly emphasises the critical role of the service departments in the preparation of MOD PESC bids (LTCs).[24] We have already seen that the major supposed instrument of central control – output budgeting – has been a chimera and this fact must lead us to a realisation that the traditional service dominated input budgeting process is still very much in operation in the MOD. Michael Hobkirk has pointed to the relatively equal distribution of resources which the services maintained for themselves (indicating 'buggin's turn').[25] It should not surprise us either because the services can be expected to want to retain a major say in defence budgeting, not only for defensive organisational reasons, but also because they are responsible for both professional advice to the government on defence matters and also for the running and administration of defence services in the field. While there may be arguments against those operationally responsible having a major say over defence budgeting allocations, it has generally been accepted in the UK that the services have the right to a major say and the Chiefs of Staff Committee and April Report are testament to this role.[26]

The central role of the services as opposed to the MOD civilian Central Staff's role is also indicated by the fact that though MOD (P & B) co-ordinates allocation decisions and sets the ceilings in conjunction with the Treasury, the actual (LTCs) are prepared by the Procurement Executive and the three service departments. The P & B division is therefore merely co-ordinating and not dominating the defence budget process centrally. Nor could it do so with a staff of six. Finally, while it might appear that centralisation is on the increase in the MOD budgeting process it is as well to bear in mind that when the MOD (P & B) division is bargaining with the Treasury over financial ceilings it is doing so in order to accommodate the bids and preferences emanating from the services, not from the MOD civilian central staffs as such.

A third omission, notably from Burt's work, has been the

analysis of fundamental policy decisions which guide annual and medium term budgeting decisions. Burt's analysis is overly concerned with the process of financial management and control and as such over-states the dominant role of the Treasury and Central Staffs in managing and controlling the defence effort in expenditure terms. Now while it is fair to argue, as Burt does,[27] that financial necessity has often generated policy reviews in Britain, this should not remove the fact that the PESC system for defence is also directed by fundamental policy decisions taken by government – often in the absence of immediate financial crises. An example of this is the 1974/5 Defence Review implemented by the Labour Government reflecting its pre-election commitment to changing the balance between social and defence expenditure. A similar, if different commitment, has been undertaken by the Thatcher Government with its decision to spend more on defence even at a time of cutting expenditure in other areas.[28] The point is that while the defence budgeting process in Britain is incremental in most respects this is not to say that fundamental policy reviews do not occur, nor that they are not important. Since 1945 there have been a number of defence reviews, as well as policy changes, indicated in the Defence White Papers, which are really the starting point for the defence budgeting process in Britain and which guide both the MOD and Treasury in its PESC and LTC deliberations. In this sense too much can be made of the decisions taken by Permanent Secretaries in PESC because, if they do their job correctly, the decisions ought to reflect the preferences specified by Ministers. In the defence field, between 1957 and 1977 at least, Ministers have generally been fairly clear that the defence commitment ought to be reduced and in this respect the Treasury and MOD have reflected this consensus.[29]

Clearly, then, the defence budgeting system cannot be understood merely by analysing the institutional processes and relationships within PESC; to understand the driving force behind these processes we need to understand the social/economic and political variables which impinge upon governments. Thus in understanding who or what shapes the defence budget in Britain, we need to consider what causes governments to shift priorities. Clearly, ideological commitments are important, but so also are strategic assumptions about 'threats' (for example, the increased 'Soviet threat' which encouraged even a Labour Government to increase defence

spending by three per cent in 1977, and the Thatcher administration to replace Polaris). Clearly, these perceptions of a threat
have always been apparent in service 'bids', but it is the
acceptance of this position by the government – which gives the
services additional expenditure – which is crucial. There are also
social and economic, as well as political, considerations of importance. The changing nature of economic circumstances will have
an impact on the defence effort. The Heath Government used
the production of more naval ships than originally intended as a
counter-cyclical method of reducing high unemployment in the
early 1970s,[30] which indicated the inter-relationship between
social and economic problems and an increased defence effort
which had little to do with the formal PESC and LTC system.
Finally, changes in the technology available within the defence
field will also play a crucial role in shaping the defence effort and
budgetary decisions, either about overall shares of expenditure or
the volume of goods to be produced.

This factor is an important one because most commentators
fail to appreciate the continuing bargaining over inter- and intra-
defence allocations which are apparent throughout the budgetary
cycle. Most commentators imply that there is no scope for
manoeuvre after the publication of the Cabinet's decision in the
Public Expenditure White Paper in September; this of course
ignores the impact of defence management problems, associated
with inflation and cash limits, in the British system.[31] At the
beginning of the annual budgeting exercise the MOD (P & B)
Division is concerned to win acceptance from the Treasury that
cash limits (imposed since 1975/76 on annual expenditure) are
not sacrosanct. In other words it is important for all departments
to ensure that the limits imposed can be adjusted if problems
arise. This problem is particularly acute for the MOD because,
while it must spend moneys allocated for any one year in that
year, there is considerable slippage in defence programmes due to
industrial/management problems or to the exigencies associated
with operating on technological frontiers which the MOD cannot
control. This means that there is a continuous potentiality for
'underspend' or 'overspend' in particular years and the MOD has
been involved in a battle with the Treasury to win acceptance
that it can carry over money voted for a particular function but
not spent in the year for which it was voted.[32]

The MOD has, however, other financial management

problems related to cash limits and inflation and high technology which appear *after* the September White Paper process has been finalised. The PESC process is conducted at constant price levels and, after deliberation by Cabinet, when the annual estimates are prepared by the GF Division, these constant prices (volume of goods and services desired) confront current prices or economic reality. It is at this point that cash limits become crucial because, if cash limits are set at fourteen per cent and inflation is running at twenty per cent plus (as in 1978/80) then unless cash limits are extended the volume production of equipment must be reduced or specific programmes, accepted by the Cabinet from LTC bids, may have to be curtailed. This problem is exacerbated of course when wage settlements for the armed forces and civilian staffs outstrip cash limits and when high technology costs exceed average inflation levels.[33] Thus when the GF Division confronts the trade-off between constant and current price levels there is a conflict and dialogue taking place with the Treasury as the MOD tries to win supplementary estimates above those agreed within the Cabinet to accommodate inflation. Clearly, while this task will have been previewed earlier in the year, the real decisions occur after the Cabinet's budgeting decisions in the summer. As John Bourn has argued however, this may well undermine efficient planning of defence because when, as has been normal in recent years, cuts have to be made to accommodate rising inflation – whatever the modification allowed in cash limits – these cuts, coming at the end of the financial year, tend to fall on what can be cut rather than what is most desirable to cut.[34] This process resembles more the 'crude axe blows' outlined by Martin than the rational planning process described by Greenwood.[35]

LEGISLATIVE OVERSIGHT AND ACCOUNTABILITY OF DEFENCE IN BRITAIN AND AMERICA

The operation of output budgeting in the DoD and the MOD has offered few of the advantages claimed for it by its supporters. There is little evidence that the respective systems have allowed political heads to establish and, if necessary, re-order priorities in relation to stated policy goals, nor that they have been able to select the most effective programmes as a result of the comprehensive comparison of programme alternatives. The process of budgeting in the DoD and MOD still involves and relies upon the bids developed and presented by the services and they are still input-based and incremental. This in itself reduces the capacity of legislatures to scrutinise or to control effectively intra-departmental or inter-governmental allocations, but it does not make impossible the task of rendering defence accountable by any means. The creation of the new Budget Committees in America and the Select Committee on Expenditure in Britain led to expectations that Congress and Parliament would be able to obtain new information on defence budgeting and would be able to use it in a way that rendered the allocations made for defence more accountable than before.

The effectiveness of holding the executive accountable depends upon the availability and the use made of information. Here the circumstances of Congress and Parliament are fundamentally different. Congressional committees traditionally suffer from information overload especially in the period after the resignation of President Nixon when shell-shocked departments made information widely available, and the Freedom of Information Act was used by Congressmen to prise out such information as was not given. SCOE and DEASC by comparison suffered from information starvation, and were denied crucially important information about defence budgeting and in some cases, such as the Chevaline development,[36] were denied any direct information at all until after the programme was nearing completion. Nevertheless, few doubted in 1970 that SCOE and DEASC would operate in a superior way to their predecessors. It is not possible to review in detail the work of these congressional and parliamentary committees; this has been done elsewhere by the authors;[37] but it is possible to identify some of the problems that led to each of these reforms falling short of the expectations of their supporters.

1. The American experience 1970–1980

In Congress the major issue was not so much the availability of information, but the use that its committees were to make of it. Even before 1974, the Armed Services Committees and the Appropriations Committees wielded great influence and were able to change the defence budget total and the line items that made it up. However, the work of the Armed Services Committees was done in isolation from the other legislative committees and the defence sub-committees of the Appropriations Committees paid scant regard to the appropriations made to other federal programmes. The Budget Committees and the new budget cycle were intended to allow Congress to oversee the separate actions of its legislative and appropriations committees so that revenues and expenditures could be compared and national spending priorities set. The Budget Committees were charged with first gathering information from the legislative committees on their spending intentions, and then assessing their effect on the economy and the size of the budget deficit. From this information the Budget Committees draw up the First Concurrent Resolution on the Budget which has to be presented to and accepted by Congress by 15 May each year. The Resolution sets spending totals for each agency budget and, after its acceptance, spending bills can be dealt with by Congress with the Budget Committees and the CBO checking that they do not breach the ceilings set in the First Resolution. Between 15 and 25 September Congress reassesses revenue, spending and debt requirements and confirms or amends the Budget Resolution. The reforms were intended to make congressional committees more responsible and allow priorities to be set.

The quantity and quality of information available to Congress appears to be sufficient to fulfil these roles. The Armed Services, Appropriation and Budget Committees in the House and the Senate are able to call upon a vast quantity of information from the DoD, from military witnesses, and from independent military analysts and experts. In the 1979 congressional budget cycle, twelve million words of oral evidence and several million more of written evidence were taken on defence issues. This evidence contained the annual posture statements of the Secretary of Defense and of the JCS, both of which were extensively examined in hearing sessions. Congress does not formally concern itself with the ten mission categories of the DoD budget, but it does receive much of the FYDP costings and the Armed Service and Appropriations Committees do review thousands of 'line items' which cover the equipment, manpower, research and development, and operations and maintenance requests for the services and take evidence on the missions for which these resources are requested.

What is crucial about the availability of information to congressional committees is that they can call before them military witnesses who are able to give, on request, their independent professional advice about needs and missions, and it is often at odds with that of the Secretary of Defense. Indeed, service heads will often not press for resources in the DoD budget cycle if they think that they can be won in Congress.[38] It is also critical that Congress has the power to alter budget requests to accommodate those needs identified by its own members or by its military and other witnesses. An outstanding example of this is the concerted congressional action by both Armed Service and both Appropriations Committees to provide the Marine Crops with the AV-8B aircraft after it had been deleted from the programme stage of the PPBs cycle in 1979 by the OSD.[39] In the case of the AV-8B, congressional committees made use of evidence from the Marine Corps. The Commandant General, Louis H. Wilson, informed the Senate Armed Services Committee and other committees that he would rather accept a fighter modernisation gap and wait for the AV-8B than accept the F/A – 18 aircraft recommended by the DoD for the Marine Corps.[40] Committees also took evidence from other military and from defence contractor witnesses and were able to assess the aircraft's capabilities against the F/A – 18 and match both to the Marine Corps' mission. Perhaps more important was that Congress was able to reconstruct the debate inside the DoD about the AV-8B, and to explode many of the misconceptions and misrepresentations about the aircraft. This example demonstrates just how well Congress can be informed, if for no other reason than that the 'losers' in the DoD budget cycle will give Congress extensive and detailed information about military needs and missions in an attempt to over-turn decisions that have gone against them.

Each committee has its own very substantial staff, 178 for the HBC in 1980 for example, as well as the resources of the GAO, the CBO, the CRS and the OTA. Altogether some 2 000 staff members and researchers are available to Congress who are able to contribute to defence issues in some way. The GAO is particularly important in reviewing the DoD's management of weapons programmes and defence services, and the CBO provides Congress with expert analysis of the President's annual budget including the defence request. Indeed the CBO estimates the effect of each element of the executive budget on the economy and analyses the cost and effect of alternative budget choices, including those for defence. The CBO negotiates with the Budget Committees each year to carry out a series of Budget Issue studies to guide Congress on budgetary choices that will come before it in the current budget cycle. Many of these studies concern defence issues.

The problem of secrecy does not loom as large for Congress as it does for Parliament. This reflects in part the willingness of the DoD to provide information to the congressional committees, including much classified information in closed session since these committees have the power to grant or deny. Of more importance is the ability of committees to call military and defence industrial witnesses who are able to give their independent professional advice. This is not to say that there is no information that is denied these committees, for when the DoD, the military and the contractor are of like mind and see no need to break ranks, they can present both a united and closed front to Congress. However, the defence experts on committee staffs and the defence specialists of the GAO, CBO and CRS maintain very close links with, and are often ex-members of, the DoD administration and are able to provide most of the committee's needs. What is not available can often be produced independently by Congress's own research facilities, such as the costings of the 'out years' of the FYDP estimated by the CBO. Those who claim that the Carter administration attempted to 'muzzle' military witnesses called before Congress committees, could point to little visible effect on the work of Congress or to a decline in the influence of the military. There is no doubt that the evidence of the JCS to the Armed Services Committees in the last years of the Carter administration was very influential in building and informing the congressional coalition that demanded and exacted from a reluctant President substantial increases in defence resources in 1979 and 1980.[41]

The quantity of information is as much a curse as it is a blessing, since there is simply too much for Congressmen to digest and it is often too technical for them to understand or to use. An example is that over eighty per cent of the GAO recommendations for savings in or changes to defence contracting and management are eventually taken up by the DoD itself rather than by Congress.[42] The complexity of the information places many Congressmen in the hands of their personal or committee staff members, and the control and supervision of the congressional bureaucracy is becoming a problem that equals the control and supervision of the executive bureaucracy.

Another feature of the information that is available to Congress is its variable and often conflicting quality. In each of the last five years of the 1970s for example, the DoD has produced an estimate for inflation and has allowed a sum for defence inflation accounting that differs from that offered by the CBO. Over and above this, independent and different assessments of inflation have been offered by the OMB, by each of the Budget Committees and by the Department of the Treasury. The CBO, OTA and GAO are supposed to be neutral and non-partisan in their gathering and presentation of information, but the CRS is consumer orientated and produces reports at the request of Congressmen; very few CRS reports are self-generated. This means that a Congressman is able to request and receive a report that argues a particular point of view and many 'partisan' defence reports have been produced by the service. The variable and conflicting nature of much of the information vital to Congress for the review and revision of the defence budget allows Congressmen to select that information which best suits their inclinations about the need for defence resources.

Another reason for the unevenness of the information available to Congress is that some of it is, or at least is regarded to be, tainted and of poor quality. Most Republicans in the House and many conservative Democrats regard the CBO as 'Keynesian' largely because its Director, Alice Revlin, is an ex-Brookings academic – and dismiss its economic and defence budgeting advice. Defence analysts on the staff of the House Armed Services Committee regarded the CBO defence staff as young and inexperienced[43] and preferred to work without their help or advice. The fact that each committee involved in the examination of the defence budget has its own staff is a further complication, since information is used to protect a committee's 'turf', and there is not always as free an exchange of information between committees, even in the same chamber of Congress, as effective examination of the defence budget requires. Because the HBC cannot muster the technical expertise on defence equipment issues that is available to the HASC, and because the HASC will not offer it, members of Budget Committees dare not challenge the HASC on the floor of the House on these issues even if they think that particular weapons programmes are not being well managed or are not necessary to fulfil defence policy goals. This typifies the HBC approach to other committees and was clearly expressed by one

HBC staff member who said, 'We're aware that we'll get killed if we take on other Committees head-to-head. All we have to work with is the goodwill of other Committees'.[44] The SBC, similarly lacking the expertise and also not willing to encroach on the work of the SASC, simply declines to examine defence line items at all, and concerns itself with the defence budget total. In the absence of a capacity to examine line items, the SBC is dependent on the SASC and the DoD for estimates of how large that total should be.

Congressional committees also use defence information for different purposes. The Budget Committees, by and large, try to use defence information in a technical way in the construction of a budget that reflects congressional priorities for public spending. The BCs are not yet seen to be central in the revision of the President's budget or in the allocation of resources for defence. They are essentially process committees which do not attract an extensive constituency. The House and Senate Armed Services Committees are special interest and constituency based, and members use information and the influence it gives them to win decisions that assist their constituents and clients. Information for them is political capital that is used for political purposes. This is increasingly the case with the House and Senate Appropriations Committees, especially in the House where, since 1976, Congressmen are voted onto committees by the party caucuses and they may select their own sub-committee assignment. It is not unusual for 'hawks' or Congressmen who represent large defence interests to become members of the defence sub-committees of appropriations and vote to express their policy preferences or to benefit their constituents, rather than to consider the balance and advisability of the appropriations of funds to the executive.

This is not to say that the reform of 1974 has had no effect on the work of Congress. There is no doubt that Congress better understands the composition and the size of the congressional budget and its effect on the economy as a whole, and the debate on the First Concurrent Resolution on the Budget is an occasion for Congress to discuss national priorities in a way that was not possible before. In May 1979 the House debated the First Concurrent Resolution for an unprecedented eight days and concentrated on the balance between spending for defence and social programmes, and upon the size of the deficit. However, this process to some extent merely concentrates and formalises the traditional conflict between the legislative committees and between them and the Appropriations Committees. Rather than discuss national priorities, the First Resolution debate expresses the struggle of the party managers to mobilise votes on the floor in support of committee programmes that have been developed very much as before 1974. It is important too that the First Resolution is compiled by the Budget Committees from information given to them by the legislative committees, and that the information provided has diminished in successive years. In the first year of the reform, the HASC provided the HBC with a lengthy document that provided a programme by programme breakdown showing outlays and budget obligations by individual account. By 1979, it provided the HBC with a two page letter that simply listed defence request totals. However good the information given to the Budget Committees and however well compiled the First Resolution, the process amounts to the presentation of budget totals rather than to their control, and a presentation of totals determined by the same sort of independent and unco-ordinated committee action as before. This reflects the most persistent problem in attempting to reform Congress so as to improve its ability to hold the executive and the DoD accountable.

There is no agreement in Congress about the purpose of the 1974 Budget Reforms. Liberal Democrats supported the reform primarily to protect welfare programmes against President Nixon's attempts to restrain them in favour of defence. Fiscal conservatives, mainly Republicans, supported the reform to restrain the growth in public expenditure, and a small group concerned with improving the congressional budget process also supported the reform. The lack of agreement about the fundamental purpose of the new system meant that its implementation has been compromised and the work of the Budget Committees frustrated. The new committees and budget cycle have been grafted onto the old system and have to work with the existing committees which were effective in denying the new process any real ability to encroach on their affairs. This means that the Armed Services and Appropriations Committees have relinquished very little of their influence and control over the defence budget. Added to this there is no effective group in Congress that is critical of defence for the simple reason that too many votes are affected by defence spending. The HASC had a number of liberal Democrats, like Robert Dellums who represented urban spending interests, but their effect upon the work of the committee was negligible. Even the Budget Committees themselves have pro-defence members and in the SBC, Ernest Hollings the last Democratic Chairman, and Pete Domenici the new Republican Chairman, are confirmed supporters of increased defence spending.

What has been missing is a desire on the part of Congress to reform the budget process in a radical sense. Defence represents big spending and has become the major 'pork barrel' in Congress, rather like the old Public Works Bill.[45] A mark of acceptance of this fact was that no Congressman saw fit to comment on the HASC 'mark up' of the Fiscal Year 1981 Department of Defence Authorisation for Appropriations Bill, which in its amended form secured for every member of the committee a new defence project that would provide jobs in their congressional district. Comment would be superfluous on an event that has become annual. With such interests at stake and with such benefits readily available, Congress is likely to continue to construct the budget piece-meal and in terms of parochial and political interests rather than centrally and in terms of national and strategic criteria. The ability to *review* the budget centrally does not detract from the fragmented and traditional way that it is formulated.

Perhaps the most invidious aspect of congressional involvement in defence budgeting is that the machinery of accountability in Congress has become a device to influence the making of defence policy and the formulation of defence budgets. Information provided for accounting and accountability purposes is used not just to review the policies and performance of the DoD, but to make substantial changes to them. This dilutes the executive's responsibility for defence decision-making and for budget formulation and management, and also undermines the detached and 'generalist' status of Congress, all of which weakens the prospects for effective accountability. The DoD can never be held fully accountable by congressional committees that share defence decisions with it. The loss is all the greater given the fact that congressional intervention is irresponsible when set against national needs and criteria, since it serves special rather than national interests, and because it makes more difficult the formulation of coherent policy by the DoD. A notorious and long-running example is the annual authorisation and appropriation for the A-7 aircraft for which the DoD has no operational requirement, but which is secured by the 'Texas lobby' in Congress and produced in uneconomic numbers by General Dynamics at Fort Worth.

2. The British experience 1970–1980

While there is no space here to discuss the work of the full SCOE and its DEASC in Britain in any detail, it is clear that both failed to live up to the highest hopes of their founders. Robinson has concluded that SCOE failed to look at public expenditure alternatives in any detail mainly because the sub-committees refused to fulfil the second tier role intended for them. Robinson also contends that this was because none of the serving MPs on the sub-committee was interested in fulfilling anything more than an enhanced scrutiny, rather than controlling, role for Parliament. Thus each of the sub-committees tended to look not at public expenditure options and priorities on a consistent basis as the Whitehall machine does in the PESC system, rather they looked at single issues which were either in the news or which were of particular interest to serving sub-committee members. This limited the SCOE role to an enhanced 'Estimates Committee' role rather than the role which many reformers had desired in the 1968/69 Procedure Committee report.[46] This criticism of the SCOE can also be laid at the door of DEASC, which was responsible for defence and foreign affairs issues.

It can be argued generally that while DEASC did more than some sub-committees by concentrating on the annual Defence White Paper and continually returning to the cumulative effects of defence cuts in the 1970s to assess priorities, there was still a tendency in its reports to consider esoteric issue areas rather than defence budgeting and financial management as intended. Reports tended to emphasise such issues as the strategic deterrent; logistic support for the front line; the future of guided weapons systems; alternatives for the cruiser programme; and reserves and reinforcement policies, rather than the relationships between missions and financial choices in the short and medium term. Centrally therefore DEASC confined its activities to scrutinising procurement policies (Chieftain tanks and MRCA/Tornado); acting as a public relations/information service to support the defence effort; and protecting the social welfare of the servicemen. These represent the areas of greatest success for DEASC, while in those areas which the sub-committee was intended to play a more effective role – questioning government priorities, scrutinising service and departmental procedures and routines and setting alternative public expenditure priorities – DEASC either played only a limited role or experienced the most fundamental opposition from the government and the civil service.

To understand why DEASC failed to fulfil the public expenditure role intended for it, it is sufficient to appreciate what information would have been necessary for it to discharge its role of making the executive (Cabinet, Treasury and MOD) more accountable. First of all, to make any sense of public expenditure policy priorities both DEASC and SCOE would have required the Treasury PESC figures and its medium term economic forecasts and models – these were not available to either of these committees which, lacking the staff to compile their own forecasts, were forced to pursue alternative and more limited goals.[47] Added to this, DEASC would have required a vast array of information from within the MOD and service departments to fulfil even its more limited individual role. To question, let alone provide, alternatives to the MOD PESC bids (which is what was intended in theory), DEASC would have required details of LTCs and all service bids; the Ledger/Target headings for each of the services and the Vote book which are controlled by civil service managers for internal accounting purposes (but which provide information on the estimated amounts for particular functions and the priority of these functions); the Joint Chiefs of Staff April Report; the P & B division studies of alternative spending scenarios prior to the PESC bid; the reports from individual project managers on time and cost; as well as volume problems in production; the FCO 'threat' perception documents; a presentation of the range of 'costed options' available to fulfil specific missions and mission functions; internal review documents such as PARs and the Rayner studies;[48] and a complete change in the information presented to Parliament in the annual Defence White Paper and supply estimates. The latter present only the most limited and anodine statements of the reasons for particular expenditure requests and are far less informative than they used to be; while the former annual document which is supposed to extend parliamentary knowledge is almost wholly presented in output/functional terms, on the basis of the element costings. While this provides useful information, the cost of particular missions, it is relatively useless information if Parliament is to fulfil a priority setting role because the element costing process does not act as a central input into the budgeting decision-making process. The relevant information on the budgetary process – apart from a short summary of the LTCs which was withdrawn by the incoming Labour Government in 1974 – was never given to Parliament. It is hardly surprising that DEASC's role should have been limited to an unsystematic scrutiny of decisions already taken even if in a more detailed manner than previously. Interestingly enough, while the explanation for this obviously rests with the defence of executive privileges by governments and civil service heads, part of the explanation for this failure also rests with both the specialist advice received by the sub-committee and the nature of British parliamentary procedures and attitudes.

Without any doubt the British civil service and the British armed forces are excessively, not to say paranoically, secretive about their activities and roles in defence budgeting when compared with the United States. Indeed, the refusal of MOD to give DEASC – a Parliamentary Committee – information which was freely available to journalists and in NATO documents is ample testament to this paranoid secretiveness.[49] Indeed, under the Labour administration – particularly under Fred Mulley – secretiveness took on an even more extreme form as the natural confidentiality of senior civil servants in Britain was heightened by a right-wing Labour Minister's fear of giving information to his left-wing opposition within his own party. This fear, of course, took the vetting of DEASC members further than the natural sensitivity towards MPs being provided with information coded SECRET by the civil service. Vetting of MPs which was undertaken in collaboration with the MOD, Cabinet Office, Whips Office, Chief Clerk's Office in the Commons, as well as by the Chairman of the SCOE was yet a further reason for the relatively non-contentious role of DEASC.[50] Indeed, there were parliamentary questions at one stage in DEASC's work over the apparent demotion of one parliamentary clerk, who assisted the sub-committee and attempted to obtain the information for DEASC which is necessary for it to fulfil an extended role.[51] This resistance to providing relevant information – which even extended to refusing permission for academic and service personnel to appear before DEASC to be asked questions[52] – is sufficient explanation of why the sub-committee failed to fulfil its highest aspirations. In a microcosm the problem for legislative oversight in Britain is that Parliament neither has the powers to change budget allocations, nor the information and research back-up to provide the legislature with the information to discharge a controlling role. The parliamentary committees in Britain are totally dependent – and particularly in defence – on information from, and the goodwill of, Whitehall. Even the specialist advisers provided for the DEASC were of former service backgrounds and themselves dependent on MOD information, there being no British equivalent of Rand, Brookings or the Ford Foundation for providing alternative information sources.

While this reliance on Whitehall for information explains much in the failure of DEASC, MPs in Britain are also likely to compound this weakness by their own abject attitude to reform and their own parliamentary role. As already indicated, backbench MPs in Britain were unprepared to take on the work required to fulfil the quasi-civil service role intended for them in the SCOE reform. MPs, while being heavily committed to constituency business and party roles, are however likely to prefer to be involved in discussing issues of media prominence or of personal interest rather than working diligently over financial management problems which are complex, time consuming and unglamorous. As a consequence MPs' own attitudes contributed to the decision to limit SCOE and DEASC's role to a scrutiny rather than controlling role over the executive. At the same time, the need for DEASC to find bi-partisan support for studies and reports also tended to force the sub-committee into relatively non-contentious areas.[53] Related, of course, were the problems associated with failing to provide the sub-committees with adequate research and staff back-up and the opposition within senior echelons of Parliament (the Clerk's Office and amongst MPs) to an enhanced parliamentary role viz-a-viz the executive.[54]

Not surprisingly therefore parliamentary control of defence budgeting was not particularly extended by the activities of either SCOE or DEASC. This was mainly because at no time did either of these committees ever obtain the important information related to the defence budgeting process which we have outlined earlier. DEASC's role was effective in providing more information about defence matters and some choices, but it failed to fulfil the brief given to it in Standing Order 87 to review public expenditure priorities and provide alternatives. Ironically, the incoming Thatcher Government, responding to a 1978 Procedure

Committee report assessing the limited success of SCOE, accepted the argument for a further innovation in 1979. This innovation abolished SCOE and its sub-committees and replaced them by twelve new departmental related committees – one of which is the Select Committee on Defence (SCOD).[55] On the face of it, the creation of a departmentally related committee ought to provide the scope for in-depth and continuous review of defence budgeting. In practice however the new department was a retrograde step because, added to the limitations already enumerated of the lack of independent information and dependence on MOD goodwill, are the structural weaknesses of this new reform. Under the new system of department-specific committees there is no scope at all in Parliament for the bringing together of all departmental decisions within Parliament to assess inter-governmental allocations in the manner of the congressional budget system. Ironically, this was what SCOE was supposed to do, but this capacity to parallel the Treasury PESC system has been replaced by a single independent committee responsible for Treasury and civil service issues. Added to this retrograde step has been the decision to divide DEASC responsibilities between autonomous Defence and Foreign Relations Committees, which are hardly likely to be able to bring together the 'threat' and strategic perceptions of the FCO and the defence capabilities of the MOD if they do not now operate in tandem. It is likely there-fore that SCOD will find its role limited, not to scrutiny of either broad policy (the aim of the new reform) or the provision of alter-native defence expenditure options (the aim of the old reform) but to the scrutiny of weapons procurement systems and 'one off' issue areas – the role formerly undertaken by the old Estimates Committee, but on a grander scale.

CONCLUSION

The development and retention of output budgeting methods in the DoD and the MOD during the 1970s have not altered substantially the way in which decisions have been made in the United States and Britain about the allocation of resources for de-fence as against other public spending programmes, nor have they affected to any marked degree the allocation of defence resources within the respective departments. An examination of the budget cycles reveals that defence budgeting is essentially input-based and incremental. In the United States the PPB system disguises the fact that the 'base' budget represented by the FYDP and the ZBB base level is in essence protected, unexamined and ongoing. DoD effort is concentrated on marginal adjustments that may be made above that level. In the MOD, the LTCs lead the budget process, and output budgeting techniques are used for presentational purposes and as an aid to the input-biased system that has always been in operation. In both departments there is little evidence to suggest that budgeting is so centralised that the political heads of departments are able to select and reorder priorities, since the services are necessarily deeply involved and retain the major responsibility for generating budget bids and in influencing how resources are allocated among them. In both systems changes in political and economic circumstances have extensive effects upon resource allocation decisions in ways that no budget system can anticipate and which therefore require substantial and irregular adjustments in planning, programming and budget decisions.

These 'failures' of output budgeting have reduced the effectiveness of congressional and parliamentary attempts to weigh the priority to be attached to defence spending and their ability to scrutinise and control the management of defence resources and programmes. These same failures show that many of the expectations current in the early 1970s, that new budgetary techniques would render central departments more accountable to the legislative branch, were optimistic. However, those expectations did help generate pressure for institutional reform in Congress and Parliament in the form of the Congressional Budget Committees and the Select Committee on Expenditure and its defence and external affairs sub-committee. A comparison of their response to new forms of defence budgeting shows that the availability of information is a necessary but by no means a sufficient condition of exercising an effective scrutiny of defence. Where the legislature shares the responsibility for national and agency budget allocations, as in the United States, the provision of information is substantial but beyond the capacity of the legislature as a whole to comprehend and manage. Those committees that specialise in handling aspects of the executive's budget, such as defence, use the information provided to share in the decision-making of the department to which it relates, rather than hold the department accountable. When the legislature has no authority to share in budget allocaton decisions, as in Britain, it also lacks power to demand that information which is necessary to render departments, and in Britain especially the MOD, fully accountable. Congress shares power, obtains information and is irresponsible; Parliament is denied both power and information and is impotent. In both the American and British cases the legislative reforms have achieved little real improvement in defence accountability, precisely because Congressmen and members of Parliament have been content to reform legislative procedure, which at best may maximise the potential for accountability that already exists, but have not been willing to confront those aspects of the legislative/executive relationship that determine the scope of the potential.

NOTES

1. See David Novick (ed.), *Program Budgeting*, 2nd edn. (Cambridge, Mass.: Harvard University Press, 1967) *passim*.
2. Aaron Wildavsky, *The Politics of the Budgetary Process*, 3rd edn. (Boston: Little Brown, 1979) p. 189.
3. David Howell, 'Public Accountability: Trends and Parliamentary Implications', in L. R. Smith and D. C. Hague (eds), *The Dilemma of Accountability in Modern Government* (London: Macmillan, 1971) p. 237.
4. Ibid., p. 236.
5. *Fulton Committee Report on the Civil Service*, Vol. 1, para. 281.
6. See for example Committee on the Budget, US House of Representatives, *Congressional Budget and Impoundment Control Act of 1974: Legislative History* (Washington, January 1979) for a list and a review of some of these reports.
7. A review of these changes can be found in Burton B. Mayer Jnr., 'Evolution of PPB in DoD', *Armed Forces Comptroller*, 18, 2 (Spring 1973) pp. 21–26.
8. Memorandum 'PPBS Schedule for the FY81–85 Cycle', from the Secretary of Defense, 13 November 1978.
9. See for example Lloyd Norman, 'The Military Chiefs and Defense Policy: Is Anybody Listening?', *Army*, 28 (April 1978) pp. 14–25.
10. See for example General Accounting Office, *Models, Data and War: A Critique for the Foundation of Defense Analysis* (Washington, 12 March 1980) ch. 3: 'The Modern Design for Defence Decision', pp. 32–48.
11. US Department of Defense, *Summary of the DoD Planning, Programming and Budgeting System*, undated, issued by DoD March 1980, p. 1.
12. Interview with Clyde O. Glaister, Director of Program and Financial Control, DoD, 1 April 1980.
13. Norman, op. cit., and Bob Gatty, 'Mr. Carter, Congress and the Generals', *Army*, 28, 12 (December 1978) pp. 28–31.

14. General David C. Jones, USAF, Chairman of the Joint Chiefs of Staff, *United States Military Posture for FY 1982*, p. iv.

15. Interview, Department of Defense, April 1980.

16. The outstanding example was the AV-8B aircraft, see p. 243 below.

17. Richard Burt, *Defence Budgeting: the British and American Cases* (London: International Institute for Strategic Studies, 1975), p. 5.

18. Maurice Wright, 'From planning to control: PESC in the 1970's', in Maurice Wright (ed.), *Public Spending Decisions* (London: Allen and Unwin, 1980) pp. 88–119.

19. On the role of the MOD see Michael Howard, *The Central Organisation of Defence* (London: RUSI, 1970); David Greenwood, *Budgeting for Defence* (London: RUSI, 1972); and Burt, op. cit. On the role of the Procurement Executive see Clive Pointing, 'The Reorganisation of Defence Procurement' (Paper presented to the Centennial Seminar, Department of External Studies, Oxford University, March 1980).

20. Burt, op. cit. and Greenwood, op. cit. This account, which relies heavily on Burt and Greenwood has been supplemented by interviews with civil servants within the MOD and FCO to take account of changes in the 1970s.

21. For a discussion of marginal/incremental conflicts see Hugh Heclo and Aaron Wildavsky, *The Private Government of Public Money* (Los Angeles: University of California, 1974), pp. 198–262.

22. Greenwood, op. cit., pp. 39–40.

23. John Bourn, 'The planning, administration and control of defence expenditure' (Paper presented to the Centennial Seminar, Department of External Studies, University of Oxford, March 1980), p. 7. Mr Bourn is Assistant Under Secretary (Programmes and Budget) MOD.

24. Greenwood, op. cit., pp. 41–42.

25. Michael Hobkirk, 'The organisation of defence policy-making in the UK and USA', in Lawrence Martin (ed.), *The Management of Defence* (London: Macmillan, 1976) pp. 12–13.

26. For this basic argument see: Sir Leo Pliatsky, 'Paying for defence: the defence budget and the public expenditure system' (Paper presented to the Centennial Seminar, Department of External Studies, University of Oxford, March 1980).

27. Burt, op. cit., pp. 32–34.

28. Pliatsky, op. cit., pp. 14–15.

29. For an introduction to the process of policy rethink see Lawrence Martin, *British Defence Policy: The Long Recessional* (London: IISS, Adelphi Paper 61, 1969).

30. Pliatsky, op. cit., p. 11.

31. On the introduction of cash limits see Maurice Wright, op. cit., pp. 101–103.

32. On this problem see *Eighth Report from the Expenditure Committee: Defence Expenditure* (Session 1977/78, H.C.600-i), paras. 6–15 and Minutes of Evidence, pp. 1–50.

33. Bourn, op. cit., pp. 4–7.

34. Ibid., p. 7.

35. Greenwood, op. cit., pp. 92–94.

36. See Lawrence Freedman, *Britain and Nuclear Weapons* (London: Macmillan, 1980), ch. 5: 'Chevaline', pp. 41–51.

37. Andrew Cox and Stephen Kirby, 'Innovations in Legislative Oversight of Defence Policies in Britain and America', *The Parliamentarian*, LXI, 4, (October 1980) pp. 215–229.

38. See 'Editorial', *Aviation Week and Space Technology*, 25 May 1981, p. 18, for comment on the USAF attempts to get funding for the B-1 bomber from Congress during the Carter Presidency.

39. US Library of Congress, CRS, *V/STOL Aircraft Development*, by Bert H. Cooper, (Washington, 13 March) *passim*.

40. Ibid., p. 7.

41. See Stephen Kirby, 'Congress and National Security', *The World Today*, July-August 1981, pp. 270–276.

42. *US General Accounting Office*, Elmer B. Staats, 'Assuring Program Accountability' (Washington, 15 November 1979), p. 9.

43. This was confirmed by several interviews with HASC staff members, one of whom described the CBO defence staff as '21 year old Vasa graduates'.

44. Quoted in Wildavsky, op. cit., p. 258.

45. See John Ferejohn, *Porkbarrel Politics* (Stanford University Press, 1974) *passim*.

46. The point is that there were disagreements within the Procedure Committee about the correct role for Parliament. These views varied between those who thought that any reforms were a waste of time without electoral reform, through those who wanted Parliament to resemble Congress, to those who felt its role should be limited to scrutiny. For details see Ann Robinson, *Parliament and Public Spending* (London: Heinemann, 1978) pp. 42–53.

47. Robinson, op. cit., pp. 26–29.

48. On the nature of PARs (Policy Analysis and Review) see Heclo and Wildavsky, op. cit., pp. 276–303. Under the Thatcher administration PARs have been abolished and replaced by internal reviews of efficiency and special studies undertaken by two special advisers to the government, Sir Derek Rayner and Paul Channon. On the MOD internal studies see Bourn, op. cit., pp. 15–18, and on the role of Rayner and Channon see Richard Norton-Taylor, 'Official paid post axed as Whitehall gets lesson in thrift', *The Guardian*, 4 July 1980, p. 22.

49. An example of this being the provision of information on the Polaris replacement in the US rather than UK: see Tony Geraghty, 'Thatcher to put British warhead in Trident', *Sunday Times*, 6 July 1980, p. 1.

50. Robinson speaks of this problem, op. cit., pp. 54–57 and it has been confirmed in interviews with Parliamentary Clerks and James Boyden, Chairman of SCOE between 1974 and 1979.

51. Martin Cooper, interview with present authors.

52. Peter Hennessy, 'Mr. Mulley angers specialists over successor to Polaris', *The Times*, 30 April 1979.

53. Masood Hyder, 'Parliament and Defence Affairs: the defence subcommittee of the Expenditure Committee', *Public Administration*, 55 (1977) pp. 59–78.

54. For further details see Cox and Kirby, op. cit.

55. *First Report from the Defence Committee: Sub-Committees*, HC455 (London: HMSO, 1979/80).

Index